The Hidden Places of
LAKE DISTRICT
and
CUMBRIA

914.27804
By
David Gerrard

OO4113 5415

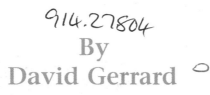

Published by:
Travel Publishing Ltd
7a Apollo House, Calleva Park
Aldermaston, Berks, RG7 8TN

ISBN 1-902-00727-1
© Travel Publishing Ltd

First Published:	*1990*	*Fourth Edition:*	*1998*
Second Edition:	*1993*	*Fifth Edition:*	*2001*
Third Edition:	*1996*		

HIDDEN PLACES REGIONAL TITLES

Cambs & Lincolnshire	Chilterns
Cornwall	Derbyshire
Devon	Dorset, Hants & Isle of Wight
East Anglia	Gloucestershire & Wiltshire
Heart of England	Hereford, Worcs & Shropshire
Highlands & Islands	Kent
Lake District & Cumbria	Lancashire & Cheshire
Lincolnshire	Northumberland & Durham
Somerset	Sussex
Thames Valley	Yorkshire

HIDDEN PLACES NATIONAL TITLES

England	Ireland
Scotland	Wales

Printing by: Scotprint, Haddington

Maps by: © Maps in Minutes ™ (2000)

Editor: David Gerrard

Cover Design: Lines & Words, Aldermaston

Cover Photographs: Wastwater; Forest in Whinlatter Pass; Whitehaven
© www.britainonview.com

Foreword

The Hidden Places is a collection of easy to use travel guides taking you, in this instance, on a relaxed but informative tour of The Lake District and Cumbria, famous for its grand, austere mountain scenery intersected by fast flowing rivers and languid lakes but also offering visitors much more – isolated hamlets and picturesque villages, quiet lanes and a deep literary and industrial heritage.

This edition of *The Hidden Places of the Lake District and Cumbria* is published *in full colour.* All *Hidden Places* titles will now be published in colour which will ensure that readers can properly appreciate the attractive scenery and impressive places of interest in this county and, of course, in the rest of the British Isles. We do hope that you like the new format.

Our books contain a wealth of interesting information on the history, the countryside, the towns and villages and the more established places of interest in the county. But they also promote the more secluded and little known visitor attractions and places to stay, eat and drink many of which are easy to miss unless you know exactly where you are going.

We include hotels, inns, restaurants, public houses, teashops, various types of accommodation, historic houses, museums, gardens, garden centres, craft centres and many other attractions throughout Cumbria, all of which are comprehensively indexed. Most places are accompanied by an attractive photograph and are easily located by using the map at the beginning of each chapter. We do not award merit marks or rankings but concentrate on describing the more interesting, unusual or unique features of each place with the aim of making the reader's stay in the local area an enjoyable and stimulating experience.

Whether you are visiting the area for business or pleasure or in fact are living in the county we do hope that you enjoy reading and using this book. We are always interested in what readers think of places covered (or not covered) in our guides so please do not hesitate to use the reader reaction forms provided to give us your considered comments. We also welcome any general comments which will help us improve the guides themselves. Finally if you are planning to visit any other corner of the British Isles we would like to refer you to the list of other *Hidden Places* titles to be found at the rear of the book and to the Travel Publishing website at www.travelpublishing.co.uk.

Travel Publishing

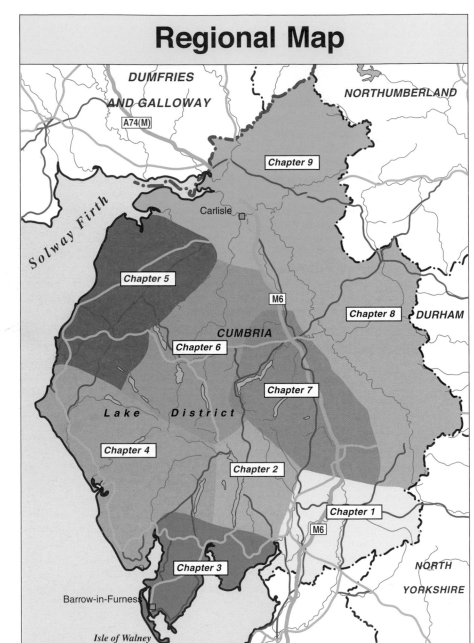

Regional Map

Contents

1 Gateway to the Lakes

Around 16 million visitors a year make their way to the Lake District, irresistibly drawn to its enchanting lakes, its picturesque villages and the most dramatic scenery in England. The highest mountain in the country, Scafell Pike (3205ft), the largest and deepest lakes, Windermere and Wast Water respectively, are all found here, along with hundreds of other mountains, another 14 lakes, challenging crags and pastoral, wooded valleys.

Despite the huge influx of visitors, most do not venture far from the main tourist "honey-pots" so it's still easy to find the peaceful glades and windswept, isolated fells celebrated by the Lake Poets, Wordsworth, Coleridge and Southey. Between them, this lyrical trio transformed the pervading 18th century perception of the most northwesterly corner of England as an intimidating wilderness into an appreciation of its majestic scenery.

Cumbria is England's second largest county but with a population (490,000) only slightly more numerous than that of the City of Leeds. Almost exactly one third of the county's 2636 square miles lies within the boundaries of the Lake District

Viaduct, Stone House

National Park, created in 1951 to protect the area from "inappropriate development and to provide access to the land for public enjoyment". Not a single mile of motorway has penetrated its borders and only the very occasional stretch of dual-carriageway - barely a dozen miles in all.

But access to the area is very easy, with the M6 running right along its eastern edge. For many people travelling from the south into Cumbria, their first experience of the county is the area around Kendal and Kirkby Lonsdale. These ancient settlements both provide an excellent introduction to the history, people, and economy of Cumbria. Ideally placed for the Lake District National Park and the south Cumbrian coast, it is easy to forget that this area is also close to the northern Pennines and the Yorkshire Dales National Park.

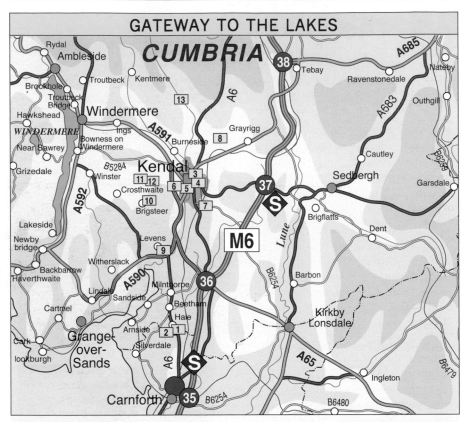

© MAPS IN MINUTES ™ (2000)

PLACES TO STAY, EAT, DRINK AND SHOP

KIRKBY LONSDALE

One fine day in 1875 John Ruskin came to Kirkby Lonsdale and stood on the stone terrace overlooking the valley of the river Lune. It was, he declared, "one of the loveliest scenes in England, therefore in the world". *He was equally enthusiastic about the busy little market town - "I do not know in all my country", he continued, "a place more naturally divine than Kirkby Lonsdale".*

Ruskin had been inspired to visit the town after seeing JMW Turner's painting of that view, and Turner himself had come in 1816 on the recommendation of William Wordsworth. All three of them made a point of going to see the **Devil's Bridge** over the Lune, a handsome, lofty structure of three fluted arches reputedly built by Satan himself in three days. According to legend an old woman, unable to cross the deep river with her cattle, had asked the Devil to build her a bridge. He agreed but demanded in return the soul of the first creature to cross but his evil plan was thwarted by Cumbrian cunning. The old woman threw a bun across the bridge which was retrieved by her dog and thus she cheated the Devil of a human soul.

The bridge is at least 700 years old and although its exact age is a mystery we do know that some repairs were carried out in 1275, making it certainly the oldest surviving bridge in Westmorland. By the 1920s, this narrow bridge originally designed for pack-horses was quite inadequate for the growth in motor traffic. A new bridge was built and this, together with one of the country's first by-pass roads, has saved the lovely old town from further destructive road-widening schemes.

Kirkby's Main Street is a picturesque jumble of houses spanning several

Kirkby Lonsdale

centuries, with intriguing passages and ginnels skittering off in all directions, all of them worth exploring. It's still a pleasure to stroll along the narrow cobbled streets bearing names such as Jingling Lane, past the 16th century weavers' cottages in Fairbank, across the Market Square with its 600-year-old cross where traders have displayed their wares every Thursday for more than 700 years, past ancient hostelries to the even more venerable **St Mary's Church** with its noble Norman doorway and massive pillars. In the churchyard, a Victorian gazebo looks across to the enchanting view of the Lune Valley painted by JMW Turner.

The town has 3 times been national winner of the "Britain in Bloom" competition and also attracts thousands of visitors for its **Victorian Fair**, held on the first full weekend in September, and

THE KINGS ARMS

Hale, nr Milnthorpe,
Cumbria LA7 7BH
Tel: 015395 63203

The Kings Arms was built in 1810 as a coaching inn along the newly created turnpike between Kendal and Lancaster and, in those days, it possessed some 80 acres of land. Today, the inn is still offering weary travellers somewhere to rest where they can be sure of finding excellent hospitality from the landlords, Rosalynd and Stanford Robinson. The couple have more than 25 years experience in the licensing trade within this area and their years of experience have certainly been put to good use at the Kings Arms which they took over in 1994.

Visitors will find an attractive and quaint pub offering a fine selection of real ales and superb food to match. The extensive menu lists a mouth-watering range of dishes culled from all over the world - a vegetarian Spinach & Ricotta Cheese Cannelloni, Cumberland Sausage, or a Spiced Cajun Chicken Fillet are just a few selections from the extensive menu. So popular has the Kings Arms become that booking is essential for weekends. For those who wish to stay in the area a little longer, there are also 2 comfortable and well-appointed double rooms available all year round. For those looking for a traditional English inn with a warm and friendly atmosphere, and good service to match, seek no further than the Kings Arms! At the time of writing, the final touches are being put to an elegant conservatory area at the side of the inn. By the time you read this, it should be up and running.

LAKELAND WILDLIFE OASIS

Hale, Milnthorpe, Cumbria LA7 7BW
Tel: 015395 63027
e-mail: mail@wildlifeoasis.co.uk
website: www.wildlifeoasis.co.uk

Opened in 1991, **Lakeland Wildlife Oasis** quickly established itself as one of the Lake District's premier visitor attractions. "Half Zoo, half Museum, and totally fascinating" the Oasis takes visitors on an amazing journey through the world of wildlife using a unique combination of live animals and imaginative

"hands-on" computer displays. Visitors can drape a snake around their neck, exchange inquisitive glances with a Ruffled Lemur or a beautifully poised Meerkat squatting on its haunches, and admire creatures rarely seen in captivity such as Flying Foxes and Poison Arrow Frogs. Or you can just relax in the tropical hall, colourful with free-flying birds, bats and butterflies. Many rare species have found a secure home here, amongst them the fossa, of which there are only 44 in captivity. Friendly staff are always on hand to answer questions and let you meet some of the inhabitants face to face! The Oasis was established by Dave and Jo Marsden, both of whom were animal keepers at Chester Zoo before setting up this popular family attraction. It is open every day of the year, (except for Christmas Day and Boxing Day), there is access throughout for the disabled, and other amenities include picnic areas, a snack bar and a gift shop. For parties of more than 30 people, it is advisable to book ahead and the Oasis will then provide a tour guide.

again in December for the Yuletide procession through streets ablaze with coloured lights and decorated Christmas trees.

AROUND KIRKBY LONSDALE

HALE
7 miles W of Kirkby Lonsdale off the A6

This tiny village surrounded by woodland and close to the Lancashire border is home to the **Lakeland Wildlife Oasis** (see panel opposite) where not only is there a wide range of animals and birds to see but also a hands-on exhibition telling the evolutionary story.

About 3 miles south of the town, **Leighton Hall** is actually in Lancashire but well worth a short diversion. Famed for its collection of Gillow furniture, the Hall has been described as the most beautifully situated house in the British Isles, with the dramatic panorama of the Lakeland Fells providing a striking backdrop. The elaborate neo-Gothic façade cloaks an 18th century mansion which in turn stands on the site of the original medieval house built in 1246 by Adam d'Avranches whose descendants still live here.

ARNSIDE
10 miles W of Kirkby Lonsdale off the B5282

This quiet town on the Kent Estuary, with its short but elegant promenade, was once a busy port with its own shipbuilding and sea salt-refining industry. As the estuary silted up during the 19th century, a process accelerated by the construction of the striking 50-arch railway viaduct, so the port declined. Today, it is a favourite retirement destination and a peaceful holiday resort.

Around Arnside itself there is a wonderful choice of country walks, particularly over and around **Arnside Knott**. This limestone headland, now a nature reserve rich in old woods and wild flowers, is part of the Arnside and Silverdale Area of Outstanding Natural Beauty. Knott comes from the Saxon word meaning 'rounded hill', which, in this case, rises 521 feet above sea level and gives extensive views of the Lakeland fells, the Pennines, and the southern Cumbrian coast. There is a beautiful path around the headland and along the shoreline past Blackstone Point.

Inland, and found down a quiet lane, is **Arnside Tower**, one of the many pele towers that were built in the area in the 14th century. This particular tower dates from the 1370s and it may have been part of the chain of towers designed to form a ring of protection around Morecambe Bay.

BEETHAM
8 miles W of Kirkby Lonsdale on the A6

Approached through a pergola of rambling roses, the **Church of St Michael and All Angels** dates from Saxon times and, during restoration work in the 1830s, a hoard of around a hundred coins, minted in Norman times, were discovered inside the building at the base of a pillar. Although badly damaged during the Civil War, when its windows were smashed and effigies broken, a glass fragment of Henry IV in an ermine robe has survived the centuries. The village is also home to an unusual 19th century Post Office with a distinctive black and white studded door.

Just outside the village lies **Heron Corn Mill**, a restored and working waterfall with fully operational grinding machinery. A fine example of a traditional corn mill which operated for trade in the Westmorland farming area, the mill only ceased trading in the 1950s. The situation

THE CASTLE INN

13 Castle Street, Kendal, Cumbria LA9 7AA
Tel: 01539 729983

Just a short walk from its namesake, **The Castle Inn** looks irresistibly inviting with its whitewashed walls set off by colourful hanging baskets and window boxes of flowers. The inn dates back to the early 1700s and a directory of 1834 lists it as a "beer house". By 1870, it had been elevated to the status of an inn. Today, mine hosts at The Castle are Christine and Geoff Metcalfe, an engaging couple who have made this traditional hostelry, hidden away in the heart of the town, a popular meeting place.

The inn has its own darts, pool and quiz teams, and the local hockey teams have made it their favoured watering hole after matches. Christine is in charge of the kitchen, offering a wide choice of quality food every lunchtime between noon and 2pm. Choose from the regular menu or from the daily specials. Christine's speciality of the house, for which she is renowned, is fish cooked in batter made to her very own secret recipe! Real ale lovers will be at home at The Castle Inn since there are always guest ales on tap, Tetleys, Jennings and Dent ales are always available. The inn is open all day, every day, and children are welcome until 6.30pm.

THE GARDEN HOUSE HOTEL & RESTAURANT

Fowl Ing Lane, Kendal, Cumbria LA9 6PH
Tel: 01539 731131 Fax: 01539 740064
e-mail: gardenhouse.hotel@virgin.net
website: www.gardenhousehotel.co.uk

Standing high on the hillside overlooking the town, **The Garden House Hotel & Restaurant** was built in 1812 by a well-known architect who also designed Kendal's striking Town Hall. The Garden House is an elegant and gracious building surrounded by several acres of mature gardens and woodland. It became a hotel some 20 years ago and is now owned and run by David and Lesley Oates who, together with their courteous and efficient staff, are always on hand to extend the warmest of welcomes.

An especially attractive feature of the hotel is its conservatory restaurant, the Garden Room, which serves outstanding cuisine, complemented by fine wines. There's a cosy bar and an adjoining lounge with a welcoming log fire. Open all year round, the Garden House has 11 guest bedrooms, (including one on the ground floor), all of them individually furnished, en suite, and provided with television, direct dial telephone, hair dryer, trouser press and hospitality tray. Children are welcome and pets too, by arrangement.

of Heron Mill is ideal as a natural shelf of rock in the River Bela forms a waterfall, providing the necessary head of water to drive the waterwheel. This made the site an obvious one when, in 1220, the Lords of the Manor of Haverback granted lands to the Canons of Coningshead for the construction of a mill. Referred to several times in archives from the Middle Ages, the land was transferred to Sir William Thorneburghe when Coningshead was destroyed in 1538. Visitors to the mill can not only see an exhibition about its history but also view the milling process.

MILNTHORPE
8 miles W of Kirkby Lonsdale on A6

Just north of the Lancashire border, Milnthorpe has been a market town since the 14th century. It originally flourished as a port on the banks of the River Bela but the harbour has long since silted up. The mill of the town's name refers to the waterfalls that once stood alongside the river. A small folly tower on St Andrew's Hill was built in the 1830s by the architect George Webster as a means of occupying his idle hours while restoring the town's unremarkable church.

SANDSIDE
9 miles W of Kirkby Lonsdale on the B5282

From this small village situated on the banks of the Kent Estuary, pack horses and drovers during the Middle Ages together with their sheep and cattle would set off across the treacherous sands into Cumbria rather than take the longer, inland route. Consequently, many lives were unnecessarily lost and the route remains as dangerous today as it was then.

KENDAL

In 1997, a survey by Strathclyde University revealed that the highest quality of life of any town in England was to be found in Kendal, the "capital" of South Lakeland. That assessment came as no surprise to the residents of this lively, bustling town which was once one of the most important woollen textile centres of northern England. The Kendal woollen industry was founded in 1331 by John Kemp, a Flemish weaver, and it flourished and sustained the town for almost 600 years until the development of competition from the huge West Riding of Yorkshire mills during the Industrial Revolution of the 19th century. The town's motto "Wool is my Bread" reveals the extent to which the economy of Kendal depended on the wool from the flocks of Herdwick sheep that roamed the surrounding fells. The fame of the cloth was so great that Shakespeare refers to archers clad in Kendal Green cloth in his play *Henry IV*.

Kendal Town Hall

ABBOT HALL ART GALLERY AND MUSEUM

Kendal, Cumbria LA9 5AL
Tel: 01539 722464
Fax: 01539 722494

Abbot Hall Art Gallery forms part of a complex within Abbot Hall park and includes work by John Ruskin and the celebrated portrait painter, George Romney, who was born nearby at Dalton-in-Furness in 1734. The permanent collection also includes a wide range of 18th, 19th and 20th century British paintings and watercolours, and the Gallery hosts regular touring exhibitions.

MUSEUM OF LAKELAND LIFE

A short walk from the Brewery Arts Centre is the **Museum of Lakeland Life and Industry** which is themed around traditional rural trades of the region, such as blacksmithing, wheelwrighting, agricultural activities, weaving, and printing. Here, too, are recreated cottage interiors, elegantly furnished period rooms, a Postman Pat room for younger visitors and a reconstruction of the study in which the celebrated author, Arthur Ransome, wrote the children's classic *Swallows and Amazons*.

KENDAL NATURAL HISTORY MUSEUM

At the other end of the town, near the railway station, is the **Museum of Natural History and Archaeology**, founded in 1796 and one of the oldest museums in the country.

Based on the collection first exhibited by William Todhunter in the late 18th century, the Museum takes visitors on a journey from prehistoric times, a trip which includes an interactive exhibit which tells the story of Kendal Castle.

The famous fellwalker and writer, Alfred Wainwright, whose handwritten guides will be found in the backpack of any serious walker, was honorary clerk here between 1945 and 1974. Many of his original drawings are on display.

These archers were the famous Kendal Bowmen whose lethal longbows were made from local yew trees culled from the nearby limestone crags. It was these men who clinched the English victories at Agincourt and Crécy and fought so decisively against the Scots at the Battle of Flodden Field in 1513.

Kendal has royal connections too. The Parr family lived at **Kendal Castle** until 1483 - their most famous descendant was Catherine Parr, the last of Henry VIII's six wives. Today, the castle's gaunt ruins stand high on a hill overlooking the town, with most of the castle wall and one of the towers still standing, and two underground vaults still complete. Castle Hill is a popular place for walking and picnicking and in summer the hillside is smothered with wild flowers. From the hilltop there are spectacular views and a panorama panel here assists in identifying the distant fells.

The largest settlement in the old county of Westmorland, Kendal has always been a bustling town, from the days when it was on the main route to Scotland. Nowadays the M6 and a by-pass divert much of the traffic away from the town centre, but its narrow main streets, Highgate, Stramongate, and Stricklandgate, are always busy during the season. The fine coaching inns of the 17th and 18th centuries, to which Prince Charles Edward is said to have retreated after his abortive 1745 rebellion, still line these streets.

Anyone wandering around the town cannot help but notice the numerous alleyways, locally known as yards, that are such a distinctive feature of Kendal. An integral part of the old town, they are a reminder that the people of Kendal used to live under a constant threat of raids by the Scots. The yards were a line of defence against these attacks, an area that could be secured by sealing the one small

THE PHOENIX

42 Stramongate, Kendal, Cumbria LA9 4BD
Tel/Fax: 01539 724130

Formerly known as The Nags Head and located right in the heart of the town, **The Phoenix** is a delightful old hostelry with a Grade II Listed Building status. It has that special atmosphere that seems to be unique to taverns run by a family, in this case the Thurlby family - landlord Phil, landlady Angela and sister Louise. They took over here in the spring of 2000 and put a lot of time, money and effort into restoring this fine old inn. Perhaps the most impressive feature in the inn is the first floor restaurant with its lofty timbered roof and handsome stone fireplace.

Here, at tables covered with crisp white cloths, customers can enjoy an à la carte menu with a predominantly English flavour, along with a selection of vegetarian choices. This striking restaurant is open every evening from 5.30pm to 9pm (9.30pm on Saturday) and there are plans under way to hold themed Medieval Evenings here. The restaurant can also be hired for small functions. Downstairs in the lounge bar, quality food is also available every lunchtime and evening. To accompany your meal there's an extensive choice that includes Tetley and John Smiths keg bitters, Guinness and Guinness Extra Cold, 3 draught lagers and a draught cider. And if you happen to be visiting on a Thursday evening, feel free to take part in the lively Quiz Night which begins at 8.30pm.

THE GLEN

Oxenholme, Kendal, Cumbria LA9 7RF
Tel: 01539 726386 e-mail: greenintheglen@btinternet.com
website: www.smoothhound.co.uk/hotels/glen2.html

Those who know the Lake District well will certainly be familiar with The Helm, a ridge-top path which opens up some wonderful views of the Cumbrian fells. Occupying a quiet location down the hillside from this popular walk but within walking distance of pub, restaurant and railway station, **The Glen** is a small, family run, non-smoking guest house standing in a third of an acre of garden and woodland. Built in 1887, it's a spacious residence with walls painted a gleaming white. The Glen is the home of Alan and Christine Green who have been welcoming guests here since 1998. The relaxed, informal atmosphere, the comfortable bedrooms and the quality of the food on offer have ensured that many visitors are keen to return.

There are 3 guest bedrooms, all spacious, all attractively decorated and furnished, all en suite with

bath and shower, and all provided with colour television and hospitality tray. If you are feeling particularly self-indulgent, ask for the room with the Jacuzzi. And if you are staying on a Friday or Saturday you would be well-advised to take advantage of the excellent food on offer in The Glen's restaurant (which is also available to non-residents who make a booking). The wide-ranging menu covers the gamut from hearty steaks to vegetarian choices such as Carrot & Mushroom Loaf. The Glen doesn't have a table licence but you are welcome to bring your own preferred beverage - glasses will be provided and there is no corkage charge.

FIELD END BARNS AND SHAW END MANSION

Patton, Kendal, Cumbria LA8 9DU
Tel: 01539 824220/0777 8596863 Fax: 01539 824464
e-mail: fshawend@globalnet.co.uk
website: www.diva-web.co.uk/fsendhols

Located on the edge of the Lake District National Park, **Field End Barns and Shaw End Mansion** enjoy an idyllic and wonderfully peaceful setting. The River Mint flows close by, a beautifully clean stream which is ideal for children to paddle in or to picnic by. There's splendid walking all around, with the Dales Way passing close by. The two stone and slate barns at Field End won an award in a prestigious national Country Landowners' Association Farm Building award scheme which praised "the skilful conversion of disused agricultural buildings". The barns now provide 5 extremely spacious and attractive 3- and 4-bedroomed cottages grouped around the old farm house and yard.

Each cottage has its own private garden, a well-equipped kitchen, separate bath and shower rooms, colour television, video, and many original features such as oak beams and wood and slate floors. The owners of Field End Barns, Edward and Karlyn Robinson, also have another self-catering complex just

10 minutes away at Shaw End Mansion. This imposing listed Georgian mansion, built in 1796, stands on a 200-acre estate and has recently been restored and converted to provide 4 luxury apartments. Two are on the ground floor, (both with 2 bedrooms); a sweeping pine staircase leads to the other two, one of them with 2 bedrooms, the other with three. The apartments all have a well equipped kitchen, a large sitting/dining room with an open fireplace and colour television - and all enjoy superb views across the Cumbrian countryside.

entrance, with the families and livestock safe inside.

Shoppers are spoilt for choice in Kendal. In addition to all the familiar High Street names, the **Westmorland Shopping Centre, Blackhall Yard** and **Elephant Yard**, all in the heart of the town, and the **K Village Factory Shopping** complex on the outskirts, make it easy to shop until you drop. One local product well worth sampling is **Kendal Mint**, a tasty chocolate-coated confection which is cherished by climbers and walkers for its instant infusion of energy. Another once-popular local medication, Kendal Black Drop, is sadly no longer available. "A more than commonly strong mixture of opium and alcohol", Kendal Black Drop was a favourite tipple of the poets Samuel Taylor Coleridge and Thomas de Quincey.

Kendal's excellent sporting facilities include the **Kendal Leisure Centre**, which offers a one-week "tourist pass", **Kendal Wall**, which is one of the highest indoor climbing facilities in the country, an artificial ski slope, 3 local golf courses and a driving range. Drama, music and the visual arts are presented in a regularly changing programme of exhibitions, live music, theatre productions and craft workshops at the **Brewery Arts Centre**. The Centre also houses Kendal's cinema which presents a mixture of mainstream, classic and art house films.

A number of interesting museums and galleries are also located in Kendal. The **Museum of Lakeland Life and Industry** which is themed around traditional rural trades of the region, **Abbot Hall Art Gallery** forming part of a complex within Abbot Hall park and **The Museum of Natural History and Archaeology**, founded in 1796 and one of the oldest museums in the country (see panel on page 8).

Adjacent to the elegant Georgian Abbot Hall is the 13th century **Parish Church of Kendal**, one of the widest in England, with five aisles and a peel of 10 bells. The church also contains a sword thought to have belonged to Robert Philipson, a Cavalier during the Civil War. Whilst away fighting in Carlisle, Cromwell's supporters laid siege to Philipson's house at Windermere. On his return, the Cavalier attacked the Kendal church when he thought the Roundheads would be at prayer. Riding his horse right into the church, he found it empty save for one innocent man whom he ran through with this very sword.

Perhaps the most unusual attraction in Kendal is the **Quaker Tapestry Exhibition** at the Friends Meeting House in the centre of the town. This unique exhibition of 77 panels of community embroidery explores Quaker history from the 17th century to the present day. These colourful, beautifully crafted tapestries are the work of some 4000 people, aged between 4 and 90, from 15 countries. A Quaker Costume Display, embroidery demonstrations, workshops and courses, and a large screen colour video combine to provide a fascinating insight into the Quaker movement and its development.

AROUND KENDAL

LEVENS
5 miles S of Kendal off the A590

Situated at the southern tip of Scout Scar, overlooking the Lyth Valley and the lower reaches of the River Kent, is **Levens Hall** and its unique topiary gardens. The superb Elizabethan mansion, (*"one of the wonders of Lakeland"*), developed from a 14th century pele tower and the garden was first laid out in 1694. They were the work of Colonel James Grahme, a keen

Topiary, Levens Hall Gardens

spread quickly and ever since they have been a popular attraction. Today, there are more 90 individual pieces, some almost 20ft (9m) high, with the ancient yew trees cut into often surreal shapes.

The interior of the house is equally rewarding - a wealth of period furniture, fine panelling and plasterwork, a dining room with walls covered in goats' leather, and

gardener, who purchased the hall in 1688 and employed a Frenchman, Guillaume Beaumont, to create the artful topiary work. (Beaumont also redesigned the gardens at Hampton Court for James II). The fame of the Levens Hall gardens

paintings by Rubens, Lely and Cuyp. The Hall is said to be haunted by three ghosts: a black dog, a lady in pink, and a gypsy woman who, legend has it, put a curse on the family saying that they would have no heir until the River Kent ceased to flow

THE GILPIN BRIDGE INN

Bridge End, Levens, nr Kendal,
Cumbria LA8 8EP
Tel: 015395 52206
Fax: 015395 52444

It was a Crusader knight, Sir Richard de Gylpin, who gave his name to the nearby river and to **The Gilpin Bridge Inn**, a charming old hostelry offering top quality food, drink and accommodation. The inn is owned by Frederick Robinson's Brewery of Stockport.

Food is available every lunchtime and evening with sandwiches and snacks served only at lunchtime. The appetising menu offers a good choice that ranges from hearty steaks, main course dishes such as the chef's Own Steak & Mushroom Pie, through vegetarian and fish dishes. There are special meals for children, or they can have a half portion of the adult meals, and the regular menu is supplemented by a choice of daily specials listed on the chalkboards. A selection of hot and cold desserts is listed on a separate menu, as well as a full A La Carte menu in the restaurant. At weekends, it is strongly advisable to book if you want to The inn is open all day during the season, with food served from 11am to 9pm, and for real ale lovers there's always a choice of two of them on tap along with draught lagers, a draught cider, Guinness extra cold and much more.

With the Lake District and the Yorkshire Dales National Parks both within easy reach, Levens provides an ideal base and the Gilpin Bridge Inn has 10 attractively furnished guest bedrooms, (7 doubles, 3 twins), all of them en suite.

and a white fawn was born in the park. In fact, after many years without a direct heir, in 1896 the River Kent froze over, a white fawn was seen, and a son and heir was born. A major location for the BBC-TV serial Wives and Daughters, the Hall's other attractions include a collection of working steam engines, a tea room, gift shop and plant centre.

Only a couple of miles north of Levens Hall, just off the A591, is another stately old residence, **Sizergh Castle**, the impressive home of the Strickland family since 1239 although the property is now administered by the National Trust. Originally a pele tower built to withstand border raiders, the house has been added to and altered over the intervening centuries to provide the family, as times became less violent, with a more comfortable home. Now boasting intricately carved chimney mantels, fine oak panelling, and a

collection of portraits of the Stuart royal family, the castle offers an additional "attraction" in the form of the ghost of a medieval lady. She is said to haunt the castle, screaming to be released from the room in which she had been locked by her fiercely jealous husband. It was here that she starved to death whilst he was away in battle. More reliable attractions at Sizergh are the well laid out gardens and 1500 acres of grounds which provide superb views over the Lakeland fells.

BRIGSTEER
3 miles SW of Kendal off A591

This tiny hamlet lies under the limestone escarpment of Scout Scar. From this pretty settlement, the road leads into the National Trust property of Brigsteer Wood where, as the climate is milder here due to its sheltered position, there are fine early flowers in the spring.

BARROWFIELD FARM

Brigsteer, nr Kendal,
Cumbria LA8 8BJ
Tel: 015395 68336

Farmhouse holidays continue to grow in popularity and for those who stay at **Barrowfield Farm**, only a ten minute drive from Kendal, it's easy to understand why. Dating back to the 1600s, the charming farmhouse is set within a 200-acre dairy and sheep farm and surrounded by many more thousands of acres of unspoilt countryside and woodland.

Barrowfield Farm is the home of Barbara and Richard Gardner who have been welcoming bed & breakfast guests here for some 14 years. And before that, Barbara's mother-in-law was doing the same. There are 3 guest bedrooms, (1 family, 1 double, 1 twin), all spacious, well decorated and furnished, and with wash basins. The rooms share a large bathroom and a separate toilet. Guests have the use of a comfortable lounge where there's a a welcoming real fire and television. A hearty Cumbrian farmhouse breakfast is included in the tariff and there are a good number of eating places locally. Children are welcome. Holiday-makers will find that there's plenty to do and see in the neighbourhood. A footpath from the farm leads up to Scout Scar from whose summit one of the finest panoramas in Lakeland can be enjoyed, while a short drive will bring you to Levens Hall with its famous topiary garden and the National Trust property of Sizergh Castle, noted for its magnificent Great Hall of 1450 and its lovely gardens.

The Punch Bowl

Underbarrow, Kendal,
Cumbria LA8 8HQ
Tel: 01539 568234
e-mail: punchbowl@kencomp.net

Not many hostelries have a history that includes being "modernised" in 1739 but **The Punch Bowl** inn at Underbarrow had been established here for at least a hundred years before that particular refurbishment. The tavern stands on the old packhorse route from Kendal to Ulverston which at that time was a deep sea port. In those days of horse-drawn traffic the Punch Bowl's landlord was also the village blacksmith, a sensible combination of trades which provided food, lodging and other services for both man and beast at the same spot.

This delightful inn has been owned by David Howarth, a former Merchant Navy officer, since 1988 and, amongst other achievements during this time, his real ales have been rated the "Best Pint in the Northwest" by the *Daily Telegraph*. Bass is always on tap, along with two rotating guest ales. The inn is also renowned for its quality food, based on fresh local produce and available every lunchtime and evening except Tuesday lunchtimes during the winter. The comprehensive menu of home cooked dishes is supplemented by daily specials. Children are welcome here, so too are dogs if they are on a lead. For special occasions, the Punch Bowl has an upstairs function room which can seat up to 60 guests and if you are planning to stay here, at the "Gateway to the Lakes", there is comfortable accommodation available in static caravans on a field adjacent to the inn.

High Gregg Hall Farm

Underbarrow, Kendal, Cumbria LA8 8BL
Tel: 015395 68318

Set in magnificent countryside only 5 miles from Kendal, **High Gregg Hall Farm** offers traditional Cumbrian hospitality to its bed & breakfast guests. The house stands on a working 100-acre beef and sheep farm and is the home of Alan and Cicely Simpson who have been providing bed & breakfast accommodation here for some 40 years! The farmhouse dates back to the late 1500s-early 1600s and has just 2 cosy and comfortable guest bedrooms, a double and a twin, with an adjoining bathroom. A truly hearty farmhouse breakfast is included in the tariff and packed lunches are available if required.

The Simpsons do not provide evening meals but close by is the local pub, The Punch Bowl, which

is also featured in this book. Rooms at High Gregg Hall Farm are available from April to October and the farm's location makes it a very convenient base for exploring both the Lake District and the Yorkshire Dales National Park which lies just a few miles to the east. Not to be missed if you are staying here is the spectacular viewpoint from the limestone escarpment of Scout Scar, about a mile and a half from High Gregg Hall Farm.

BURNESIDE
2 miles N of Kendal off the A591

There has been a settlement here since the Stone Age and the remains of a stone circle can be seen close by on Potter Fell. By the 15th century Burneside was a settled agricultural area and a rich variety of mills sprang up along the River Sprint - fulling, corn, cotton, wool, bobbin, and the original rag paper mill at Cowan Head.

The River Sprint, which meets the River Kent just south of the village, has its own remarkably beautiful Longsleddale Valley which curves past Garnett Bridge deep into the high fell country. A bridle path climbs from the head of the valley into Kentmere, another spectacularly beautiful walk.

GRAYRIGG
5 miles NE of Kendal on the A685

This is a fine village with a cluster of alms houses, cottages, and a simple church found in a lovely rural setting. It was the birthplace of Francis Howgill (1610-69) who was responsible for introducing George Fox to the Westmorland Seekers, a group of radical Christians from the area. It was this meeting that led directly to the establishment of the Quaker Movement.

SEDBERGH

In 1974 Sedbergh was brusquely removed from the West Riding of Yorkshire and became part of Cumbria. However, it still lies within the Yorkshire Dales National Park and the surrounding scenery certainly belongs to the Dales with the mighty **Howgill Hills** - great pear-shaped drumlins shaped by glaciers - soaring to more than 2200ft (670m). **Winder Hill**, which provides a dramatic backdrop to the little market town, is half that height, but with its sleek grassy flanks and domed top, seems much loftier. Four valleys and

HIGH SWINKLEBANK FARM

Longsleddale, nr Kendal,
Cumbria LA8 9BD
Tel: 01539 823682

Rather surprisingly, Longsleddale provided the inspiration for the rural scenes in John Cunliffe's *Postman Pat* stories. This beautiful dale provides some glorious walking and from the fell tops there are superb views into 7 different valleys.

Located near the head of the dale, **High Swinklebank Farm** is a working hill sheep farm offering quality self-catering accom-

modation in an attractively converted stone barn. The cottage is completely self-contained and can sleep up to 4 guests, plus a cot. On the ground floor, there's a living room with colour TV, and a well-fitted kitchen with fridge, microwave, spin drier, toaster, electric cooker along with a full complement of crockery and cooking utensils. Upstairs there are 2 bedrooms - 1 double and one with 3ft bunk beds, also a shower room with electric shower and heater. All bed linen and towels are provided and a travel cot is available if required. Electricity is supplied by a 50p coin meter. Outside, there's a pleasant garden in front of the cottage, with tables and chairs, and also ample parking. Children are very welcome here and a dog is acceptable by arrangement. Quiet and secluded though it is, the farm is only 4 miles from the old market town of Kendal, the main lakes are all within easy driving distance, and both the Yorkshire Dales and the Scottish Borders are only a little further away.

four mountain streams meet here and for centuries Sedbergh (pronounced Sedber) has been an important centre for cross-Pennine travellers. During the golden age of stage coach travel, the town became a staging post on the route between Lancaster and Newcastle-upon-Tyne. The complete journey between Lancaster and Newcastle took from 4 o'clock in the morning to 7 o'clock at night: fifteen hours to cover a distance of about 120 miles, an average speed of 8mph. At the King's Arms hotel, the four horses would be swiftly changed before the equipage rattled off again across the moors to Teesdale, Durham and Newcastle.

In those days, the stage-coach would have been used frequently by the boys attending Sedbergh's famous **Public School**. Its founder was Roger Lupton, a Howgill boy who rose to become Provost of Eton: he established the school because he felt that one was desperately needed *"in the north country amongst the people rude in knowledge"*. In later years, Wordsworth's son studied here and Coleridge's son, Hartley, became a master. The school's extensive grounds, through which visitors are welcome to wander, seem to place the olde-worlde town within a park.

That impression is reinforced if you follow the path beside the River Rawthay to Brigflatts where you'll find the **Quaker Meeting House** built in 1670 and the oldest in the north of England. This area is filled with Quaker history and Firbank Knott, on nearby Firbank Fell, can be said to be the birthplace of Quakerism for it was here, in 1652, that the visionary George Fox gave his great sermon to inspire over a thousand "seekers" from the whole of the north of England. This meeting was to lead to the development of the Quaker Movement. The simple boulder on the fell, from which Fox delivered his momentous words, is

marked by a plaque and is now known as **Fox's Pulpit**.

Sedbergh seems a very friendly town. At **St Andrew's Church**, for example, Protestants and Roman Catholics take turns to use the building for their own services, an arrangement believed to be unique in England.

Much of the heart of the town has been deemed a Conservation Area and fortunately many of the older buildings have survived. In particular, the stone-built cottages on both sides of the cobbled yard, known as **The Folly**, just off Main Street, have not only survived unscathed but remain dwellings and have not had the misfortune to be converted to other uses.

To the east of the town, on a small wooded hill top, lies **Castlehaw**, the remains of an ancient motte and bailey castle. Built by the Normans in the 11th century, the castle guarded the valleys of the River Rawthey and the River Lune against the marauding Scots.

AROUND SEDBURGH

BRIGFLATTS
2 miles S of Sedbergh off the A683

Close to where George Fox stayed overnight with his friend Richard Robinson is the oldest Quaker Meeting House in the north of England. Built in 1675, and still with its original oak interior, this beautiful, simple building has changed little over the years.

DENT
4 miles SE of Sedbergh off the A684

This charming village, the only one in Dentdale - one of Cumbria's finest dales - has a delightful cobbled main street with tall cottages lining the road. Visitors to

Sedgwick Memorial Fountain, Dent

Cambridge University and also a friend of Queen Victoria and Prince Albert. The fountain of pinkish Shap granite in the village centre is Dent's memorial to this great geologist.

The little valley of Dentdale winds from the village up past old farms and hamlets to **Lea Yeat** where a steep lane hairpins up to **Dent Station**, almost five miles from the village. This is a marvellous place to begin a ramble into Dentdale or over the Whernside. Dent is the highest railway station in Britain, over 1,100 feet above sea level, and it lies on the famous Settle-Carlisle railway line.

this tranquil place will find it hard to believe that, in the 18th century, Dent was of greater importance than nearby Sedbergh. The impressive **St Andrew's Church** is Norman in origin though it underwent an almost complete rebuilding in the early 15th century. Inside can not only be seen the Jacobean three-decker pulpit that is still in use but also the local marble which paves the chancel.

Farming has, for many years, dominated the local economy but knitting, particularly in the village, has too played an important part. During the 17th and 18th centuries, the women and children, on whom this work fell, became known as the "Terrible Knitters of Dent" which, today, sounds uncomplimentary but the local use of the word terrible meant quite the opposite. Large amounts of dressed wool were turned by the knitters into stockings and gloves which were then exported out of the dale to local towns.

Dent's most famous son is undoubtedly the "Father of Geology", Adam Sedgwick. Born the son of the local vicar in 1785, Sedgwick went on to become the Woodwardian Professor of Geology at

GARSDALE
5 miles E of Sedbergh on the A683

Lying just north of Dentdale, Garsdale is both a dale and a village and they are overlooked by the dramatic Baugh Fell. The River Clough follows down the dale from **Garsdale Head**, the watershed into Wensleydale, where a row of Midland Railway cottages lies alongside the former junction station on the Settle-Carlisle line. This is now a surprisingly busy little place during the summer months when preserved steam locomotives pause to take water from a moorland spring.

CAUTLEY
3 miles NE of Sedbergh on the A683

This quiet village is situated on a stunning stretch of road which, for a couple of miles, follows the River Rawthey and is one of those beautiful routes through the high fells that only a few people find. To the west of the road loom the **Howgill Fells**, a series of magnificent, open hills and ancient common land, which provide some of the most spectacular countryside in the north of England for the dedicated hill walker. Several tracks and old greenways lead across them. The most spectacular feature of the Howgills is **Cautley Crag**, a great cliff several hundred feet high, alongside which a beautiful narrow waterfall, **Cautley Spout**, tumbles. For campers and walkers this area is a perfect place to be based for a holiday, surrounded on all sides by the best English walking country, with the Lake District and the Yorkshire Dales National Parks to choose from.

2 Around Windermere and Ambleside

Windermere Lake, Bowness-on-Windermere

This southeastern corner of the Lake District National Park is Cumbria's best known and most popular area, with the main resort towns of Windermere, Bowness-on-Windermere, and Ambleside and, of course, Lake Windermere itself. They are certainly busy with tourists during the summer months but their charm and attraction remains for all to see. Also, with the unpredictability of Lakeland weather, they provide a whole host of indoor amusements which can be an advantage.

The whole area opened up to tourism as a result of the Victorians growing interest in the natural landscape and their engineering ability in providing a railway service. So these villages, once little more than places where the fell farmers congregated to buy and sell their livestock and exchange gossip, have grown into inland resorts with fine Victorian and Edwardian villas, houses, and municipal buildings.

Elterwater

There are, also, many beautiful places close to the bustling and crowded towns that provide solitude. To the southeast lies Cartmel Fell while further north is isolated Kentmere.

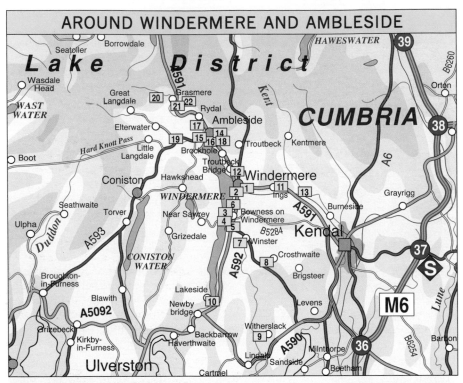

© MAPS IN MINUTES ™ (1999)

PLACES TO STAY, EAT, DRINK AND SHOP

Sunset over Windermere

WINDERMERE

Birthwaite village no longer features on any map, thanks to the Kendal and Windermere Railway Company which built a branch line to it in 1847. With an eye on tourist traffic, and considering the name Birthwaite had little appeal, they named the station "Windermere" even though the lake is over a mile distant. In the early days carriages and, in later years, buses linked the station with the landing stages in the village of Bowness on the shores of the lake. As the village burgeoned into a prosperous Victorian resort, it became popularly, and then officially, known by the name of its station, while Windermere water was given the redundant prefix of Lake.

The Victorian heritage still predominates in the many large houses here, originally built as country retreats for Manchester businessmen - the railway made it possible for them to reach this idyllic countryside in just over two hours. Hotels, boarding houses, comfortable

PINETHWAITE

Lickbarrow Road, Windermere, Cumbria LA23 2NQ
Tel: 015394 44558 Fax: 015394 44556
e-mail: legge@pinethwaite.freeserve.co.uk
website: www.pinecottages.co.uk

Only a mile from Windermere and Bowness villages, **Pinethwaite** is a quite unique holiday venue with cottages, apartments and a house set in 10 acres of natural woodland in the heart of the country. The enterprise was started some 30 years ago by the Legge family who still live here and are always on hand to suggest places to visit, recommend walks to suit your particular wishes and can also provide a list of their favourite local pubs. Inspected annually by the Cumbria Tourist Board, all of the accommodation is of 3 Star standard. Each is totally self-contained, attractively furnished and decorated and comprehensively equipped for between 2 and 7 people. Pinethwaite has plenty of parking for cars and boats and has a launderette and a sauna which may be booked for private sessions. The extensive grounds provide an idyllic environment and are a haven for wildlife, including red squirrels and roe deer.

Nearby is a farm little changed in a hundred years and the surrounding fellside has a network of footpaths with stunning mountain views. The resident owners are local guides and can arrange a variety of outdoor activities, including riding, sailing and even para-gliding. For a small fee, guests may use the swimming pool, spa, squash and badminton courts, sun beds and bar at the nearby Parklands Country Club. In a nutshell, Pinethwaite is in a secluded location, yet close to village facilities and only 20 minutes drive from the M6.

villas and shops sprang up around the station and spread rapidly down the hill towards the lake until Birthwaite and Bowness were linked together.

Windermere's railway is still operating, albeit now as a single track branch line. **The Lakes Line** is now the only surviving Railtrack line to run into the heart of the Lake District. Modern diesel railcars provide a busy shuttle service to and from the main line at Oxenholme. The route, through Kendal, Burneside and Staveley, is a delight and provides a very pleasant alternative to the often crowded A591.

Within a few yards of Windermere Station, just across the busy main road, is a footpath that leads through the woods to one of the finest viewpoints in Lakeland, **Orrest Head**. This spectacular vantage point provides a 360° panoramic view that takes in the ten mile length of Windermere, the Cumbrian hills and even the fells of the Yorkshire Pennines. In a region where glorious views open up at

THE WOODLANDS HOTEL

New Road, Windermere, Cumbria LA23 2EE
Tel: 015394 43915

A handsome Edwardian villa located on the peaceful side of the village, **The Woodlands Hotel** offers guests comfortable bed and breakfast accommodation in truly charming surroundings. The owners, Ann and John, are a friendly and welcoming couple who arrived here in September 2000 and have refurbished the hotel to a very high standard. The 15 guest rooms, (14 of them en suite, the other with a private bathroom), include a choice of single, double and twin rooms, with 2 of them located on the ground floor.

All rooms are well equipped with colour television, radio alarm clocks, hairdryer and

tea/coffee-making facilities. Two of the rooms have 4-poster beds and, if you really want to impress, flowers and/or champagne can be waiting for you in the room. A family room is also available but please note that Woodlands does not have the facilities for catering to children under 5. There's a bar and residents' lounge where you can relax with a drink, and breakfast is served in the light and airy dining room with its large windows overlooking the garden. Woodlands is open all year round and special midweek breaks are available. There's ample off road parking and credit cards are accepted.

The hotel is ideally located for visiting the many attractions of this glorious area. It's just a short walk to Bowness and the host of activities on Lake Windermere where you can also take a trip on the famous old steamboat and visit the Steamboat Museum. The World of Beatrix Potter is a popular visitor attraction and a vehicle ferry will take you across the lake to the famous writer's home at Near Sawrey. Woodlands Hotel is also close to the National Park Visitor Centre at Brockhole, the Wordsworth Museum at Grasmere and, in whichever direction you travel from Windermere you are surrounded by some of the most spectacular scenery in England.

every turn, the vista from Orrest Head remains exceptional. In Victorian times, visitors wandered through such ravishing scenery carrying, not cameras, but small, tinted mirrors mounted in elaborate frames. Arriving at a picturesque spot, they placed themselves with their back to the view, held the mirrors above them and so observed the view framed as in a painting. The image they saw recalled the romantic landscapes of Claude Lorraine: the mirrors accordingly were known as *"Claude glasses"*.

Remembrance Drinking Fountain, Bowness-on-Windermere

AROUND WINDERMERE

BOWNESS-ON-WINDERMERE
2 miles S of Windermere on the A592

It is from this attractive, if busy, town right on the edge of Windermere that most of the lake cruises operate. Lasting between 45 and 90 minutes, the cruises operate daily and provide connections to the **Lake District Visitor Centre** at Brockhole, the **Lakeside & Haverthwaite Steam Railway** and the **Fell Foot Country Park**. There are evening wine/champagne cruises during the summer months, and rowing boats and self drive

motor boats are also available for hire all year round.

Not only is **Windermere** the largest lake in Cumbria but it is, at 11 miles long, the largest in England. Formed in the Ice Age by the action of moving glaciers, the lake is fed by the Rivers Brathay and Rothay, at the northern end, whilst the outlet is into the River Leven, at Newby Bridge. Windermere is actually a public highway or, more correctly, waterway and this stretch of water, with its thickly wooded banks and scattered islands, has been used since Roman times as a means of transport. Roman Legionnaires used it for carrying stone to their fort at Galava, near present day Ambleside, at the head of the lake. Later, the monks of Furness Abbey fished here for pike and char. The

BLACKWELL
Bowness-on-Windermere, Cumbria LA23 3JR
Tel: 01539 722464 Fax: 01539 722494
e-mail: info@blackwell.org.uk website: www.blackwell.org.uk

Located about a mile and a half south of Bowness, and occupying a superb position overlooking Lake Windermere and the Coniston fells, **Blackwell** is a treasure trove of the Arts and Crafts movement. Completed in 1900, the house was the work of the architect M.H. Baillie Scott who designed every last detail of this outstanding house, creating a symphony of art nouveau stained glass, oak panelling, intricate plasterwork and fanciful metalwork. As well as being a perfect work of art in itself, Blackwell provides the perfect setting for changing exhibitions of the highest quality applied arts and crafts. Other attractions here include a licensed restaurant with an outdoor terrace and a book & gift shop.

STORRS GATE HOUSE

Longtail Hill, Bowness-on-Windermere,
Cumbria LA23 3JD
Tel: 015394 43272
e-mail: enquiries@storrsgatehouse.co.uk
website: www.storrsgatehouse.co.uk

One of the many delights for bed & breakfast guests at **Storrs Gate House** is the delightful decor. Throughout the house there are exquisite hand-sewn furnishings, picture and china collections, together creating an ambience of Olde Worlde charm. The framed cross-stitching and tapestries are the work of Shirley Byrne who, together with her husband Vince, runs this welcoming guest house located on the fringes of the old village.

Built in 1896 and standing in its own quiet and secluded gardens, Storrs Gate is only minutes from Lake Windermere, close to the Marina and only a stone's throw from the Hawkshead ferry. Guests can stay on either a bed & breakfast, or dinner, bed & breakfast basis but, as one satisfied diner wrote in the Visitors' Book: "Eat out and miss out!". The delicious 4-course dinners are prepared from fresh local ingredients, vegetables and herbs from the Byrnes' garden, and complemented by a selection of wines at reasonable prices. At breakfast time the wide choice includes free range eggs and Shirley's home made jams and marmalade. With just 4 guest bedrooms, Shirley and Vince are able to offer a personal service appropriate to the high level of comfort. All the rooms have colour TV, hospitality trays, en suite or private facilities, and all overlook the gardens. One of the rooms boasts a splendid king size four-poster bed. This outstanding establishment, which is entirely non-smoking, enjoys a 4-Diamond rating from the English Tourism Council, welcomes children over 8 but regrets it cannot accommodate pets other than guide dogs.

THE SHIP INN

Glebe Road, Bowness-on-Windermere,
Cumbria LA23 3HE
Tel: 015394 45001 Fax: 015394 45983
e-mail: theshipinn@bownessbay.com

Occupying a superb position on the shores of Lake Windermere, **The Ship Inn** is a popular and lively hostelry with a reputation for serving excellent food and well-maintained ales. A mere 20 years or so ago on this site, there was only a wooden hut selling cups of tea. Then in 1981 Ian Wilson and his brother Kevin had a stylish, 3-storey restaurant built here which they named The Quarterdeck Restaurant. A few years later, when they acquired a full licence, the building became The Ship Inn.

The inn is open all day, every day, serving a wide range of quality beers which includes a minimum of 3 real ales,

(Theakstons, Courage Directors and Jennings), along with draught keg bitters, stout, lagers and cider. A menu of wholesome and appetising food is available throughout the day, from 11.30am until 10pm. Children are welcome and there are non-smoking areas. During the season, Ian and Kevin lay on live entertainment. Late in the evening the third floor rooms serve as a night club from 10pm until 2am, Monday to Saturday. The Ship doesn't have guest rooms of its own but has a close liaison with local guest houses and hotels and staff will be happy to arrange suitable accommodation for you.

Windermere, Bowness-on-Windermere

on another campaign. In 1774, the island was bought by a Mr English who constructed the round house which, at the time, caused such consternation that he sold the property and the island to Isabella Curwen, who planted the surrounding trees.

Fishermen, too, find great enjoyment practising their skills on this well-stocked lake. Once considered a great delicacy in the 17th and 18th centuries, the char, a deep-water trout, is still found here though catching it is a special art.

name Windermere, however, comes from Viking times and is derived from Vinand's Mere, Vinand being the name of a Nordic chief.

Across from Bowness, the lake is almost divided in two by **Belle Island** which is believed to have been inhabited by the Romans. During the Civil War, it was owned by Colonel Phillipson (the Royalist supporter who disgraced himself by riding into Kendal Parish Church) and his family had to withstand an 80 day siege, successfully, whilst the colonel was away

Away from the marinas and car parks is the old village where **St Martin's Church** is of particular interest. It has a magnificent east window filled with 14th and 15th century glass, and an unusual 300-year-old carved wooden figure of St Martin depicted sharing his cloak with a beggar.

On the lake shore just to the north of the village is the **Windermere Steamboat Museum**. The Museum grounds also includes a model boat pond, shop, tea room, picnic area, a self-catering flat for 2 persons, and free parking (see panel below).

WINDERMERE STEAMBOAT MUSEUM

Rayrigg Road, Windermere, Cumbria LA23 1BN
Tel: 01539 445565

On the lake shore just to the north of the village is the **Windermere Steamboat Museum**, a unique collection of Victorian and Edwardian steam launches which includes the *SL Dolly*, the oldest mechanically powered boat in the world. *Dolly* celebrated her 150th birthday in 2000 and still has her original engine in working order despite its having lain on the bed of Ullswater for more than 60 years before being recovered. Guided tours of the museum are available and also around the Esperance, the inspiration for Captain Flint's boat in Arthur Ransome's Swallows and Amazons. Some of the launches are still in working order and occasional cruises in one of these wonderful vintage craft are possible. Private charters of an Edwardian steam launch for up to 12 passengers can also be arranged, with catering provided if required. The Museum grounds also includes a model boat pond, shop, tea room, picnic area, a self-catering flat for 2 persons, and free parking.

THE BROWN HORSE

Winster, nr Bowness-on-Windermere,
Cumbria LA23 3NR
Tel: 015394 43443
website: www.brownhorse.com

For many years **The Brown Horse** has
been the focal point of this picturesque
village and until the beginning of the
20th century it was in its large upstairs
room that many of the local dances and
social events were held. In particular,
there was the Auld Wife's Aik, a much
anticipated social event at which
everyone did a turn - singing, dancing
or reciting, and the bar stayed open all
night.

Today, this free house is still a popular local meeting place and the owners, Cath and Ric Musetti,
with the help and experience of Ric's father, Mario, ensure that the tradition continues. Well known
for the excellent range of well-kept real ales that are on offer in the bar, the Brown Horse has also
gained a fine reputation for the delicious and rather different menu that is sure to excite even the
most jaded palate. The inn was one of the first pubs to begin serving basket meals back in the 1960s
but things have certainly moved on since then. The unusual and exotic dishes served here would put
a lot of restaurants to shame. The recently completed new restaurant, which has level access from the
car park, has seating for 60 diners, while the non-smoking Winster Room upstairs can accommodate
another 50 guests. Children are welcome at this warm and friendly inn and, with an outside patio
where visitors can sit and enjoy the sunshine, this is a great place for all the family.

THE PUNCH BOWL INN

Crosthwaite, nr Kendal,
Cumbria LA8 8HR
Tel: 015395 68237 Fax: 015395 68875
e-mail: enquiries@punchbowl.fsnet.co.uk
website: www.punchbowl.fsnet.co.uk

In the half-dozen years since Steven and
Marjorie Doherty took over **The Punch
Bowl Inn** they have been showered with
awards. "Cumbria's Dining Pub of the
Year"; "Lake District Pub of the Year", two
AA rosettes and a "Red Bib" from the
Michelin Guide are just some of them.
Steven arrived at The Punch Bowl to
continue a glittering career that has
included working as a Commis Chef at Albert Roux's Le Gavroche where he later became Head Chef,
then Group Executive Chef for Roux Restaurants, finally closing his association with the legendary
chef by opening The Grand Hotel in Amsterdam.

He and his wife Marjorie now devote their attentions to providing outstanding cuisine at this
charming 16th century inn just across from the village church. Food is available every lunchtime and
evening, (except Sunday evenings and all day Monday during the winter), and despite Steven's fame
the prices remain eminently reasonable - a 3 course lunch for around £11 for example, and a main
dinner course costing about the same. Meals are served throughout the pub which seats 60 but booking
ahead is strongly recommended. The inn's lovely location, just a few minutes drive from Lake
Windermere, makes this an excellent place to stay. The Punch Bowl has 3 double rooms, all en suite
and guests can stay on either a bed & breakfast, or dinner, bed & breakfast basis.

Just down the road from the Steamboat Museum is the Old Laundry Visitor Centre, the home of **The World of Beatrix Potter**, one of the top ten most popular visitor attractions in the country. Here visitors can enjoy fascinating recreations of the Lakeland author's books, complete with the sounds, sights and even smells of the countryside. Open all year, the complex also includes the Tailor of Gloucester Tea Room and the Beatrix Potter shop.

A little further south, just past the steamer piers, **Amazonia, World of Reptiles** contains a wonderful collection of creepy crawlies, some of which are for sale. Boa constrictors, an 8ft Nile alligator, a deadly puff adder are just some of the residents, along with tarantulas and a snapping turtle. Amazonia also offers an on site café and gift shop.

WINSTER
4 miles S of Windermere on the A5074

This charming hamlet has an old post office, originally built in the early 17th century as a cottage, that is much photographed. South from the village runs the Winster Valley which provided Wordsworth with one of his favourite walks. It was at **Low Ludderburn**, a couple of miles to the south, that Arthur Ransome settled in 1925 and here that he wrote his classic children's novel *Swallows and Amazons*. The house is still there but is not open to the public.

WITHERSLACK
9 miles S of Windermere off the A590

On the edge of the village is the **Latterbarrow Reserve** of the Cumbrian Wildlife Trust, a relatively small reserve that is home to some 200 species of flowering plant and fern. Butterflies and

The Derby Arms

Witherslack Village, South Lakes, Cumbria LA11 6RH
Tel: 015395 52207
e-mail: gregers@supanet.com

Dating back to the early 1800s, **The Derby Arms** is a charming country inn with a cosy, warm atmosphere. Open every session and all day Saturday and Sunday during the season, the inn serves a superb range of fine, traditional ales which includes 4 real ales and a good selection of draught keg bitters, lager and cider.

Tasty, home cooked food is available every lunchtime, (noon until 2pm), and evening (6pm to 9pm) with local produce such as Cumbrian fell-bred meats, Ullswater Trout and Cartmel Smoked Salmon featuring prominently on the menu. Meals can be enjoyed in the non-smoking restaurant while for smaller appetites snacks and light meals are served in the bar. Booking is strongly advised for Saturday evening and the traditional Sunday lunch. Comfortably furnished throughout and with open fires adding to the olde worlde atmosphere, the inn is not only the ideal place for a drink and a meal but music lovers will delight in the live musical entertainment every Saturday evening from 8.30pm, and quiz addicts should make sure they don't miss the Quiz Night, held every Thursday.

The Derby Arms is also a residential inn, offering guests a high standard of comfort in each of the 4 guest bedrooms, (2 family rooms en suite; 1 twin en suite; and 1 double standard room). The tariff includes a hearty Cumbrian breakfast. Children and pets are welcome, and all major credit cards are accepted apart from American Express.

birds, including the spotted flycatcher, are common amongst the plants that grow in the thin soil between the rocky outcrops. Further from the village is **Witherslack Hall**, once the summer residence of the Earls of Derby and now a school.

NEWBY BRIDGE
8 miles S of Windermere on the A592

The bridge here crosses the River Leven which runs from the southern tip of Windermere to Morecambe Bay. According to geologists, the mass of end moraines seen here show clearly that the village lay at the southernmost point of Windermere since they were deposited by the glacier whilst it paused having carved out the lake. Today, however, the village is some distance from the water's edge which can be reached on foot, by car, or by taking the steam train on the Lakeside and Haverthwaite Railway. As the village lies at the junction of two major south Cumbrian roads it is also a popular tourist destination.

To the north of the village, **Fell Foot Park** (NT) is a delightful 18-acre site of landscaped gardens and woodland laid out in late-Victorian times. Admission is free, (although there's a car parking charge), and the grounds include picnic areas, a children's adventure playground, a splendid rhododendron garden, a gift shop and a tea room with outside tables where you can watch the lake traffic and

also the steam trains chugging into Lakeside on the western bank. Rowing boats can be hired at the piers from which there are regular ferries across to Lakeside and pleasure cruises operate during the summer school holidays.

BACKBARROW
9 miles S of Windermere on the A592

This small village in the valley of the River Leven, which drains Windermere, was a hive of industry at one time. In 1711, the most ambitious iron furnace in Cumbria was built here and the remains can still be seen along with the relics of the heyday of water power in the village.

LAKESIDE
10 miles S of Windermere off the A590

Located at the southwestern tip of Windermere, Lakeside sits beneath gentle wooded hills. It's the northern terminus of the **Lakeside & Haverthwaite Railway**, a 4-mile route through the beautiful Leven valley which was once part of a line stretching to Ulverston and Barrow in Furness. Throughout the season, hard-working steam locomotives chug along the track, their departure times set to co-incide with boat arrivals from Bowness - a joint boat and train return ticket is available.

Nearby lies the **Aquarium of the Lakes** with shops, "Café at the Quay" and a

THE AQUARIUM OF THE LAKES

Lakeside, nr Ulverston, Cumbria LA12 8AS
Tel: 01539 530153

Nearby, the **Aquarium of the Lakes** boasts the largest collection of freshwater fish in the UK. A walk-through tunnel along a re-created lake bed provides great views of char, perch and diving ducks, whilst in the Morecambe Bay displays, visitors come face to face with sharks and rays from around the local coast. The mischievous otters are a special favourite with children and for the more earnest visitor there are educational displays

on anything from leeches to lobsters. "The Quay" shop stocks a good range of quality gifts and souvenirs, and the "Café at the Quay" offers light refreshments and a good view of the lake.

good view of the lake (see panel on page opposite).

A mile or so north of Lakeside, **Stott Park Bobbin Mill** (English Heritage) is a must for anyone interested in the area's industrial heritage. One of the best preserved in the country, it's a genuine working 19th century mill and stands in a lovely woodland setting. Visitors can join the inclusive 45-minute tour and browse over the informative exhibition.

INGS
3 miles E of Windermere off the A591

A pleasant little village set alongside the River Gowan, Ings owes its fine Georgian church and charming almshouses to a certain Robert Bateman who was born here in the late 1600s. Wordsworth commemorated Bateman in a rather pedestrian poem which recounts how the villagers made a collection so that the young boy could travel to London. He

prospered greatly, became a major ship owner and devoted a sizeable portion of his wealth to the benefit of his native village. Sadly, he never saw the completed church - less than a year after building began, he was murdered by Italian pirates.

TROUTBECK BRIDGE
1 mile N of Windermere on the A591

This small village in the valley of Trout Beck takes its name from the bridge here over the beck, just before the water runs into Windermere. During the 17th century, Calgarth Hall was owned by Myles Phillipson, a local JP who wished to gain possession of nearby farmland. So he invited the landowner and his wife to a banquet at the Hall and then, having hidden a silver cup in their luggage, accused them of stealing.

At the resulting trial, Phillipson was the presiding judge and he sentenced the

MEADOW CROFT COUNTRY HOTEL

Ings Village, Staveley, Cumbria LA8 9PY
Tel: 01539 821171

Located in the hamlet of Ings, only 10 miles from Exit 36 of the M6, **Meadow Croft Country Hotel** stands in an area of outstanding natural beauty with Windermere and its lake just a couple of miles to the west. Built in 1932 and extended in the 80s, Meadow Croft is stylishly and comfortably furnished and has a fully licensed lounge bar, a 40-seater restaurant offering the

very best of top quality local fare, and a residents' TV lounge where guests can sink into the luxurious Chesterfield settees.

There are 8 bedrooms, all with a very individual character and seven of them en suite. The eighth has its own private bath/shower room. All rooms are centrally heated and provided with complimentary tea/coffee-making facilities. At breakfast time, guests have the choice of either a hearty full Cumbrian

breakfast which will set you up for the day, or continental croissants. Children are welcome and guests can stay on either a bed & breakfast, or dinner, bed & breakfast basis.

Meadow Croft is owned and run by Ian and Rosalie Clenahan, a friendly and welcoming couple who do everything they can to ensure their guests have a relaxed and comfortable stay. They can guide to the many places of interest in the area and to the many activities available - from walking to water sports, bird watching to pony trekking, as well as fishing, cycling and climbing.

couple to death as well as appropriating their land. As she was led away, the wife placed a curse on the judge saying that not only would his victims never leave him but that his family would also perish in poverty. The couple were executed but their skulls reappeared at Calgarth Hall and, no matter what Phillipson did (including burning them and throwing them into Lake Windermere) the skulls kept returning to the Hall. Moreover, the Phillipson family grew poorer and poorer until, in 1705, the family died out altogether.

Just north of the village, the Royal Horticultural Society's 4-acre garden at **Holehird** (free, but donations welcome) contains a wide variety of habitats, ranging from rock and alpine gardens to rose gardens and shrubberies.

TROUTBECK
3 miles NE of Windermere off the A592

Designated a conservation area, Troutbeck has no recognisable centre as the houses and cottages are grouped around a number of wells and springs which, until recently, were the only form of water supply. Dating from the 16th, 17th, and 18th centuries, the houses retain many of their original features, including mullioned windows, heavy cylindrical chimneys, and, in some cases, exposed spinning galleries, and are of great interest to lovers of vernacular architecture. **Troutbeck Church**, too, is worthy of a visit as there is a fine east window, dating from 1873, that is the combined work of Edward Burne-Jones, Ford Maddox Brown, and William Morris.

However, perhaps the best known building at Troutbeck is **Townend** (NT), an enchanting example of Lake District

THE SUN HOTEL

Troutbeck Bridge, Windermere, Cumbria LA23 1HH
Tel: 015394 43274 Fax: 015394 47443

With its 3-storey tower and huge bay windows **The Sun Hotel** is an impressive-looking building which has a history going back some 300 years to the era when it was a busy coaching inn. Mine hosts Angela and Tony Wood took over here in late 2000 and in a very short space of time have restored the inn's flagging fortunes. They undertook a comprehensive programme of refurbishment and introduced an appetising menu which is available every weekday lunchtime (noon until 2.30pm) and evening (6pm to 8.30pm), and from noon until 8pm on Saturday and Sunday.

The Sun is also well known for its quality ales which include 4 real ales, (Tetleys, Marston Pedigree

and Castle Eden, plus a guest brew), and a good range of draught keg bitters, stout, lagers and cider.

The inn has 11 guest bedrooms, (more than half of which are currently en suite with more to follow), and guests are welcome on either a bed & breakfast or dinner, bed & breakfast basis.

From the summer of 2001, The Sun offers another amenity for its guests. Angela's brother, Malcolm Brown, is a master fisherman and he will be looking after the inn's private beach and fishing expeditions.

Troutbeck Village

KENTMERE
8 miles NE of Windermere off the A591

This hamlet, as its name implies, lies in part of the valley that was once a lake; drained to provide precious bottom pasture land. A large mill pond remains to provide a head of water on the River Kent for use at a paper mill. Inside **St Cuthbert's Church** is a bronze memorial to Bernard Gilpin who was born at Kentmere Hall in 1517 and went on to become Archdeacon of Durham Cathedral. Known as The Apostle of the North, Gilpin was also a leader of the Reformation and, in 1558, he travelled to London to face charges of heresy against the Roman Catholic Church. During the journey, Gilpin fell and broke his leg but, fortunately, whilst he was recovering Catholic Queen Mary died and was succeeded by Protestant Queen Elizabeth. The new queen restored him to favour and saved Gilpin from being burnt at the stake.

vernacular architecture. Built in 1626 it contains some fine carved woodwork, books, furniture and domestic implements collected by the Browne family, wealthy farmers who lived here for more than 300 years until 1944. Open from April to October, the house runs a regular "living history" programme, so if you visit on a Thursday you can meet Mr George Browne - circa 1900.

The beautiful valley of the River Kent is best explored on foot. A public footpath runs up its western side, past **Kentmere Hall**, a fortified pele tower that is now a private farmhouse. Following the river southwards, the **Dales Way** runs down into Kendal and on into the Yorkshire Dales.

Long Green Head Farm, Troutbeck

WILF'S CAFÉ

Mill Yard, Back Lane, Staveley,
Cumbria LA8 7HG
Tel: 01539 822329
e-mail: food@wilfs-cafe.co.uk
website: www.wilfs-cafe.co.uk

Housed in a former wood mill, **Wilf's Café** offers outstanding food in unusual surroundings. In good weather, customers can enjoy their refreshments on the wooden deck outside which overlooks the weir on the River Kent and the old salmon trap. Inside, some of the old mill machinery is still in place while the attractive pine tables and chairs were made at this very mill which now houses a number of interesting small businesses.

One of them provides fresh bread daily for the café. 'Wilf' is actually the school days' nickname of Iain Williamson who runs the café with his business partner Charlotte Webb. Their wholesome and appetising menu starts with a choice of 3 hearty breakfasts, (one of them vegetarian), and includes Wilf's famous Veggie Chilli, a variety of Rarebits, jacket potatoes, salads and home made cakes. The café is open every day from 10am to 5pm but there are regular speciality evenings, (French, Mexican, for example). Also popular are the "slide and supper" evenings held during the winter months when guest speakers give a talk on a wide range of subjects. Since 1991, when Wilf's catered for an Orienteering event in Eskdale, Wilf and Charlotte have catered at a variety of events although Orienteering (including 3 Mountain Marathon events) and Mountain Bike challenges remain the backbone of their outside catering business.

STAMPERS

The Old Stamp House,
Church Street, Ambleside,
Cumbria LA22 0BU
Tel: 015394 32775

As the address indicates, **Stampers** restaurant occupies Ambleside's former Stamp House, a Grade III listed building which still has its original beams, slate floor and walls 4 feet thick. The restaurant is actually in the cellar of the attractive old building, a cosy ambience with tables and chairs of warm-coloured pine.

Stampers has been owned and run by Heather Tennant since 1984, ably assisted since 1995 by her "right hand man", Geoff Jones. Heather is the chef, offering a menu of local specialities on extensive seasonal à la carte menu. The à la carte menu changes two or three times a year and is supplemented by a specials board which changes at least once a week. Special diets are also catered for. A typical specials board might include a fresh halibut dish, Moroccan lamb, chicken supreme, as well as vegetarian choices. Most of the restaurant is non-smoking. Stampers is open most evenings, from 6pm until last orders at 10.45pm, but do telephone first as bookings are essential. The restaurant is closed at lunchtime except for pre-booked parties of 10 or more. Stampers is licensed, with an interesting wine list, and all major credit cards are accepted.

BROCKHOLE
3 miles NW of Windermere off the A591

The **Lake District Visitor Centre** at Brockhole provides enough activities for a full family day out. Lake cruises depart from the jetty here for 45-minute circular trips and groups of more than 20 can even organise their own private boat. Within the beautifully landscaped grounds visitors can join a guided walk, dispose of their children in the well-equipped adventure playground, enjoy a lakeside picnic or visit the rare breeds of sheep. A wide variety of events takes place during the season - amongst them a Medieval Living Weekend, a Taste of Cumbria Food Fair, a Christmas Craft Fair and much more. Brockhole itself is a fine Victorian mansion, originally built for a Manchester silk merchant. Here visitors can watch an audio visual presentation about the area, browse in the gift shop which stocks an excellent range of books, guides and maps, or take a break in the comfortable café which has an outdoor terrace overlooking the lake.

Ambleside

AMBLESIDE
5 miles NW of Windermere on the A591

Standing less than a mile from the head of Lake Windermere, Ambleside is one of the busiest of the Lakeland towns, a popular centre for walkers and tourers, with glorious walks and drives radiating from the town in all directions. Ambleside offers a huge choice of pubs, restaurants, cafés, hotels and guest houses, as well as art galleries, a 2-screen cinema and a mix of traditional family-run shops supplemented by a modern range of retailers in the new **Market Cross** centre. Because of its many shops specialising in outdoors clothing, the town was recently described as "the anorak capital of the world" and it would certainly be hard to find a wider selection anywhere of climbing, camping and walking gear.

Many of Ambleside's buildings are constructed in the distinctive grey green stone of the area which merges attractively with the green of the fields and fells all around. The centre of the town is now a conservation area and perhaps the most picturesque building here is **The Bridge House,** a tiny cottage perched on a packhorse bridge across Stock Ghyll. Today it's a National Trust shop and information centre, but during the 1850s it was the home of Mr and Mrs Rigg and their six children. The main room of this one-up, one-down residence measures just 13 feet by 6 feet. Close by, at **Adrian Sankey's Glass Works,** visitors can watch craftsmen transform molten material into glass in the age-old way and also purchase the elegant results - wine glasses, perfume bottles, lampshades, huge bowls and much more. The studio stands next to an 18th century water mill which Adrian Sankey, together with other local craftsmen, restored in 1995. Now, water flow permitting, you can watch the wheel

ELDER GROVE

Lake Road, Ambleside, Cumbria LA22 0DB
Tel: 015394 32504
e-mail: info@eldergrove.co.uk
website: www.eldergrove.co.uk

Only a short stroll from the head of Lake Windermere, **Elder Grove** is a striking Victorian building which is the home of Paul and Vicky McDougall. They took over this stylish guest house in 1999 from Vicky's mum and dad who had been welcoming guests here for more than 20 years. The visitor's day begins with breakfast in the dining room with its walls of attractive Lakeland greenstone. A traditional full Cumbrian breakfast as well as lighter fare is available and the McDougalls are happy to provide packed lunches or picnic hampers to see you through the day. Vegetarians and special diets are catered for. Guests at Elder Grove have the use of an elegant, tastefully furnished

lounge, (well supplied with information on local attractions and activities), and can also enjoy a drink from the bar. There are 10 guest bedrooms, all beautifully furnished with central heating, colour TV, radio, complimentary hot drinks tray and internal telephone link as well as private bathrooms with bath/shower, toilet and hand basin. Some bedrooms also enjoy glorious views over the surrounding fells. If you are celebrating a honeymoon or anniversary, or just want to indulge yourself, there's also a Special Occasions room which will help to make your stay especially memorable! (Please note that Elder Grove is non-smoking throughout).

COTTAGES ON THE GREEN

The Haven, The Green, Ambleside, Cumbria LA22 9AU Tel: 015394 32441
e-mail: twosparrows@havengreen.fsbusiness.co.uk   website: www.amblesideonline.co.uk

Only a minute's walk from the centre of Ambleside, **Cottages on the Green** are three charming cottages, part of a late-19th century terrace built of Lakeland green stone. They stand in a quiet private road and each cottage is fully equipped for up to 4 self-catering guests with fridge, toaster etc., and with a colour television. Rocklea and Wilwyn cottages have a 3-piece bathroom suite of bath, hand basin and WC, while Sunnydene has a shower cubicle, hand basin and WC. Children are welcome, with a cot and high chair available on request. The cottages share a pleasant rear garden looking on to Loughrigg Fell and there is easy access to open countryside.

The owners of Cottages on the Green, Bryan and Fiona Sparrow, welcome guests all year round. During the season, there is a minimum let of one week, but from November to Easter, the cottages can be hired on a minimum two night basis. The Sparrows also have another attractive self-catering property to let, Ellers Fold, which is part of a mid-19th century farmhouse set in idyllic countryside close to Loughrigg Tarn, about 2 miles west of Ambleside. Ellers Fold is fully equipped for up to 6 guests, has a living room with wood-burning stove, bathroom with bath, shower, hand basin and WC, and outside there is a small garden.

in full working order and enjoy a coffee in the café-restaurant housed in a restored 15th century building.

A short walk from the mill brings you **The Armitt Museum** and library dedicated to the area's history since Roman times and to its most famous literary luminaries, John Ruskin and Beatrix Potter (see panel below).

The popular panoramic view of Ambleside, looking north from the path up **Loughrigg Fell**, reveals the town cradled within the apron of the massive Fairfield Horseshoe which rises to nearly 3000ft. Within the townscape itself, the most impressive feature is the rocket-like spire, 180ft high, of **St Mary's Church**. The church was completed in 1854 to a design by Sir George Gilbert Scott, the architect of London's St Pancras Station and the Albert Memorial. Inside the church is a chapel devoted to the memory of William Wordsworth and an interesting 1940s mural depicting the ancient ceremony of rush-bearing. The mural was painted by Gordon Ransome of the Royal College of Art during World War II when the college was evacuated to the town. The ceremony, dating back to the days when the floor of

View from Loughrigg Fell

the church was covered by rushes, is still held on the first Saturday in July. Some 400 children process through the town bearing colourful decorated rushes and singing the specially commissioned Ambleside Rushbearer's Hymn.

A few weeks later the famous **Ambleside Sports** take place, an event distinguished by the variety of local traditional sports it features. In addition to carriage-driving, ferret or pigeon racing, and tugs of war, the Sports include

THE ARMITT MUSEUM

Rydal Road, Ambleside, Cumbria LA22 9PL
Tel: 01539 431212

A short walk from the mill brings you to **The Armitt**, an attractive new building which contains a museum and library dedicated to the area's history since Roman times and to its most famous literary luminaries, John Ruskin and Beatrix Potter. Visitors can "talk" to John Ruskin, watch a 19th century lantern slide show, and marvel at Beatrix Potter's pre-Mrs Tiggywinkle watercolours - exquisite scientific studies of fungi and mosses. Other exhibits include a lock of Ruskin's hair, a life mask of Harriet Martineau, the political writer and author of an early *Guide to the Lakes*, and a fascinating collection of photographs by Herbert Bell (1856-1946), an Ambleside chemist who became an accomplished photographer, concentrating on lakeland scenes. The Armitt hosts regular exhibitions, lectures and concerts, and also has its own shop selling items produced exclusively for sale only at the museum.

Ambleside Pier

Cumberland and Westmorland wrestling, (a little like Sumo wrestling without the rolls of fat), muscle-wrenching fell racing, and hound trailing.

Another experience not to be missed while staying at Ambleside is a boat cruise on Lake Windermere to Bowness. There are daily departures from the pier at Waterhead, about a mile south of the town. At Bowness, there are connections to other lakeland attractions and, during the summer months, evening wine cruises. Rowing boats and self drive motor boats can also be hired. Just to the west of the pier is Borrans Park, a pleasant lakeside park with plenty of picnic spots, and to the west of the park, the site of Galava Roman Fort. There is little to be seen of the fort but the setting is enchanting. Also well worth a visit is nearby **Stagshaw Garden** (NT), a spring

woodland garden which contains a fine collection of shrubs, including some impressive rhododendrons, azaleas and camellias. Parking is very limited so it's best to park at Waterhead car park and walk.

Perhaps the most unusual visitor attraction in Ambleside is **The Homes of Football**, described by the *Sunday Times* as "a national treasure". It began as a travelling exhibition of football

River Brathy, Ambleside

GARDEN ROOM CAFÉ,

Zeffirellis Complex, Compston Road,
Ambleside, Cumbria LA22 9AD
Tel: 015394 31612

Located on the ground floor of Zeffirellis Shopping Gallery, the **Garden Room Café** is definitely the place to seek out for quality home made teas, coffees and confectioneries. In the stylish, non-smoking conservatory with its potted palms, Dorothy and Graham Smith have been serving excellent vegetarian food for more than 8 years. This is a delightful place to meet friends, have a cappuccino or a complete lunch, and is open daily from 10am to 5.30pm.

photographs and memorabilia but now has a permanent home in Lake Road. Photographer Stuart Clarke recorded games and grounds at every kind of venue from the Premier League down to amateur village teams. There are now 60,000 photographs on file and a massive selection on show, framed and for sale. Some of the memorabilia retails for £200 or more but a free picture postcard of your favourite soccer ground is included in the modest entrance fee.

From Ambleside town centre, a steep road climbs sharply up to the dramatic **Kirkstone Pass** and over to Ullswater. The pass is so called because of the rock at the top which looks like a church steeple. Rising to some 1,489 feet above sea level, the road is the highest in the Lake District and, though today's vehicles make light work of the climb, for centuries the Pass presented a formidable obstacle. The severest incline, known as **The Struggle**,

Kirkstone Pass

necessitated passengers to step out of their coach and to make their way on foot, leaving the horses to make the steep haul with just the carriage.

RYDAL
7 miles NW of Windermere on the A591

In 1813, following the deaths of their young children Catherine and Thomas, William and Dorothy Wordsworth were too grief-stricken to stay on at the Old

ELTERWATER PARK COUNTRY GUEST HOUSE

Skelwith, Ambleside, Cumbria LA22 9NP
Tel: 015394 32227 Fax: 015394 31768
e-mail: enquiries@elterwater.com
website: www.elterwater.com

Surrounded by magnificent scenery, **Elterwater Park Country Guest House** stands high on the hillside above Langdale. Bordering its parkland is Elterwater, the Lake of Swans, which is a leisurely 10 minute walk away. The house itself, built of the lovely local stone, dates back to the 1700s and the owners, Caroline and Murdoch Macaulay, have taken great care to preserve traditional features along with all modern amenities.

There are two comfortable guest lounge areas, one of which has window seats overlooking the garden, and a terrace for fairweather days. For the other kind of day, there's also a drying room!

Guests can stay on either a bed & breakfast, or dinner, bed & breakfast basis. The breakfasts are lavish, with plenty of choice and, like the dinners, prepared from fresh local ingredients wherever possible. Meals are served in the spacious dining room with its large tables, widely spaced, and traditional Lancashire rush-seated chairs. Elterwater has a full residential licence and a wine list chosen for quality and value. The Macaulays always make sure that the evening meal is never the same twice during your stay. The accommodation comprises four elegantly furnished rooms, spacious and airy, all of them enjoying glorious views. All the bedrooms are en suite and provided with colour television, radio, hair dryers, hospitality trays, lots of storage space and, a really nice home-from-home touch, fresh flowers.

Rectory in Grasmere. They moved a couple of miles down the road to **Rydal Mount**, a handsome house overlooking tiny Rydal Water. By now, the poet was well-established and comparatively prosperous. A salaried position as Westmorland's Distributor of Stamps (a tax official), supplemented his earnings from poetry. Although Wordsworth only ever rented the house, it is now owned by his descendants and has been open to the public since 1970. The interior has seen little change, retaining a lived-in atmosphere. It contains first editions of the poet's work and many personal possessions, amongst them the only surviving portrait of his beloved sister, Dorothy. William was a keen gardener and the 4-acre garden remains very much as he designed it.

Wordsworths House, Rydal Mount

GRASMERE
9 miles NW of Windermere on the A591

In 1769 Thomas Gray described Grasmere as "*a little unsuspected paradise*". Thirty years later, Wordsworth himself called it "the loveliest spot that man hath ever found". Certainly, Grasmere enjoys one of the finest settings in all Lakeland, its small lake nestling in a natural scenic amphitheatre beside the compact, rough-stone village.

For lovers of Wordsworth's poetry, Grasmere is the pre-eminent place of pilgrimage. They come to squeeze through tiny **Dove Cottage** where Wordsworth lived in dire poverty from 1799 to 1808, obliged to line the walls with newspaper for warmth. The great poet shared this very basic accommodation with his wife Mary, his sister Dorothy, his sister-in-law Alice and, as almost permanent guests,

Rydal Water

Grasmere Lake

Coleridge and De Quincey. (Sir Walter Scott also stayed, although he often sneaked off to the Swan Hotel for a dram since the Wordsworths were virtually teetotallers). Located on the outskirts of the village, Dove Cottage has been preserved intact: next door is an award-winning museum dedicated to Wordsworth's life and works. Dove Cottage, Rydal Mount, another of the poet's homes near Grasmere, and his birthplace, Wordsworth House at Cockermouth, are all owned by the

LANCRIGG VEGETARIAN COUNTRY HOUSE HOTEL

Easedale, Grasmere, Cumbria LA22 9QN
Tel: 015394 35317 Fax: 015394 35058
website: www.lancrigg.co.uk

Once a meeting place for the Lakeland Poets, **Lancrigg Vegetarian Country House Hotel** stands in 30 acres of gardens and woodland overlooking the peace and tranquillity of Easedale. The oldest part of the house dates back to the 1600s when it was a modest farmhouse. In 1840, Elizabeth Fletcher asked her friend William Wordsworth to find a house for her "summer refreshment". William and Dorothy had discovered Lancrigg only four days after arriving in Grasmere and the poet took a great interest in renovating and enlarging the house. Elizabeth was prominent in the intellectual, artistic and political life of the times, and a fervent lover of revolutions - American, French, Greek, Hungarian, she supported them all.

Dickens and Wilkie Collins stayed at Lancrigg on their regular trips to Southern Scotland. In 1985 this historic house was opened by Robert and Jane Whittington as an elegant hotel serving only vegetarian wholefood home cooking. The kitchen uses a wide range of the very best fresh and natural ingredients, organic where possible and always free of artificial additives. All cheeses are vegetarian and the bread, croissants and cakes are made from organic stone ground flour in a wood fired brick oven by a local award-winning baker. Meals are served in the elegant chandelier-lit dining room

which enjoys superb views across the valley. The menu changes every evening, Vegan alternatives are always available, and to complement your meal Lancrigg has an extensive wine list with a choice of organic and fruit wines as well as all the usual bar refreshments. The accommodation is outstanding, with 12 rooms in the main house, (3 of them on the ground floor), and a cottage nearby. Some have 4-poster beds, whirlpool baths and antique furniture, and all rooms have their own private bathrooms, colour television, tea-making facilities and telephone. Lancrigg's brochure gives individual descriptions of each room as no two rooms are the same. Anyone who stays at this exceptional hotel will surely agree with the artist William Heaton Cooper who described Lancrigg as "a perfect example of a gracious country house".

DOVE COTTAGE TEA ROOMS & RESTAURANT

Town End, Grasmere, Cumbria LA22 9SH
Tel/Fax: 015394 35268

Taking its name from the famous cottage nearby in which William and Dorothy Wordsworth lived from 1799 to 1808, **Dove Cottage Tea Rooms and Restaurant** would surely have been welcomed by the celebrated couple after one of their long walks across the fells. The tea rooms are housed in an unusual building which was erected in the 1930s as an antique shop. Since 1997, the business has been owned and run by Michael and Kate Metcalfe, with Michael in charge of the excellent cooking. The tea rooms are open every day, February to December, from 10am to 5pm, serving breakfasts (until 11.30am), snacks, filled rolls, soups, salads, hot dishes and, of course, an appetising choice of tea breads, scones and cakes. In the evenings,

Tuesday to Saturday, the restaurant is open from 6.45pm until last orders around 9pm. A typical menu might include Venison Terrine or "Nero's Vegetarian Antipasti Salad" among the starters, main courses such as Steak au Poivre, Roasted Salmon Parcel or Mushroom-filled Ravioli with a tarragon cream sauce, to be followed by a wonderful choice of desserts. And if you are planning to stay in this popular village, Michael's parents run a charming guest house, Howfoot Lodge, located just to the rear of the restaurant. There are 6 very comfortable guest rooms - 3 doubles and 3 twins.

BROADRAYNE FARM COTTAGES & GRASMERE HOSTEL

Broadrayne Farm, Grasmere, Cumbria LA22 9RU
Tel: 015394 35055 Fax: 015394 35733
e-mail: jo@grasmere-accommodation.co.uk
website: www.grasmere-accommodation.co.uk

Standing in the geographical centre of the Lake District, **Broadrayne Farm Cottages & Grasmere Hostel** are surrounded by spectacular countryside with glorious views in every direction. Footpaths from the farm provide instant access to the fells, and if touring by car visitors can reach all point of the lakes within an hour. Set one field back from the road, the farm enjoys a sunny, elevated position and the three stone-built cottages with deep set windows nestle around a picturesque farmyard. They can accommodate between 2 and 5 people but, in combination, up to 10. The Lodge and Broadrayne Cottage are both 3 Stars, while The Wooloft, a splendid conversion of the old barn , has 4 Stars rating. All three are fully equipped with modern amenities and have the benefit of both central heating and

open fires. Children and pets are welcome. For those travelling on a budget, the farm's owners, Bev and Jo Dennison Drake, opened the Grasmere Hostel in 2000 (no membership required). Standing only 100 metres from the Coast to Coast Path, the Hostel (non-smoking), has family sized bunk bedded rooms sleeping 3-6 people, private showers and washing facilities, a common room with stunning views of the valley, two self-catering kitchens, laundry, drying room, pay phone and sauna. There's a car park adjacent as well as a bike store, and only 400 metres away is an excellent pub serving real ales and fine bar meals.

Wordsworth Trust which offers a discount ticket covering entrance to all three properties.

In 1808, the poet moved to The Rectory (private) opposite St. Oswald's Church. In his long poem, *The Excursion*, he describes the house and its lovely garden beside the River Rothay. In 1850, the Poet Laureate was buried beneath yew trees he himself had planted in St Oswald's churchyard. He was joined here by his sister Dorothy, in 1885, and his wife Mary, in 1889.

Like Ambleside, Grasmere is famous for its **Sports**, first recorded in 1852, which still take place in late August. The most

Grasmere Church

celebrated event in the Lake District, they attract some 10,000 visitors and feature many pursuits unique to Cumbria such as Cumberland and Westmorland wrestling as well as the more understandable, though arduous, fell running.

Collectors of curiosities who happen to be travelling north on the A591 from Grasmere should look out for the vintage black and yellow AA telephone box on the right hand side of the road. Still functioning, **Box 487** was recently accorded Grade II listed building status by the Department of the Environment.

Dove Cottage, Grasmere

3 The Cartmel and Furness Peninsulas

These two peninsulas, which form the southernmost coast of Cumbria, are often overlooked by visitors to the county. This is a great pity as both have much to offer the tourist including a rich history as well as splendid scenery. Lying between the lakes and mountains of the Lake District and the sandy estuaries of Morecambe Bay, this is an area of gentle moorland, craggy headlands, scattered woodlands, and vast expanses of sand.

It was once a stronghold of the Cistercian monks whose influence can still be seen in the buildings and fabric of the landscape. This is Cumbria's ecclesiastical centre and there were several monasteries here but two in particular are well worth visiting today. There is little left of Cartmel Priory except the church and gatehouse which lie in the heart of this charming old market town. However, the remains of Furness Abbey, once the second richest in England, are extensive and occupy a particularly pleasant site.

Bridgefield, Spark Bridge

Before the great boom of the local iron ore mining industry, the peninsula villages and market towns relied on farming and fishing and, before some of the river estuaries silted up, there was also some import and export trade. The rapid growth of Barrow-in-Furness, which will be forever linked with the shipbuilding industry, changed the face of much of the area but as the iron industry declined so did the town.

The arrival of the railways, in the mid-19th century, however, saw the development of genteel resorts such as Grange-over-Sands overlooking the treacherous sands of Morecambe Bay. Grange is still an elegant little town and has been spared the indignity of vast amusement parks and rows of slot machines, retaining its character as a quiet and pleasant holiday centre.

THE CARTMEL AND FURNESS PENINSULAS

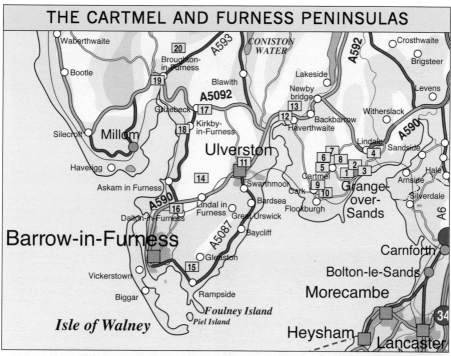

© MAPS IN MINUTES ™ (1999)

PLACES TO STAY, EAT, DRINK AND SHOP

1	Cumbria Grand Hotel, Grange-over-Sands	Hotel and restaurant	Page 44
2	The Lancastrian, Grange-over-Sands	Pub with food	Page 45
3	Clare House, Grange-over-Sands	Hotel and restaurant	Page 46
4	Greenacres Country Guest House, Lindale	Country guest house	Page 46
5	Beckside Farm, Cartmel	Self catering	Page 48
6	The Cavendish at Cartmel, Cartmel	Inn, restaurant & accommodation	Page 49
7	Priory Hotel, Cartmel	Hotel and restaurant	Page 50
8	Uplands Country House Hotel, Cartmel	Country house hotel & restaurant	Page 50
9	Lakeland Motor Museum, Cark-in-Cartmel	Motor museum	Page 52
10	Old Park Wood Caravan Park, Cark-in-Cartmel	Caravan park	Page 53
11	The Tinner's Rabbit, Ulverston	Gallery, delicatessen & fashion shop	Page 54
12	The Lakeside & Haverthwaite Railway	Steam railway	Page 56
13	White Hart Inn, Bouth	Pub, food & accommodation	Page 56
14	New Inn, Marton	Pub and restaurant	Page 57
15	The Copper Dog, Leece	Pub and restaurant	Page 59
16	The Brown Cow Inn, Dalton-in-Furness	Pub, restaurant & self catering	Page 61
17	Ashlack Cottages, Grizebeck	Self catering	Page 63
18	The Greyhound Inn, Grizebeck	Pub, restaurant & accommodation	Page 64
19	The Old Kings Head, Broughton-in-Furness	Inn, restaurant & accommodation	Page 64
20	Rose Cottage, Broughton-in-Furness	Self catering	Page 65

CUMBRIA GRAND HOTEL,

Lindale Road, Grange-over-Sands,
Cumbria LA11 6EN
Tel: 01539 532331 Fax: 01539 534534
e-mail: cumbria@cgrandhotel.freeserve.co.uk

Originally built in 1880 as the Hazlewood Hydro, the **Cumbria Grand Hotel** really lives up to its name. It stands in 20 acres of beautifully maintained grounds where there's a woodland nature walk you can follow without stepping outside the hotel's boundaries. Also within the grounds are a tennis court, putting green and children's play area, and right next door there's a golf course.

The Cumbria Grand is one of the Strathmore family of quality hotels which enjoy a well-deserved reputation for providing excellent hospitality accompanied by courteous and efficient service. This is immediately evident in the elegant restaurant which seats up to 250 diners. The hotel's experienced executive chef has developed an excellent kitchen and along with the well stocked bar and wine cellar ensures that guests have a truly memorable

meal. The restaurant is open every evening, while at lunchtime there's a choice of bar snacks and a carvery.

As one might expect, accommodation at the Cumbria Grand is also top of the range. All the 128 bedrooms have an en suite bathroom, colour television, radio, tea tray, telephone, central heating and most have views over the bay or woodland. Mini suites and executive bedrooms are also available. As well as the above facilities, they are equipped with hair dryer, trouser press and an additional telephone/modem point. There's even a 4-poster bed for that special occasion.

Live entertainment is available on some evenings and the hotel also has a full size snooker table and table tennis. There was a billiard room here as early as 1891. Residents at that time were also entertained by concerts, dances and games of progressive whist. There was even a dark room for the new hobby of photography. Back then, cars were still a rarity, (today, the hotel has parking for 150 vehicles), but cycling was very popular so a special cycle house was installed where machines were "stored at a charge of 1/- (5p) a week, a fee which included "free insurance against burglary or fire".

Located only 12 miles from Junction 36 of the M6, the Cumbria Grand is ideally situated for meetings of all kinds -wedding receptions, dinner dances, residential and day conferences. There's a wide choice of rooms of different sizes, accommodating anything from 20 to 300 people. Whatever your requirements, there are extensive facilities to suit your individual need.

The Cumbria Grand is also well-placed for all kinds of activities - facilities for golf, fishing, water sports, climbing and pony trekking are all within easy reach. Other attractions nearby include cruising on Lake Windermere, the Lowther Leisure and Wildlife Park, The World of Beatrix Potter, the "Cars of the Stars" Motor Museum, the Wordsworth Museum and the Eskdale Steam Railway.

GRANGE-OVER-SANDS

Grange, as it's known locally, is an attractive little town set in a natural sun-trap on the north shore of Morecambe Bay. Much of its Victorian charm can be credited to the Furness Railway Company which developed the town after building the Lancaster to Whitehaven line in 1857. At that time, the whole of the Cartmel and Bowness Peninsulas were part of Lancashire, a detached area whose main link with the rest of the county was the dubious route across Morecambe Sands. The railway provided a safe alternative to this hazardous journey. At Grange the company built an elegant mile-long promenade (now traffic free) and set out the colourful ornamental gardens. Prosperous merchants built grand country homes here and it wasn't long before local residents began referring to their town as the "Torquay of the North".

Though Grange doesn't have a beach to rival that of its brash neighbour across Morecambe Bay, it does enjoy an exceptionally mild climate, the mildest in the northwest, thanks to the Gulf Stream. It is still a popular place particularly with people who are looking for a pleasant and quiet place to retire. It was a favourite with Beatrix Potter who recorded that on one visit to the town she met a "friendly porker" which inspired *The Tale of Pigling Bland*. There's no connection of course but today the town does boast a butcher's shop, Higginsons, which was recently voted the Best Butcher's Shop in England.

The route to Grange, across the sands of Morecambe Bay, is a treacherous one though it was used not only by the Romans but also by the monks of Furness Abbey and, later, even by stage coaches looking to shorten their journey time. Avoiding the quicksands of the bay, which have taken many lives over the centuries,

THE LANCASTRIAN

Main Street, Grange-over-Sands,
Cumbria LA11 6AB
Tel: 015395 32455

Built in the early 1900s, **The Lancastrian** has had a rather unusual history for a hostelry. For many years this impressive stone building served the town as The Palace Cinema and Dance Hall. Today, the inn is owned and run by the father and son team of Tony and Jonathan Entwhistle who arrived here in the autumn of 1999. They renamed the tavern The Lancastrian but many locals still refer to the premises as "Flooks", or flukes - a tasty kind of small flatfish caught locally and from which the nearby village of Flookburgh also takes its name.

An interesting feature of The Lancastrian's interior is the series of quotations inscribed on the beams and taken from sources as various as Shakespeare's *Coriolanus* and Tennessee Williams' *Cat on a Hot Tin Roof*. Open all day, every day, the inn is noted for the quality of its food and ale. There are always at least 3 real ales on tap, with Boddingtons and Castle Eden as permanent fixtures, along with keg bitter, Stella and Heineken draught beer, Strongbow cider and Guinness. Excellent food is served every lunchtime (noon until 3pm) and evening (5.30pm to 8pm), except Monday lunchtimes and Sunday evenings. Customers can choose from the extensive regular menu or from the daily specials listed on the board. If you are visiting this hospitable hostelry on a Friday evening, you'll find live entertainment from 9pm.

is a difficult task. Back in the 16th century, the Duchy of Lancaster appointed an official guide to escort travellers over the shifting sands and also provided him with a house at Grange. The town still has an official guide who takes groups on a 3-hour walk across the bay. The sands are extremely dangerous since "the tide comes in with the merciless speed of a galloping horse" - a crossing should never be attempted without the help of a qualified guide.

Away from the hotels, shops, and cafés of the town there are some lovely walks and none is more pleasant than the path behind Grange which climbs through magnificent limestone woodlands rich in wild flowers. The path finally leads to

CLARE HOUSE

Park Road, Grange-over-Sands, Cumbria LA11 7HQ
Tel: 015395 33026 (Residents: 015395 34253)

Occupying a beautiful position overlooking the bay and close to Grange's famous mile-long promenade, **Clare House** provides all the charm of "country house " hospitality together with all modern amenities and facilities. The Read family have owned this spacious Victorian house for more than 30 years and during that time have built up a loyal following of guests, many of whom return year after year. One reason is the food, which is renowned throughout the area. Son Andrew, and second chef Mark, offer a superb dinner menu of traditional and speciality dishes - cuisine which has earned Clare House an AA Rosette and a quality grading of 78%. The hotel has a residential licence so visitors can enjoy wines and spirits with their meals and at other times. A comprehensive English breakfast is served between 9 and 9.30am and light lunches and afternoon teas are also available.

All the 17 bedrooms have private bathrooms, (with the exception of one single room which is let at a reduced rate), central heating, colour TV, direct dial telephones, and hospitality trays. Most enjoy views over the bay and some have balconies, including 2 ground floor twin bedded rooms. Children are welcome but the Reads regret that dogs are not allowed in the house. Never crowded with conferences, Clare House is always full of like-minded people seeking a restful retreat and a perfect base for exploring the breathtaking scenery of this spectacular corner of the Lakes.

GREENACRES COUNTRY GUEST HOUSE

Lindale, Grange-over-Sands, Cumbria LA11 6LP
Tel/Fax: 015395 34578
website: www.accomodata.co.uk/091098.htm

A small, family-run guest house, **Greenacres Country Guest House** offers quality bed and breakfast accommodation in a completely non-smoking environment. Barbara Pettit has been providing a warm welcome, good food and hospitality here since 1998 and already has many repeat visitors. The 4 guest bedrooms are all en suite, decorated and furnished to a very high standard, and fully equipped with TV, clock radio, hair dryer, hospitality tray and lots of other little extras. Evening meals are available on request, with a choice of wines to complement your meal, and afterwards guests can relax in the lovely conservatory or the lounge with its log fire in winter.

Morecombe Bay, Grange-over-Sands

Hampsfell Summit and **The Hospice**, a little stone tower from which there are unforgettable views over the bay and, in the opposite direction, the craggy peaks of the Lake District. The Hospice was provided by Grange's Vicar, the Revd. Thomas Remington, in 1834 to provide a refuge for travellers who found themselves stranded on the fell overnight. An external flight of stairs leads to a flat roof and, as the Vicar observed in a poem attached to the wall:

"The flight of steps requireth care,
The roof will show a prospect rare".

A natural curiosity just outside the town is the extraordinary **Bowder Stone** which provides a very good photo-opportunity. A massive 50ft square and weighing some 2000 tons, it stands precariously on one corner apparently defying gravity. A wooden staircase on one side provides easy access to the top.

Grange is also the starting point of the **Cistercian Way**, an exceptionally interesting 33 mile long foot path through Furness to Barrow which takes in, naturally, many Cistercian sites.

AROUND GRANGE-OVER-SANDS

LINDALE
2 miles NE of Grange-over-Sands off the A590

This small village was the birthplace of a man who defied the scepticism of his contemporaries and built the first successful iron ship. "Iron Mad" John Wilkinson also built the first cast iron barges and later created the castings for the famous Iron Bridge at Coalbrookdale. After his death in 1808 he was buried in an iron coffin, naturally, and the lofty **Wilkinson Obelisk** to his memory that stands near the village

Wilkinson Obelisk, Lindale

crossroads is also cast in iron. The admirers who erected it however omitted to provide the iron column with a lightning conductor. A few years later it was struck to the ground by a lightning bolt. The obelisk lay neglected in shrubbery for some years but has now been restored and towers above the village once again.

CARTMEL
2 miles W of Grange-over-Sands off the B5278

One of the prettiest villages in Furness, Cartmel is a delightful cluster of houses and cottages set around a square from which lead winding streets and arches into back yards. The village is dominated by the famous **Cartmel Priory**, founded in 1188 by Augustinian canons. According to legend, it was originally intended to be sited on nearby Mount Bernard but St Cuthbert appeared in a vision to the monastic architect and ordered him to build the priory between two springs of water, one flowing north and the other south. The next morning, water was found to be trickling in two different directions from the foundation

BECKSIDE FARM

Cartmel, Grange-over-Sands, Cumbria LA11 7SP
Tel/Fax: 015395 36141
e-mail: beckside@dircon.co.uk website:
www.beckside.co.uk

Only a mile outside the delightful village of Cartmel, **Beckside Farm** provides quality self-catering accommodation in two charmingly converted old farm buildings. Beckside Barn and Beckside Dairy are both built in the attractive local stone and have been fully restored with modern facilities while retaining many of the original features. They stand is beautiful gardens with a stream rippling by and with the unspoilt scenery of south Lakeland all around.

Beckside Barn sleeps 5 and to take advantage of the peaceful views across the fields the lounge has been created on the first floor and is equipped with a woodburning stove, television and VCR. Also on the first floor is a spacious dining area and a kitchen with oven, gas hob, microwave, dishwasher, fridge and separate laundry room. On the ground floor is a double bedroom with en suite shower room, spacious twin and single rooms and a family bathroom with shower. Outside, there's an enclosed garden and a raised patio. Beckside Dairy sleeps 4 and owes much of its character to the charming open-plan layout of the living area. Equipped to the same high standards as Beckside Barn, the Dairy also has an enclosed patio which is perfect for alfresco dining.

The owners of Beckside Farm, Jeremy and Mary Ratcliff, have furnished and decorated the Barn and Dairy, like their own house, in the Shaker style which combines beautiful simplicity combined with every modern comfort. Children are welcome at Beckside Farm but pets cannot be accommodated and please note that both properties are non-smoking.

Cartmel Priory

stones and this is where the church stands today.

Like all monastic institutions, the priory was disbanded in 1537 and several of its members were executed for participating in the Pilgrimage of Grace. Today, substantial remains of the 12th century Gatehouse (NT) survive, but the rest of the Priory was cannibalised to build many of the village's cottages and houses. After the Dissolution, only the south aisle of the **Church of St Mary and St Michael** was still standing but, in 1620, George Preston of Holker began restoring the entire building and the richly carved black oak screens and stall canopies date from this restoration. St Mary & St Michael's has recently been described as "the most beautiful church in the northwest".

Inside, in the southwest corner of the church, is a door known as Cromwell's Door. The holes in it are said to have

THE CAVENDISH AT CARTMEL

Cartmel, Cumbria LA11 6QA
Tel: 015395 36240 Fax: 015395 36243

Located in the heart of this historic town, **The Cavendish at Cartmel** is a picturesque establishment which dates back to the 15th century. Full of charm and character, the inn has retained many original features, including the low-beamed ceilings and creaky floorboards! The Cavendish has an established reputation for its warmth of welcome, excellence of food and its own traditional

beers. At least 4 real ales are always available, two of which are permanent, (Theakston's Pedigree and Theakston's Best), the other two are rotating guest ales. The non-smoking restaurant delights customers old and new with meals skilfully prepared to suit all tastes. It's open every lunchtime (noon until

2.15pm) and evening (6pm to 9.15pm), and food is also served in the lounge bar. On Sunday, the roast is prepared on an open spit and is very popular, indeed booking is strongly advised for all meals at the weekend. On Sunday evenings in the winter, mine hosts Paul and Sandra Lester, lay on a Quiz which everyone is welcome to join in. If you are staying in Cartmel, The Cavendish has a choice of 7 tastefully furnished bedrooms, some dating from the 16th century, others of more recent date. There are 5 doubles, 1 twin and 1 family room, and all have en suite facilities, television and hospitality tray.

PRIORY HOTEL

The Square, Cartmel, Cumbria LA11 6QB
Tel: 015395 36718

The beautiful priory church stands majestically over the most enchanting of Lakeland villages. In the heart of Cartmel stands the prestigous Georgian building of the **Priory Hotel**, formerly part of the original village walls. Smothered in Virginia Creeper, the Priory Hotel stands in the market square of this delightful village. For a stress free break, Cartmel is the ideal holiday or short break location. The village allows you to leave all worries and problems outside as mobile phones do not work here, thus creating a relaxed, peaceful atmosphere. Recently the proprietor Mr George Broadhurst and his daughter Adele have completely redecorated and refurbished the hotel, in keeping with it's elegant Georgian origins. George - Cartmels answer to Basil Fawlty - is an entertaining character to say the least.

He is a legend in the local area and is renowned for his sudden outbursts of Pavarotti, and reciting Cumbrian poetry. It is clear from her recent success that Adele has inherited Georges singing talents and can regularly be found mid performance in the local public houses. Together the Broadhursts have established a reputation for fine food, top of the range accomodation and a happy atmosphere. Open all year round, the Priory has five guest bedrooms, all spacious, en suite and decorated to the same high standard as the rest of the hotel. Definitely a place not to be missed.

UPLANDS COUNTRY HOUSE HOTEL

Haggs Lane, Cartmel, Cumbria LA11 6HD
Tel: 015395 36248 Fax: 015395 36848
e-mail: uplands@kencomp.net

Standing in two acres of truly delightful gardens, with magnificent panoramic views over the Leven estuary, **Uplands Country House Hotel** provides its guests with a memorable combination of an outstanding setting, excellent cuisine, stylish accommodation and, perhaps best of all, a warm, friendly and informal atmosphere. Uplands was opened in 1985 by Tom and Diana Peter with John Tovey of the renowned Miller Howe Hotel in Windermere. John retired in 1998 and Uplands is now in the sole ownership of Tom and Diana. Naturally, the food here is terrific. The dinner and lunchtime menus change daily and Tom uses only the freshest ingredients to prepare the mouth-watering dishes served in the elegant restaurant with its

lovely garden and countryside views. Not surprisingly, the restaurant has received a 2 Rosettes award from the AA for its food. Located a few miles south of the Lake District proper, this area is much more peaceful and tranquil, an ideal place to stay for a restful holiday. Uplands has just 5 guest bedrooms, all with either bath or shower, comfortably furnished and prettily decorated, and all are equipped with television, telephone and hair dryer as well as books and magazines. Well behaved dogs are welcome. The hotel is open from March 1st to January 1st, serves dinner every evening except Monday, and lunch from Thursday to Sunday.

Cartmel Gatehouse

River Eea, on which meetings are held on the last weekends of May and August. Located close to the village, the course must be one of the most picturesque in the country and it is certainly one of the smallest. A holiday atmosphere descends on the village for race day and, though the competition is fierce, it is a wonderful and relaxing day out.

FLOOKBURGH
3 miles SW of Grange-over-Sands on the B5277

An ancient Charter Borough, Flookburgh is still the principal fishing village on Morecambe Bay. Roads from the square lead down to the shore where fishermen still land their catches of cockle, shrimps and (less often nowadays) flukes, the tasty small flat fish from which the village takes its name.

CARK-IN-CARTMEL
3 miles SW of Grange-over-Sands on the B5278

Cumbria's premier stately house, **Holker Hall** is one of the homes of the Cavendish family, the Dukes of Devonshire. An intriguing blend of 16th century, Georgian and Victorian architecture, "Hooker", as

been made by indignant parishioners firing at Parliamentarian soldiers who had stabled their horses in the nave. Cromwell's troops were certainly in the area in 1643 and, to further establish the story, fragments of lead were found in the wood during restoration work in 1955.

Other features of interest include the glorious 45ft high east window (inspired by York Minster), the 14th century tomb of Lord and Lady Harrington, a fine Jacobean screen and some floor tablets referring to people who had drowned trying to cross the sands of Morecambe Bay.

Cartmel is also famous for its attractive **Racecourse**, set beside the

Holker Hall

LAKELAND MOTOR MUSEUM

Holker Hall and Gardens, Cark-in-Cartmel,
Grange-over-Sands, Cumbria LA11 7PL
Tel/Fax: 015395 58509

A nostalgic reminder of transport bygones, the **Lakeland Motor Museum** has more than 100 vehicles on show ranging from pioneer vehicles of the early 1900s through to the exuberant models of the swinging 40s and fabulous 50s. As well as these classic cars, the Museum also houses a fascinating collection of "magnificent motorbikes, superb scooters, bygone bicycles and triumphant tractors!" Also amongst the 10,000 exhibits, probably the most extensive presentation of automobilia on display in the UK, are "Authentic automobilia, reminiscent rarities, micro cars and mechanical marvels". This unique and carefully maintained collection is housed in a quaint former

Shire horse stable and its courtyard. Prominent contributors to 20th century motoring are all honoured - amongst them Walter Owen Bentley, Colin Chapman, Henry Ford, Cecil Kimber, William Lyons, Alec Issigonis and Frederick Henry Royce. The world of agriculture is not neglected either, with Henry Ferguson and the horticultural reformer Charles H. Pugh both featured. Interpretive displays and strategically positioned push-button narrative centres, together with a well-researched exhibit listing, provide added interest and enjoyment.

The recent recovery of Donald Campbell's *Bluebird* from the depths of Coniston Water gives an added interest to the Campbell Legend Bluebird Exhibition which pays tribute to Sir Malcolm Campbell and his son Donald who between them

captured 21 world land and water speed records for Britain. Highlights of the exhibition include full size detailed replicas of the 1935 *Bluebird* car and the famous jet hydroplane, *Bluebird K7*. There's even a replica of Donald Campbell's lucky mascot, teddy bear Mr Whoppit, together with a continuous video detailing the lives, careers, failures and achievement of these two sporting celebrities.

Also on site is an exhibition celebrating Britain's horticultural heritage, a comprehensive display of vintage mechanical rotavators, trimmers, cutters and rollers, plus a fine collection of historical lawnmowers. The Potting Shed contains a display of gardening hand tools and other equipment of the past, as well as a re-creation of a pre-war glasshouse. Other attractions include the Coach House Café and a gift shop.

it's known to locals, is a visitor-friendly place with no restraining ropes keeping visitors at a distance, a fire burning in the hearth and a "lived-in", family atmosphere. There's an impressive cantilevered staircase, a library with some 3,500 leather bound books, (plus a few dummy covers designed to hide electricity sockets), and an embroidered panel said to be the work of Mary, Queen of Scots.

Holker's 25 acres of award-winning gardens have featured in BBC-TV's *An English Country Garden*, and each year host the Holker Garden Festival which has been hailed as the "Chelsea of the North".

The Holker Hall estate contains a wide variety of other attractions - formal gardens, water features, a 125-acre deer park, picnic and children's play areas, a gift shop and café. Also within the grounds is the **Lakeland Motor Museum** (see panel opposite) which, as well as boasting a completely restored 1920s

garage, has more than 100 vehicles on show. Amongst them are 1880 tricycles, wartime ambulances, and 1980s MGs. A special exhibit is devoted to the attempts of Sir Malcolm and Donald Campbell to beat the world water speed record on Coniston Water.

ULVERSTON

It was way back in 1280 that Edward I granted Ulverston its market charter: more than seven centuries later, colourful stalls still crowd the narrow streets and cobbled market square every Thursday. It's a picturesque scene but for an even more striking view of the town, follow the walk up nearby **Hoad Hill**. The great expanse of Morecambe Bay with a backdrop of the Pennines stretches to the south, the bulk of Ingleborough lies to the east, Coniston Old Man and the Langdale Pikes lie to the

OLD PARK WOOD CARAVAN PARK

Holker, Cark-in-Cartmel, Cumbria LA11 7PP
Tel: 015395 58266 Fax: 015395 58101

Overlooking the estuary of the River Leven and enjoying exceptional views of the Cumbrian hills, **Old Park Wood Caravan Park** stands in 35 acres of beautifully maintained grounds. Most of the static caravans are privately owned but there are also hard and soft standings for up to 52 touring caravans and camper vans. (Tents are not permitted). Established in the 1960s, the Park's amenities have been continually upgraded over the years and now include a covered heated swimming pool, a fully stocked self service shop and adventure playground as well as a 42 electric hook-ups, a launderette, toilets and showers.

Because of its splendid position and excellent facilities, the Park is one of the most popular in the Lake District and it is essential to book well in advance to avoid disappointment. The Park is situated

only one mile from Holker Hall with its many attractions and special events, Windermere lies about 8 miles to the north, and the small seaside resort of Grange-over-Sands is just 5 miles to the east.

The golf course at Grange has arrangements for visitors and horse riding is also available locally. The Park notice board displays details of other attractions and activities in the area. The resident managers, Bill and Pauline O'Brien, have been at the Park for some 20 years and make sure that all visitors receive prompt and efficient service at all times.

Market Street, Ulverston

as a Lord of the Admiralty for more than forty years, his naval reforms contributing greatly to England's success in the Napoleonic Wars.

An even more famous son of Ulverston was Stanley Jefferson, born at number 3, Argyle Street on June 16th, 1890. Stanley, of course, is far better known to the world as Stan Laurel. His thirty-year career in more than one hundred comedy films with Oliver Hardy is celebrated in the town's **Laurel and Hardy Museum** in King Street. The museum was founded in 1976 by the late Bill Cubin who devoted his life to the famous duo and collected an extraordinary variety of memorabilia,

west and north. Crowning the hill is a 100ft-high **replica of the Eddystone lighthouse**, raised here in 1850 to commemorate one of Ulverston's most distinguished sons, Sir John Barrow. Explorer, diplomat and author, he served

The Tinner's Rabbit

48 Market Street, Ulverston, Cumbria LA12 7LS
Tel: 01229 588808 Fax: 01229 586585
e-mail: chris@tinnersrabbit.freeserve.co

Looking out onto the cobbles of Market Street, the attractive frontage of **The Tinner's Rabbit** conceals no fewer than four different, very interesting enterprises. The first to be established was the gallery and craft shop at No. 48 which Chris Benefield opened in 1998. The gallery has hosted a series of exhibitions by important artists, but as Chris says, the space available was "to say the least, challenging". So when No. 50 became available in 1999, he purchased the property to provide a stage for art and crafts "not only from Great Britain but also Europe". No 48 is now Liz Drew's "The Bookshop" with a beautiful interior by local craftsman Duncan Copley, providing a quiet and welcoming place to relax and browse. Visitors will find a wide selection of local guides, maps and holiday reading.

The complex also includes Lou's Delicatessen in King Street, run by Louise Corbett, which stocks an appetising range of quality items, and Two by Two which sells distinctive clothes and accessories for women. In just one location, visitors can examine the works of noted painters and photographers, both national and local, choose from the wide range of ceramics, jewellery, sponge-ware, pottery, Highland stoneware and much more. Also on site are six studios, occupied by a diverse range of painters and crafts people all of whom are happy to talk with visitors about their work and to accept commissions.

Laurel and Hardy Museum, Ulverston

believed to be the largest in the world. Everything is here, including letters, photographs, personal items, and even furniture belonging to the couple. The museum is now looked after by Bill Cubin's daughter Marion who continues to extend its amenities. A large extension has been added to the modest 17th century house and there is also a small cinema showing films and documentaries throughout the day. The museum is open seven days a week all year round except during January.

Yet another great man associated with the town is George Fox, founder of the Quakers. Despite an extremely rough reception from the citizens of Ulverston when he preached here in the 1650s, Fox later married Margaret, widow of Judge Fell of nearby Swarthmoor Hall. This lovely 17th century manor house, set in extensive gardens, still stands and was acquired by the Society of Friends in 1954.

Ulverston itself, with its fascinating ginnels and cobbled streets, is a delightful place to wander around. The oldest building in the town is the **Church of St Mary** which, in parts, dates from 1111. Though it was restored and rebuilt in the

mid-19th century and the chancel was added in 1903, it has retained its splendid Norman door and some magnificent stained glass, including a window designed by the painter Sir Joshua Reynolds. The present tower dates from the reign of Elizabeth I as the original steeple was destroyed during a storm in 1540.

Ulverston also boasts England's shortest, widest and deepest **canal**. Visitors can follow the towpath walk alongside which runs dead straight for just over a mile to Morecambe Bay. Built by the famous engineer John Rennie and opened in 1796, the canal ushered in a half-century of great prosperity for Ulverston as an inland port. At its peak, some 600 large ships a year berthed here but those good times came to an abrupt end in 1856 with the arrival of the railway. The railway company's directors bought the canal and promptly closed it.

The town's other attractions include a wide range of interesting specialty shops, Heron Glass and Cumbrian Crystal at **The Lakes Glass Centre**, for example, which also houses the **Gateway to Furness Exhibition**, providing a colourful snapshot of the history of the Furness Peninsula. There's more history at the **Ulverston Heritage Centre** which also has a gift shop selling souvenirs and crafts made in Cumbria, while modern entertainment is provided at the Coronation Hall theatre complex and the traditional Roxy Cinema.

Two other snippets of information about Ulverston: the open area to the north of the town, known as **The Gill**, is the starting point for the 70-mile-long

Cumbria Way - and the town claims to have originated the sport of pole vaulting!

AROUND ULVERSTON

HAVERTHWAITE
5 miles NE of Ulverston off the A590

Haverthwaite is the southern terminus of the **Lakeside and Haverthwaite Railway**,

a branch of the Furness railway originally built to transport passengers and goods to the steamers on Lake Windermere. It was one of the first attempts at mass tourism in the Lake District. Passenger numbers peaked in the 1920s but the general decline of rail travel in the 1960s led to the railway's closure in 1967. However, a group of dedicated rail enthusiasts rescued this scenic stretch, restored its engines

The Lakeside & Haverthwaite Railway

Haverthwaite Station, nr Ulverston, Cumbria LA12 8AL
Tel: 015395 31594

From the Victorian station at Haverthwaite, beautifully restored steam locomotives of the **Lakeside & Haverthwaite Railway** haul comfortable coaches through the Leven Valley. With connections at Lakeside by way of Windermere Lake Cruises, the train offers a unique perspective from which to enjoy the every-changing lake and river scenery of this picturesque part of the Lake District. This former Furness Railway branch line runs for 3.5 miles, with a journey time of around 20 minutes, giving passengers a leisurely and relaxing trip. Whilst at Haverthwaite, visitors can sample a delicious home baked scone in the licensed Station Restaurant - an ideal way to start or end the journey.

White Hart Inn

Bouth, Ulverston, Cumbria LA12 8JB
Tel: 01229 861229
website: www.whitehartbouth.co.uk

A charming 16th century hostelry, the **White Hart Inn** offers visitors quality cuisine, comfortable accommodation and a well-stocked bar that boasts some 50 different malt whiskies. Kath and Nigel Barton are "mine hosts" at this welcoming old inn with its olde worlde beams, open log fires and, decked around the ancient walls, an interesting collection of bygone agricultural tools. The inn offers a varied menu that includes old favourites such as the home made Steak & Guinness Pie as well as Pasta Siciliana and a vegetarian Bean Burger. Specialities of the house include dishes made from locally bred rare breed meats. Start your meal with the home made soup of the day, perhaps, and conclude with one of the delicious home made sweets. A free house, the White Hart stocks a wide range of beverages. There are always 6 real ales on tap, (including Jenning's

Cumberland, Black Sheep, Boddington's and Tetley's), a good choice of draught lagers and cider, and of course those 50 malt whiskies. Food is served every lunchtime (noon until 2pm) and evening (6pm to 8.45pm) and can be enjoyed either in the upstairs non-smoking restaurant, in the spacious bar or, weather permitting, in the pleasant beer garden. Booking at weekends is essential. Children are welcome but please note that credit cards are not accepted. The inn also has 4 guest bedrooms, available all year round. Two of the rooms are en suite and each has a double and a single bed; one is a double, the other a twin.

and rolling stock to working order and now provide a full service of steam trains throughout the season. (see panel below).

SWARTHMOOR
1 mile S of Ulverston off the A590

This small village of white-washed cottages, now almost entirely incorporated into Ulverston, also has a curious 16th century hall. **Swarthmoor Hall** stands in well-kept gardens and, although a cement rendering disguises its antiquity, the mullioned windows and leaded panes give a clue to its true age. It was built in around 1586 by George Fell, a wealthy landowner. It was his son, Judge Thomas Fell, who married Margaret Askew, who, in turn, became a follower of George Fox after hearing him preach in 1652. At that time, many people were suspicious of Fox's beliefs but Margaret was able to persuade her husband to use his position to give Fox protection and shelter, and the hall became the first

settled centre of the Quaker Movement. Missionaries were organised from here and the library was stocked with both Quaker and anti-Quaker literature. Judge Fell died in 1658 and, 11 years later, Margaret married George Fox. The hall is open during the summer and it gives a fascinating insight into the history of the early Quakers.

LINDAL-IN-FURNESS
3 miles SW of Ulverston on the A590

The Colony Country Store combines the aromatic character of an old-fashioned country general stores with the cost-cutting advantages of a Factory Shop. There's a huge range of textiles, glassware, ceramics and decorative accessories for the home, but the Colony is also Europe's leading manufacturer of scented candles, supplying millions of scented and dinner candles every year to prestigious stores around the world. The 30 fragrances include classic Rose, fruity Fresh Peach

NEW INN

Silver Street, Marton, Ulverston, Cumbria LA12 0NQ
Tel: 01229 463237 e-mail: the _croppers@lineone.net

During its heyday as a mining village in Victorian times, the village of Marton boasted no fewer than seven hostelries. By the late 1990s, the **New Inn** was the only survivor and *it* was in a pretty parlous state. Then Deborah and Paul Cropper arrived on the scene and spent a great deal of time, money and energy brightening up the old tavern.

Within a very short time they had not only transformed the look of the place but also established a reputation for serving excellent food. Meals are served in the charming restaurant with its large

windows, primrose walls, stained wood floor and vintage fireplace. Paul is an accomplished chef and delights in creative imaginative dishes that are wholesome, appetising and also very good value for money. His menus change every month or so, but a typical menu might include Sautéed Prawns in Lemon & Ginger amongst the starters; main dishes such as Medallions of Duck and Venison or Lamb Henry (minted marinated lamb knuckle joint, pot roasted and served with a minted orange and redcurrant jus-lie); and a good choice of desserts, including Sweet of the Moment - "basically whatever Paul decides to make". The New Inn is a very customer-friendly hostelry so if you are hankering after a particular dish not on the menu, give Paul some notice and he'll be happy to cook it for you! Children are welcome here up to 9.30pm and if you are planning to eat on a weekend evening or Sunday lunchtime, you should definitely book ahead.

and French Vanilla. From a viewing gallery visitors can watch the traditional skills of hand pouring and dipping being used to create a variety of candle styles. And for a small additional fee, you can try your hand at dipping your own candle. Open daily all year round, The Colony has a restaurant serving hot meals and snacks, and free parking.

GREAT URSWICK
3 miles S of Ulverston off the A590

The ancient village **Church of St Mary and St Michael** is noted for its unusual and lively woodcarvings that were created by the Chipping Campden Guild of Carvers. As well as the figure of a pilgrim to the left of the chancel arch, there are some smaller carvings in the choir stall of winged children playing musical instruments. Also worthy of a second look is the 9th century wooden cross which bears a runic inscription.

Lying between Great Urswick and Bardsea and overlooking Morecambe Bay is **Birkrigg Common**, a lovely area of open land. Here, on the east side of the common, is the Druid's Circle, with two concentric circles made up of 31 stones up to three feet high. The cremated human remains found around the site in 1921 indicate that is was used for burials. There are also several other prehistoric sites in the area.

BARDSEA
2 miles S of Ulverston off the A5087

The village stands on a lovely green knoll overlooking the sea and, as well as having a charming, unhurried air about it, there are some excellent walks from here along the coast either from its Country Park or through the woodland.

Just up the coast, to the north, lies **Conishead Priory**, once the site of a leper colony that was established by

Augustinian canons in the 12th century. The monks from the priory used to act as guides across the dangerous Cartmel Sands to Lancashire. After the Dissolution, a superb private house was built on the site and the guide service was continued by the Duchy of Lancaster. In 1821, Colonel Braddyll demolished the house and built in its place the ornate Gothic mansion that stands here today. He was also responsible for the atmospheric ruined folly on **Chapel Island** that is clearly visible in the estuary.

Latterly, Conishead Priory became, firstly, a rest home for Durham miners but it is now owned by the **Tibet Buddhist Manjushri Institute**. During the summer months, visitors are welcome to the house, which is open for tours, and there is a delightful woodland trail to follow through the grounds.

BARROW-IN-FURNESS

Undoubtedly the best introduction to Barrow is to pay a visit to the **Dock Museum** (free), an impressive glass and steel structure which hangs suspended above a Victorian Graving Dock. Audio-visual displays and a series of exhibits describe how Barrow grew from a tiny hamlet in the early 1800s to become the largest iron and steel centre in the world and also a major shipbuilding force in just 40 years. The original population of just 200 had, by 1874, increased to over 35,000.

The museum has some spectacular models of ships of every kind, a recently opened Art Gallery hosts both permanent and travelling exhibitions, and a high tech interactive film show where characters from Barrow's history come to life to tell the town's story. Other attractions at the museum include a themed adventure playground, a Museum

Shop and a coffee shop.

It was James Ramsden who established the first Barrow Iron Ship Company in 1870, taking advantage of local steel production skills. In 1896, the firm was acquired by Vickers, a name forever linked with Barrow, and for a number of years was the largest armaments works in the world.

Today, Barrow is the Peninsula's prime shopping centre, with all the familiar High Street stores mingling with local specialist shops, and the largest indoor market in the area which is open every day except Thursdays and Sundays. The town also boasts a wide range of entertainment facilities - multiplex cinema, 10-pin bowling, fitness centre and leisure club, and three first class golf courses all within easy reach.

Barrow is also the western starting point of the **Cistercian Way**, a 33-mile-walk to Grange-over-Sands through wonderfully unspoilt countryside. En route it passes Furness Abbey in the Vale of Deadly Nightshade, prehistoric sites on the hills surrounding Urswick Tarn and many other historical places of interest. The Way is marked on public roads and footpaths, and a fully descriptive leaflet is available from Tourist Information Centres.

AROUND BARROW-IN-FURNESS

GLEASTON
3 miles E of Barrow-in-Furness off the A5087

This village is typical of the small, peaceful villages and hamlets that can be found in this part of the peninsula. Here, standing close by the ruins of Gleaston Castle, can be found **Gleaston Water**

THE COPPER DOG

Leece, Ulverston, Cumbria LA12 0QP
Tel: 01229 877088 / 877463

With its whitewashed walls and a dazzling floral display of tubs, window boxes and hanging baskets, **The Copper Dog** looks irresistibly inviting. Walkers along the Cistercian Way know it well since the long-distance footpath passes through this small village. Gillian and Morton Richardson bought the inn in 1996. It was then known as the Queen's Arms and had been closed for a year. They gave the inn a new name and a new lease of life so that today the Copper Dog is well-known for the quality of its food and ales. Morton is the chef and his extensive evening menu is available Friday and Saturday evenings and offers around 7 starters, 18 main courses (including two vegetarian options), plus salads and a children's menu. Morton's speciality is sea food, with dishes such as Oysters with Stilton and wonderfully fresh Dressed Crab amongst the most popular choices. At Sunday lunchtime a traditional roast meal is served, as well as a selection of the evening meals. Booking is advisable at all times. To accompany your meal, there's a good selection of beverages, including 2 real ales, Calders, Tetley Dark Mild, draught lager and cider. An additional attraction at the Copper Dog is the live entertainment on Friday evenings, from 9pm, and also on some Saturday evenings. Please note that the pub is closed lunchtimes, Monday to Friday, apart from Bank Holidays, but open all day on Saturdays and Sundays.

Mill. The present buildings date from 1774, with original wooden gearing from the 1700s. The machinery is operational most days - an 18ft water-wheel and an 11ft wooden pit wheel serviced by an intriguing water course. Evening tours with supper are available by prior arrangement.

FOULNEY ISLAND
5 miles E of Barrow-in-Furness off the A5087

The island, like its smaller neighbour Roa Island, is joined to the mainland by a causeway. The site of the local lifeboat station, the island is small and sheltered from the Irish Sea by Walney Island.

PIEL ISLAND
5 miles SE of Barrow-in-Furness via foot ferry from Roa island

Though this tiny island was probably visited by both the Celts and the Romans, its first recorded name is Scandinavian - Fotheray - from the Old Norse meaning "fodder island". In 1127 the islands were given to the Savignac Monks by King Stephen and, after the order merged with the Cistercian monks in the middle of the 12th century, the monks of Furness Abbey began to use Piel Island as a warehouse and storage area.

Piel Castle, on the island, was a house fortified in the early part of the 14th century and at the time it was the largest of its kind in the northwest. Intended to be used as one of the abbey's warehouses and to offer protection from raiders, in later years the castle also proved to be a useful defence against the King's Customs men and a prosperous trade in smuggling began. The castle has, over many years, been allowed to fall into ruin and now presents a stark outline on the horizon.

One of the most exciting events in Piel's history occurred on 4th June 1487 when a man claiming to be the Earl of Warwick, one of the Princes in the Tower allegedly murdered by Richard III, landed on the island. If true, the Earl was indisputably the true King of England. In reality, this "Earl of Warwick" was Lambert Simnel, the son of a joiner. Supported by an army of German and Irish mercenaries, Simnel set out across Furness to march on London. However, when he arrived in the capital it was as the prisoner of Henry VII who had defeated Simnel's troops at Stoke. Somewhat contemptuously, Henry gave Simnel employment in the royal kitchens.

WALNEY ISLAND
2 miles W of Barrow-in-Furness on the A590

This 10-mile-long island is joined to the Furness Peninsula by a bridge from Barrow docks and is home to two important nature reserves that are situated at either end of the island. **North Walney National Nature Reserve** covers some 350 acres within which are a great variety of habitats including sand dunes, heath, salt marsh, shingle, and scrub. As well as having several species of orchid and over 130 species of bird either living or visiting the reserve, there is also an area for the preservation of the Natterjack toad, Britain's rarest amphibian. Unique to the Reserve is the Walney Geranium, a plant that grows nowhere else in the world. North Walney also boasts a rich prehistoric past, with important archaeological sites from mesolithic, neolithic, Bronze, and Iron Age times.

Situated on the island's long foot, **South Walney Nature Reserve** is home to the largest nesting ground of herring gulls and lesser black-backed gulls in Europe. It is also the most southerly breeding ground of such species as the oyster catcher, tern, and ringed plover. A stopover for many migratory birds, the reserve has considerable ecological interest with mudflats, sandy beaches, rough pasture, and fresh water.

The island's southernmost tip, Walney Point, is dominated by a 70ft lighthouse which was built in 1790 and whose light was, originally, an oil lamp.

DALTON-IN-FURNESS
5 miles N of Barrow-in-Furness off the A590

Lying in a narrow valley on the part of Furness which extends deep into Morecambe Bay, it is difficult to imagine that this ancient place was once the leading town of Furness and an important centre for administration and justice. The 14th century pele tower, **Dalton Castle**, was built with walls six feet thick to provide a place of refuge for the monks of Furness Abbey against Scottish raiders and it still looks very formidable. Over the centuries, in its twin role as both prison and court, it has been substantially altered internally although it still retains most of its original external features. It is now owned by the National Trust and houses a small museum with an interesting display of 16th and 17th century armour, along with exhibits about iron mining, the Civil War in Furness, and the life and work of George Romney, the 18th century portrait painter who was born and is buried in Dalton.

Dalton became established as a market town in the 13th century when the Cistercians began to hold fairs and markets in the town. Indeed, the influence of the monks was great here as, before the Dissolution, it was the Abbot who held court and administered justice. Not surprisingly, Dalton's decline coincided with the departure of the monks and also with the growing importance of Ulverston and Greenodd as ports.

The red sandstone **Church of St Mary** was designed by the celebrated Victorian

THE BROWN COW INN

10 Goose Green, Dalton-in-Furness,
Cumbria LA15 8LQ
Tel: 01229 462553 Fax: 01229 468881

Standing close to the parish church, **The Brown Cow Inn** is a delightful traditional inn whose history stretches back to the 1300s. That was when Dalton Castle was being built and housing for the workmen was provided on this spot. Today, the inn is owned and run by Chas Bell and his son Paul. Chas has been here for some 17 years and during that time has established a well-merited reputation for the quality of the food and ales on offer here. The inn is open all

day, every day, and real ale lovers will be pleased to find a choice of at least 4 brews on tap, as well as an array of other beverages. The Brown Cow serves excellent food every day from noon until 9pm. The inn has no fewer than 3 separate dining rooms, (one non-smoking), which between them can seat 100 people. But such is the fame of the food on offer that you should definitely book if you want to eat here at the weekend. The inn has a large screen TV in the bar and outside there's an attractive beer garden. You may well feel like lingering at this charming old inn. In that case, the Brown Car has a self-catering flat which sleeps up to 4 people and is available all year round.

architects Paley and Austin and, in the graveyard, lies George Romney who was best known in his day for his many portraits of Nelson's mistress, Lady Hamilton, with whom he was infatuated. Also worth seeking out in the graveyard is the plaque which outlines the devastating effect of the bubonic plague which swept through the town in 1631.

Visitors to Dalton will find that it is time well spent looking around the many fascinating façades in and close to the market place, such as the unique, cast-iron shop front at No 51, **Market Street**. In the market place itself is an elegant, Victorian drinking fountain with fluted columns supporting a dome of open iron work above the pedestal fountain. Nearby stands the market cross and the slabs of stone that were used for fish-drying in the 19th century.

From the mostly pedestrianised Tudor Square visitors can board a bus to the award-winning **South Lakes Wild Animal Park** which has been designated the Region's Official Top Attraction by the Cumbria Tourist Board. It's the only place in Britain where you can see rare Amur and Sumatran tigers. At feeding time (14.30 each day) they climb a 20ft vertical tree to "catch" their food. Ring-tailed lemurs wander freely through the park, visitors can walk with emus and hand feed the largest collection of kangaroos in Europe. The 17 acres of natural parkland are also home to some of the rarest animals on earth, amongst them the Red Panda, maned wolves and tamarin monkeys as well as some 150 other species from around the world, including the ever-popular meerkats. Other attractions include a Safari Railway, adventure play area, many picnic spots, a gift shop and café.

To the south of the town lies **Furness Abbey** (EH), a magnificent ruin of eroded red sandstone set in fine parkland, the focal point of south Cumbria's monastic heritage. Amongst the atmospheric ruins can still be seen the canopied seats in the presbytery and the graceful arches overlooking the cloister, testaments to the abbey's former wealth and influence. Furness Abbey stands in the Vale of Deadly Nightshade, a shallow valley of sandstone cliffs and rich pastureland. The abbey itself was established in 1123 at Tulketh, near Preston, by King Stephen. Four years later it was moved to its present site and, after 20 years, became absorbed into the Cistercian Order. Despite its remoteness, the abbey flourished, with the monks establishing themselves as guides across the treacherous sands of Morecambe Bay. Rich endowments of land, including holdings in Yorkshire and Ireland, led to the development of trade in products such as

Furness Abbey

The Cloisters, Furness Abbey

wool, iron, and charcoal. Furness Abbey became the second wealthiest monastery in Britain after Fountains Abbey in Yorkshire. After Dissolution, in 1537, the abbey became part of Thomas Cromwell's estate and it was allowed to decay into a picturesque and romantic ruin. It is now owned by English Heritage who have a small Interpretative Centre nearby detailing its history.

GRIZEBECK
15 miles N of Barrow-in-Furness on the A595/A5092

This small village on the edge of the Lake District National Park nestles against the flanks of the **Furness Fells**. Although it stands at the junction of roads leading to the Furness Peninsula and the South Cumbria coast, the village and the area around is peaceful and unhurried, offering the visitor an inviting alternative to some of the busier and more crowded Lakeland towns.

ASHLACK COTTAGES

Ashlack Hall, Grizebeck, Cumbria LA17 7XN
Tel: 01229 889108 Fax: 01229 889111
website: ashlackcottages.co.uk

Beautifully located in idyllic countryside, **Ashlack Cottages** offer quality self-catering accommodation in a peaceful, "get-away-from-it-all" setting which nevertheless is only a 40-minute drive from Junction 36 of the M6. The cottages stand on a working farm where in spring the fields are full of sprightly lambs and young calves, a captivating sight for young visitors.

All the properties have been imaginatively converted from traditional Lakeland farm buildings dating back to the 17th century, and furnished and decorated to a very high standard. Two of the cottages, The Carthouse, located just 200 yards from the main farmhouse, and Beckstones Cottage, a short drive away, are available now. Two more, Old Beckstones and Beckstones Farmhouse, will be ready for occupation in July 2001. Guests at the Carthouse enjoy free membership of the well-equipped Cascades Leisure Club at the Whitewater Hotel only a few miles away. The cottages are ideal for a lazy holiday but if you are feeling more active there are facilities for cycling, swimming and water-skiing all within easy reach. The local pub is a 10-minute walk away and the lively market towns of Ulverston and Barrow-in-Furness about 6 and 8 miles respectively. Even closer are the stone hut circles on Woodland Fell which date back to the Bronze Age.

THE GREYHOUND INN

Grizebeck, Kirkby-in-Furness, Cumbria LA17 7XJ
Tel/Fax: 01229 889224
e-mail: greyhound@grizebeck.fsbusiness.co.uk

Located on the edge of the Lake District National Park, **The Greyhound Inn** looks very inviting with its green shutters and whitewashed walls and the hills rising behind it. There are many scenic walks across the surrounding fells and the Cumbria Coastal Way passes by just a mile or so to the south. The building, which is believed to date back some 300 years, was originally a farmhouse, then an alehouse, before becoming an inn.

Today, The Greyhound is owned and run by Lee and Mike Mawby who have made their traditional tavern with its low-beamed rooms and open log fire a popular venue with locals and visitors alike.

The inn enjoys an exceptional reputation for its food - Lee is a Cordon Bleu chef and her menu offers an excellent choice of wholesome and appetising dishes. Quality home made food is available every lunchtime and evening, and the regular menu is supplemented by daily specials. Enjoy your meal either in the 30-seater restaurant, in the lounge or, on fairweather days, on the outside patio. The Greyhound is a place where you may well want to linger, if so, take advantage of the accommodation on offer. There are 4 guest bedrooms, all of them en suite and one with a 4-poster bed. Visitors are welcome to stay on either a bed & breakfast, or bed, breakfast & dinner basis.

THE OLD KINGS HEAD

Church Street, Broughton-in-Furness, Cumbria LA20 6HJ
Tel: 01229 716293   website: www.oldkingshead.co.uk

With its gleaming white walls, window-boxes and hanging baskets, **The Old Kings Head** looks irresistibly inviting. It's believed to be the oldest building in the village, first recorded in 1666 when it was known as Kirk, or Church, House. During the 1800s, the inn was a recognised posting house and one of the original mangers is still in place, set in the wall of the dining room.

In fact, there are 2 restaurants here, with food available every day for most of the year from noon until 9pm (Sunday, until 8.30pm). Gary McClure, who runs this delightful hostelry with his wife Jacquelyn, is an accomplished chef with an enviable reputation for his freshly prepared dishes. These include vegetarian options and there's a separate full menu for younger guests. Real ale fans will be in their element here since there are always at least 7 brews available in the relaxed and informal bar, along with a full selection of lagers, spirits and soft drinks.

Outside, there's a secluded garden with seating, an activity playground and an aviary. This charming old inn also has accommodation for up to 15 guests in the 6 bedrooms, two of which are doubles and en suite, 2 are family rooms, and two more are standard double rooms. All rooms have central heating, tea/coffee-making facilities, hair dryers and hand basins.

BROUGHTON-IN-FURNESS
19 miles N of Barrow-in-Furness on the A595/A593

At the heart of this attractive, unspoilt little town is the Market Square with its tall Georgian houses, commemorative obelisk of 1810, village stocks, fish slabs and some venerable chestnut trees. The original **Market Hall**, occupying the whole of one side, dates back to 1766 and now houses the town's Tourist Information Centre and the Square Gallery which exhibits paintings, ceramics, mirrors and glassware. On August 1st each year, Broughton's Lord of the Manor comes to the Square to read out the market charter granted by Elizabeth I, while Councillors dispense pennies to any children in the crowd.

One of the town's famous short-term residents was Branwell Brontë who was employed here as a tutor at Broughton House, a splendid double-fronted, 3-storey town house just off the Square. Branwell apparently found time to both enjoy the elegance of the town and to share in whatever revelries were in train. Wordsworth often visited Broughton as a child. Throughout his life he loved this peaceful corner of Lakeland and celebrated its charms in some 150 poems; his 20th century poetical successor, Norman Nicholson, was similarly enchanted.

Some of the Lake District's finest scenery - the Duddon Valley, Furness Fells, Great Gable and Scafell are all within easy reach, and about 3 miles west of the town is **Swinside Circle**, a fine prehistoric stone circle, some 60ft in diameter, containing 52 close-set stones and two outlying "portal" or gateway stones.

About 3 miles north of the town, the peaceful hamlet of **Broughton Mills** will attract followers of the **Coleridge Trail**.

ROSE COTTAGE

Lane End Farm, Broughton Mills,
Broughton-in-Furness, Cumbria LA20 6AX
Tel: 01229 716332

Dating back to the late 1600s, **Rose Cottage** is located in the peaceful hamlet of Broughton Mills, in the Lickle Valley which is next to Duddon Valley, one of Wordsworth's most favoured parts of the Lake District. The cottage has been sympathetically refurbished and remains full of character with its old beams, open fire and deep window seat.

It now provides quality self-catering accommodation for up to 6/7 people in its 3 bedrooms: - a family room with double bed and a single divan, a small room with bunk beds, and another room with a double bed. Downstairs, there's a spacious lounge equipped with TV and video, and with that open fire with its splendid stone surround. Also on the ground floor is a large kitchen-dining room, fully fitted with modern units, microwave, refrigerator, cooker, dishwasher, stainless steel sink and plenty of pans, cooking utensils and crockery. A washing machine and tumble dryer is available in a separate utility room nearby. All heating and bedding is included in the tariff. An attractive feature at Rose Cottage is the small garden and patio provided with table and seats. Please note that the cottage is non-smoking and that pets cannot be accommodated. Children are welcome. From Easter 2001, the owner of Rose Cottage, Mrs Harrison, will have a second property available for self-catering guests, Honeysuckle Cottage, which sleeps just 2 people.

During the course of his famous "circumcursion" of Lakeland in August 1802, the poet stopped to refresh himself at the Blacksmith's Arms where he "Dined on Oatcake and Cheese, with a pint of Ale, and 2 glasses of Rum and water sweetened with preserved Gooseberries". The inn, built in 1748, is still there and barely changed since Coleridge's visit.

4 Coniston and Southwest Cumbria

Three distinct areas lie within the southwest quarter of Cumbria. The enchanting scenery around Coniston Water and its environs is very much

Little Langdale

on the tourist trail, and also has strong literary connections. John Ruskin, the 19th century author, artist, and critic made his home at Brantwood on the shore of Coniston and the lake is also the setting for many of the adventures recounted in *Swallows and Amazons* as told by Arthur Ransome. Wordsworth went to school in Hawkshead where the desk he defaced with his name can still be seen. But probably the most popular of Coniston's literary denizens is Beatrix Potter who, after holidaying at Near Sawrey as a child, later bought a house at Hill Top as well as many acres of farms which she bequeathed to the National Trust. Further west is Cumbria's "Empty Quarter", a vast terrain of magnificent mountains and desolate fells beloved of climbers and walkers. England's highest mountain, Scafell Pike, rises here; the country's deepest lake, Wast Water, sinks to a depth of some 200ft and is surrounded by sheer cliffs soaring up to 2000ft, and the village of Wasdale Head claims to have the smallest church in England.

Bordering this untamed landscape is the narrow coastal strip, stretching from Whitehaven down to Millom, which has its own identity as well as a quiet charm. The coastline is dominated by small 18th and 19th century iron mining communities set between the romantic outline of the Lakeland fells and the grey-blue waters of the Irish Sea. The famous Ravenglass and Eskdale Railway carries many visitors from the coast up one of Cumbria's most picturesque valleys. There are also several genteel Victorian resorts along the coast, including the popular village of Seascale. One of the area's most controversial sites is the visitor centre at Sellafield, the nuclear power station, which has defied all predictions to become one of the most popular visitor attractions in Cumbria.

Ulpha

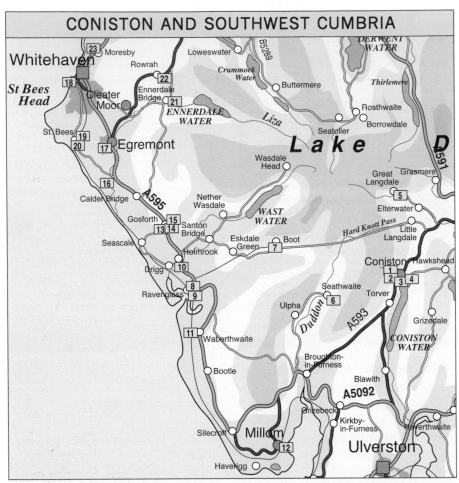

CONISTON AND SOUTHWEST CUMBRIA

© MAPS IN MINUTES ™ (1999)

PLACES TO STAY, EAT, DRINK AND SHOP

CONISTON

Beatrix Potter, John Ruskin, Arthur Ransome, Sir Donald Campbell - all of them have strong connections with Coniston Water, the third largest and one of the most beautiful of the central Cumbrian lakes. Beatrix Potter lived at Sawrey near Lake Windermere but she owned the vast Monk Coniston estate at the head of Coniston Water. On her death, she bequeathed it to the National Trust, a body she had helped establish and to which she devoted much of her time and fortune.

Ruskin came to Coniston in 1872, moving into a house he had never seen. "**Brantwood**", on the eastern side of the lake, is open to the public and enjoys superb views across the water to the great crumpled hill of the "**Old Man of Coniston**", 800 metres high. From its summit there are even more extensive vistas over Scotland, the Isle of Man, and on a clear day as far as Snowdonia.

Arthur Ransome's *Swallows and Amazons* has delighted generations with its tales of children's adventures set in and around the Lake District. As a child he spent his summer holidays near Nibthwaite at the southern end of the lake and recalled that he was always "half-drowned in tears" when he had to leave. Later he bought a house overlooking Coniston Water and many locations in his books can be recognised today: Peel Island, for example, at the southern end of the lake, is the Wildcat Island of his books.

Sir Donald Campbell's associations with the lake were both glorious and tragic. In 1955 he broke the world water speed record here; twelve years later, when he was attempting to beat his own record, his boat, *Bluebird*, struck a log while travelling at 320mph. Campbell's body was never recovered but in March 2001 his widow, Tonia Bern-Campbell, watched tearfully as the tailfin of the boat

Coniston Lake from Nibthwaite

THE SUN HOTEL

Coniston, Cumbria LA21 8HQ
Tel: 015394 41248 Fax: 015394 41219
e-mail: TheSUN@hotelconiston.com
website: www.smoothhound.co.uk/hotels/sun.html

About 100 years ago, the local brewery decided to
build a hotel on the hill leading up to The Old Man
of Coniston. They already owned a 16th century pub
there so they built **The Sun Hotel** right next to it.
Today, the delightful 400-year-old inn is gradually
being uncovered. It's a real gem, with flagstone floor,
beamed ceiling, a beautiful old range in the fireplace,
and piped music is banned! With 5 real ales on tap,
the pub "is ideally suited for walkers and talkers" says
its owner, Alan Piper. He bought the hotel in March
2000 and has his sights firmly set on raising standards
generally and the quality of what he and his staff
provide in particular.

In the restaurant just about everything is prepared and cooked on site and Alan has a policy of
buying locally wherever possible. The meat for example comes from locally reared or fell-bred traditional
English or Scottish breeds. The restaurant, like the lounge, overlooks the terrace and the large mature
garden that stretches away down the hill towards the lake and village. The views are spectacular - no
wonder Donald Campbell stayed at The Sun during his later attempts at the Water Speed Record. The
hotel has 11 guest bedrooms, all en suite or with private bathrooms, and with the old inn next door,
provides a relaxed, inexpensive, pet-friendly venue for all age groups. As one guest put it, "everyone
from twinklies to wrinklies!"

THE COPPERMINES

The Estate Office, The Bridge, Coniston, Cumbria LA21 8HJ
Tel: 015394 41765
website: www.coppermines.co.uk

The scenic beauty of Coniston Water may be the major attraction for visitors
nowadays, but during the Bronze Age and while the Romans occupied
Cumbria, and again from the 1600s to Victorian times, the only reason
anyone came here was to extract copper from the hillsides. Hence the name
of Philip Johnston's cluster of self-catering cottages, **The Coppermines** -
four charming cottages in spectacular mountain scenery. All of the cottages
are built of local stone, a material which displays an astonishing range of
hues - anything from near-charcoal to gleaming white. Inside, the cottages
are just as attractive as they look from outside, with lots of vintage
architectural features still in place. Each of the cottages can accommodate
from 2 to 8 guests but, if you ingeniously link them together, up to 27

visitors can enjoy a high old
time here. All of the cottages are
provided with every up-to-date
amenity. The kitchens (stylishly designed with oak or
chestnut surrounds) are comprehensively equipped with
electric cooker, dish washer, microwave, fridge/freezer and
washing machine. Every cottage at The Coppermines also
has a comfortable sitting/dining room warmed, (if
necessary), by log fire central heating and provided with
a colour television. Should you get bored by the television
programmes, just step to the window and marvel at the
mountain views.

Gondola Steam Yacht, Coniston Lake

mountain, and some of the surrounding hills, that copper was extracted. Mined from the days of the Romans, the industry's heyday in Coniston took place in the 18th and 19th centuries but, with the discovery of more accessible deposits, the industry went into decline and the village returned to pre-boom peacefulness. At 2,631 feet, the Old Man of Coniston is a considerable climb but many make the effort and the summit can be bustling with fell walkers enjoying the glorious views.

was at last hauled up to the surface. For 34 years the 15ft rear section had lain on a bed of silt, 140ft down and right in the middle of the lake. Plans are currently under way for the boat to be restored and placed on display at the Ruskin Museum.

Nowadays, boats on **Coniston Water** are restricted to a 10 mph limit which is an ideal speed if you're travelling in the wonderful old steamship, the *Gondola*. So called because of its high prow which enabled it to come in close to shore to pick up passengers, Gondola was built in 1859, abandoned in 1937 for many years and then restored by the National Trust in 1980. Up to 86 passengers can now travel in opulent comfort on its regular trips around the lake. Coniston Launch also offers lake cruises in its two timber launches, and at the boating centre craft of every kind are available to rent.

Coniston village was once an important copper mining centre and was also widely known for the beautiful decorative green slate, quarried locally, which is used on so many of the public buildings. The great bulk of the **Old Man of Coniston** overlooks the village and it was from this

Just south of the village and beside the lake is Coniston Hall, the village's oldest building. Dating from the 16th century, it was the home of the Le Fleming family, the largest landowners in the area. Coniston's most famous inhabitant was, however, John Ruskin, the 19th century author, artist, critic, social commentator and one of the first conservationists. He lies buried in Coniston churchyard and the **Ruskin Museum** nearby contains many of his studies, pictures, letters, and photographs as well as his collection of geological specimens. You can also see a pair of his socks, his certificate of matriculation from Oxford, and his funeral pall made of Ruskin lace embroidered with wild flowers. The lace was so called because Ruskin had encouraged the revival of flax hand-spinning the area. Lace pieces made to his own designs and based on the sumptuous ruffs worn by sitters in portraits by Titian, Tintoretto and Veronese, were attached to plain linen to make decorative cushions, table covers and bedspreads - many of these are on display.

JUMPING JENNY AT BRANTWOOD

Coniston, Cumbria LA21 8AD
Tel: 015394 41715 Fax: 015394 41819

Occupying the former stables of John Ruskin's home, Brantwood House, **Jumping Jenny at Brantwood** is an outstanding coffee house and licensed restaurant which also boasts stunning views from its terrace across the enchanting lake that Ruskin loved so much. Jumping Jenny, incidentally, is the name of Ruskin's rowing boat. The boat has survived intact and is on display nearby in the Coach House.

Chris and Gillie Addison took over here in 1991 and readily admit that they had little previous experience of running a food operation - "which we think is an advantage!" Chris was a City/West End lawyer whose dinner parties were memorable affairs. He's in charge of the savoury menu. Gillie was in Executive Recruitment but had mastered

baking at an early age at home in New Zealand. So she looks after the sweets and cakes. Everything they serve, apart from the bread which comes from local bakers, they cook themselves. Jumping Jenny is open every day, (except Mondays and Tuesdays from December to February), from 11am until 6pm (earlier in winter), but the evenings are available for pre-booked parties of 10 or more. You would be well-advised to book well in advance.

As a very special prelude to your meal, Chris and Gillie can arrange for your party to enjoy a cruise around the lake first, with drinks and delicious canapés served on board.

CONISTON LODGE PRIVATE HOTEL

Sunny Brow, Coniston, English Lakes,
Cumbria LA21 8HH
Tel/Fax: 015394 41201
e-mail: infor@coniston-lodge.com
website: www.coniston-lodge.com

One regular visitor to the **Coniston Lodge Private Hotel** calls it his "little piece of heaven on earth" and tourism organisations have been equally enthusiastic. The RAC awarded the Lodge their "Small Hotel of the Year" (Northern Region) in 1993, the English Tourism Council gives it 4 diamonds and a Gold Award, while the AA rating is Premier Select QQQQQ. The Lodge is owned and run by Anthony and Elizabeth Robinson, the third generation of Lakeland hoteliers. They built the Lodge in 1989, hoping to create "something just a little different, a small hotel, with that very special feeling of staying in someone's beautiful home, but with the facilities you would expect in a modern hotel". There are 6 beautifully furnished guest bedrooms, (3 doubles, 3 twins), all en suite and one with a 4-poster bed.

The Dining Room enjoys an excellent reputation for its traditional home-cooked English and Lakeland

dishes, presented with flair and originality and based on fresh local produce. There's a small but very carefully chosen wine list with some interesting entries and with something to complement every dish. Guests have the use of a comfortable residents' lounge which overlooks the garden and where one of the intriguing features is a plaque, carved in Lakeland Green Slate, which depicts *Bluebird,* the world speed record breaking boat. The plaque was commissioned in memory of Donald Campbell whose family always stayed with the Robinsons when making their record attempts on Lake Coniston.

Brantwood

From the jetty at Coniston, a short ferry trip takes you to John Ruskin's home, **Brantwood**, which occupies a beautiful setting on the eastern shores of Coniston Water. It was his home from 1872 until his death in 1900. When he arrived for the first time he described the house, which he had bought for £1500 without ever seeing it, as "a mere shed". He spent the next 20 years extending the house, by adding another 12 rooms, and laying out the gardens. The view from the Turret Room he had built was, Ruskin declared, "the best in all England". Sadly, Ruskin's later years were blighted by mental illness, "He was" said a biographer "at times quite mad".

Visitors today can wander around rooms filled with Ruskin's watercolours, paintings by Turner (who was one of his heroes), see his study which is lined with wallpaper he designed himself, and watch a 20-minute video which provides a useful introduction to his life and works. Every Thursday during the season there are lace-making demonstrations and readings from Ruskin's works are performed regularly in the study. There's also a well-stocked bookshop, a craft gallery, an excellent tea room, the Jumping Jenny (see panel opposite), and 250 acres of grounds where there are well-marked nature trails and where a theatre season is held during the summer.

AROUND CONISTON

GRIZEDALE
3 miles SE of Coniston off the B5285

The village lies at the heart of the 9000-acre **Grizedale Forest** which was acquired by the Forestry Commission in 1934 and is famous for its Theatre and Sculpture. The Commission's original intention of chiefly cultivating the forest for its timber met with much resistance and, over the years, many pathways have been opened and a variety of recreational activities have been encouraged. The Visitor Centre vividly illustrates the story of the forest as well as showing how the combination of wildlife, recreation, and commercial timbering can work together hand in hand. The forest, too, is famously the home of some 80 tree sculptures commissioned since 1977. All are created from natural materials found in the forest and they have been made by some of Britain's best known contemporary artists, including Andy Goldsworthy, as well as by artists from all over the world. The great beauty of these

Brantwood

On the Sculpture Trail, Grizedale

sculptures is their understated presence: there are no signposts pointing to the exhibits and visitors are left entirely on their own to discover these wonders though there is a printed map obtainable from the Visitor Centre.

The **Theatre-in-the-Forest** has an excellent programme throughout the year of musical and theatrical events of the highest quality, and the Visitor Centre now includes an art gallery and workshop which is also open to the public, where the artists in residence will happily take a break from their work to describe their experiences of living and working in this unique environment.

NEAR SAWREY
4 miles E of Coniston on the B5285

Though this little village will not be familiar to many visitors to the Lake District, its famous inhabitant, Beatrix Potter, almost certainly will be. After holidaying here in 1896, the authoress fell in love with the place and, with the royalties from her first book, *The Tale of Peter Rabbit*, she purchased **Hill Top** in 1905. After her marriage in 1913 to a local solicitor, she actually lived in another house in the village, Castle Cottage (private), and used the charming 17th century cottage as her study. Oddly, she wrote very little after the marriage, spending most of her time dealing with the management of the farms she had bought in the area.

Following Potter's death in 1943, the house and the land she had bought on the surrounding fells became the property of the National Trust and, in accordance with her will, Hill Top has remained exactly as she would have known it. One of the most popular Lakeland attractions, Hill Top is full of Beatrix Potter memorabilia, including some of her original drawings. Bear in mind that the house is very small - so it is best avoided at peak holiday times.

HAWKSHEAD
3 miles E of Coniston on the B5285

There are more Beatrix Potter connections in the enchanting little village of Hawkshead. Her solicitor husband, William Heelis, worked from an office in the Main Street here and this has now been transformed into **The Beatrix Potter Gallery.** The gallery features an exhibition of her original drawings and illustrations alongside details of the author's life.

Hawkshead has specific Wordsworth connections too. **Hawkshead Grammar School** was founded in 1585, and between 1779 and 1787 the young William Wordsworth was a star pupil. The earliest of his surviving poems was written to celebrate the school's 200th year. The

St Michael's Church, Hawkshead

school is open from Easter to September and visitors can inspect the classrooms during the summer holidays, see the desk where William carved his name and have a look around the headmaster's study. Ann Tyson's cottage, where Wordsworth lodged while he attended the school, has

also survived. It stands in Wordsworth Street and is now a guest house.

Situated at the head of **Esthwaite Water**, enjoying glorious views of Coniston Old Man and Helvellyn, Hawkshead has a history that goes back to Viking times. Its name is Norse in origin, derived from Haukr who built the original settlement. It's a delightful village of narrow cobbled lanes with a pedestrianised main square dominated by the Market House, or Shambles, and another square linked to it by little snickets and arched alleyways which invite exploration. The poet Norman Nicholson observed that *"The whole village could be fitted into the boundaries of a large agricultural show; yet it contains enough corners, angles, alleys and entries to keep the eye happy for hours"*.

Hawkshead was once an important market town serving the surrounding area and at that time most of the land here was owned by the monks of Furness Abbey. The only building to remain from those monastic times is the **Courthouse**, to the north of the village, part of a medieval manor house built by the monks.

St Michael's Church, with its massive 15th century tower, seems rather grand for the village but it too was built at a time when Hawkshead was a wealthy town. Inside, there are some remarkable wall paintings from the late 1600s and also look out for the "Buried in Woolen" affidavit near the vestry door. In 1666 the Government had decreed that corpses must not be buried in shrouds made from *"flaxe, hempe, silke or hair, or other than what is made of sheeps wool onely"*. The idea was to help maintain the local woollen industry and this was one way of

Hawkshead Centre

THE OLD DUNGEON GHYLL HOTEL

Great Langdale, Ambleside, Cumbria LA22 9JY
Tel/Fax: 015394 37272
e-mail: neil.odg@lineone.net website: www.odg.co.uk

Mike Harding is just one of many fell walkers and rock climbers for whom the Great Langdale Valley is a favourite area, "both because the round of the Pikes, Bowfell and Crinkle Crags is a great day and because the **Old Dungeon Ghyll Hotel** is a wonderful pub with music and singing in the old bar". Most visitors call in first at the Hiker's Bar where there's a selection of real ales on tap.

Occupying a superb position at the head of the Great Langdale Valley, the hotel has been providing hospitality for some 300 years. In the old days the horse-drawn "charas" bringing visitors over Blea Tarn Pass would pause at the top, and the coachman would blow his horn as a signal for the landlord to prepare lunch or tea - the number of blasts indicating the number of passengers requiring a meal! Since 1983 this grand old inn has been owned and run by Neil and Jane Walmsley who have continued

to improve and develop its amenities. They both enjoy cooking so the emphasis is very much on home made meals served in the comfortable dining room. An excellent wine list is available. The hotel has a spacious residents' lounge with an open fire, a quiet residents' bar and, an essential amenity for Lake District walkers, a drying room! There are 14 attractive bedrooms, 4 of which have en suite facilities, while an abundance of hot water supplies the bathrooms for a well-earned soak.

THE NEWFIELD INN

Seathwaite, Duddon Valley,
Broughton-in-Furness,
Cumbria LA20 6ED
Tel: 01229 716208
e-mail: paul@seathwaite.freeserve.co.uk

Located on the country road leading to the dramatic Wrynose Pass and Langdale, **The Newfield Inn** dates back to the 1600s and during its long history has served as a farmhouse, alehouse and Post Office. There's even some evidence that Manorial Courts were held here.

Today, this welcoming old inn is run by Paul and Alwyn Batten who only took over in the winter of 2000 but since Paul's parents ran the inn from 1974 to 1990 he knows it well - and also has an excellent knowledge of this spectacularly scenic area. An interesting feature of the inn is its unique slate floor, made with slate quarried from the nearby Walner Scar Quarry which closed some 80 years ago. The Newfield is open all day, every day, with appetising food available daily. The varied choice of dishes can be enjoyed either in the bar or in the stylish grill room which seats 26. Booking is strongly recommended for Fridays and Saturdays. (Please note, credit cards are not accepted). Beverages on offer include a minimum of 3 real ales, with Theakston's Old Peculier and Coniston Bluebird as regulars, Younger's Scotch Bitter, Guinness, plus draught lagers and cider.

For those planning to stay in the area, The Newfield has 2 holiday flats available, one accommodating 2 to 4 guests, the other up to 6. They are adjacent to the inn, comfortably furnished and equipped with cooker, fridge, microwave oven and television.

ensuring that even the dead got to help out.

Some lovely walks lead from Hawkshead to Roger Ground and Esthwaite Water, possibly the least frequented of the Lakes, and also to the nearby hamlet of **Colthouse** where there's an early Quaker Meeting House built around 1690.

Langdale Pikes

GREAT LANGDALE
9 miles N of Coniston on the B5343

One of the most dramatic of the Lake District waterfalls is **Dungeon Ghyll** which tumbles 60ft down the fellside. The "dungeon" is actually a natural cave. Nearby is the well known Old Dungeon Ghyll Hotel (see panel on page) which makes an excellent starting point for walks in this spectacularly scenic area where the famous peaks of Crinkle Crags, Bowfell and the Langdale Pikes provide some serious challenges for hikers and ramblers.

SEATHWAITE
5 miles W of Coniston via minor road off the A593

A mere 5 miles or so from Coniston as the crow flies, by road Seathwaite is nearly three times as far. It stands in one of the Lake District's most tranquil and least known valleys, **Dunnerdale**. Little has changed here since the days when William Wordsworth, who knew the area as Duddon Valley, captured its natural beauty in a sequence of sonnets. In his poem *The Excursion*, he wrote about the Revd. Robert Walker, the curate of Seathwaite. Nicholas, or "Wonderful Walker" as Wordsworth referred to him, served the church here for some 67 years though he also filled various other jobs such as farm labourer and nurse as well as spinning wool and making his own clothes. Fell walkers and hikers who prefer to escape the masses will delight not only in the solitude of this glorious valley but also in the wide variety of plant, animal, and birdlife that have made this haven their home.

HARDKNOTT PASS
5 miles W of Coniston off the A593

Surrounded by the fell of the same name, this pass is one of the most treacherous in the Lake District yet it was used by the Romans for the road between their forts at Ambleside (Galava) and Ravenglass (Glannaventa). Of the remains of Roman occupation, **Hardknott Fort** on a shoulder of the fell, overlooking the Esk Valley, is the most substantial and also provides some of the grandest views in the whole of the Lake District.

BOOT
8 miles W of Coniston off the A595

Lying at the eastern end of the **Ravenglass and Eskdale Railway**, this is

BROOK HOUSE INN & RESTAURANT

Boot, Eskdale, Cumbria CA19 1TG
Tel: 019467 23288 Fax: 019467 23160
e-mail: stay@brookhouseinn.co.uk
website: www.brookhouseinn.co.uk

A delightful way of arriving at the **Brook House Inn & Restaurant** is by way of the Ravenglass & Eskdale light railway - "La'al Ratty". The station is only 200 metres from the inn and someone from the Thornley family will pick you up there by prior arrangement. There are three generations of the Thornley family involved in the running of this relaxed and friendly hotel.

Built around 1870, Brook House enjoys glorious views of the spectacular scenery of Eskdale and provides an ideal base for exploring the unspoilt western fells and valleys. (A drying room is provided

at the inn for those occasional rainy days!) Delicious home-made food is served all day until last orders at 8.30pm, and the imaginative menu includes vegetarian options, a children's menu, and some famous puddings. Daily specials are available, and you can complement your meal with a selection from the wide range of real ales or from the varied wine list. Devotees of the amber nectar will find a huge choice of malt whiskies, currently 75 brands and rising! If you plan to stay in this enchanted corner of the county, Brook House has 8 guest bedrooms, all beautifully furnished and decorated, all en suite and with central heating, colour TV, radio, and grand views of the local fells.

HOLLY HOUSE HOTEL

Ravenglass, Cumbria CA18 1SQ
Tel: 01229 717230

A small privately-run hotel, **Holly House Hotel** occupies a peaceful position in this quiet village overlooking the broad estuary where the rivers Esk, Irt and Mite flow into the Irish Sea. Anita Jackson arrived at Holly House in 1995 and her friendly personality has made the hotel a favourite eatery with both visitors and locals alike. Wholesome home-made food is available throughout the day, served either in the bar or in the intimate dining room. The menu provides

for all tastes and pockets, including vegetarians, and there's also a special children's menu. The cosy public bar, with its welcoming log-burning stove, offers a wide selection of wines, spirits and beers, including real ale. Once a month, Anita hosts a Theme Night when she and her staff dress up and encourage customers to do the same. Food and drink appropriate to the occasion are served - and at a specially reduced rate.

Holly House has 6 comfortable guest rooms, three of them en suite, the other three with wash basins, and all with TV. Three of the rooms enjoy views across the estuary, a popular spot for sailing. Fishermen are spoiled with a choice of beach or river fishing virtually on the doorstep and railway buffs will be delighted to find the Ravenglass and Eskdale narrow gauge railway nearby. At Ravenglass station, there's an interesting museum which records the history of the 7-mile long railway which many believe provides one of the most scenic rail journeys in the country.

a wonderful place to visit whether arriving by train or car. A gentle walk from the station at Eskdale brings you to this delightful village with its pub, post office, museum, waterfall and nearby St Catherine's Church in its lovely secluded riverside setting. Perhaps because of the rugged walking country to the east, the village is well supplied with both a campsite and bunkhouse available.

ESKDALE GREEN
10 miles W of Coniston off the A595

One of the few settlements in this beautiful and unspoiled valley, the village lies on the route of the Ravenglass and Eskdale Railway. Further up the valley lies a group of buildings that make up **Eskdale Mill** where cereals have been ground since 1578. The original machinery for grinding oatmeal is in full working order and operated daily. Power for the two waterwheels is provided by Whillan Beck which surges down from England's highest mountains, the Scafell range. Visitors can enjoy a picnic in the picturesque mill grounds, browse in the gift shop or explore the Mill's history in the informative exhibition.

RAVENGLASS

Lying at the estuary of three rivers - the Esk, the Mite, and the Irt - as well as enjoying a sheltered position, it is not surprising that Ravenglass was an important port from prehistoric times. The Romans built a naval base here around AD78 which served as a supply point for the military zone around Hadrian's Wall. They also constructed a fort, Glannaventra, on the cliffs above the town, which was home to around 1,000

Eskdale Green

THE RATTY ARMS

Ravenglass, Cumbria CA18 1SN
Tel/Fax: 01229 717676 e-mail:
rattyarms@aol.com

New patrons of **The Ratty Arms** naturally want to know how it acquired its unusual name. The answer lies in the narrow gauge Ravenglass & Eskdale Railway which here meets the main West Cumbrian railway line. To local people, the narrow gauge railway was always affectionately known as the "laal Ratty". So when the privately-owned Ravenglass & Eskdale company bought the old main line railway station in 1974 and converted it into a tavern, The Ratty Arms was the obvious name to choose. The former platform provides a splendidly spacious patio for eating out on fine summer days and inside, as you might expect, the decor has a railway theme with lots of railway memorabilia on show. Mine hosts, Beverley and Gordon, have even added Gordon's old model railway to the display!

The inn enjoys an excellent reputation for the quality of the food on offer. The daytime menu includes a wide range of main dishes, vegetarian choices, children's meals, light meals, salads and sandwiches. A popular feature is the half-portion option for those with lighter appetites. In the evening, a selection of starters, steak and other grilled dishes is also available. Four real ales are always on tap, along with a wide range of other beverages. The inn has non-smoking areas, children and dogs are welcome, and there's a ramp and toilets for the disabled and baby changing facilities.

MUNCASTER CASTLE

Ravenglass, Cumbria CA18 1RQ
Tel: 01229 717614 Fax: 01229 717010

Muncaster Castle is an impressive castellated mansion which has been owned by the Pennington family since 1208. Back in 1464 the Penningtons gave shelter to King Henry VI after his defeat at the Battle of Hexham. On his departure Henry presented them with his enamelled glass drinking bowl saying that as long as it remained unbroken the Penningtons would live and thrive at Muncaster. It remains intact and the Penningtons are indeed still here - your audio tour guide is narrated by Patrick Gordon-Duff-Pennington, the present owner, who enlivens the tale with old legends and family anecdotes. The tour also introduces visitors to the many Muncaster treasures (including tapestry, silver, and porcelain collections), the stunning Great Hall, Salvin's octagonal library and the barrel ceiling in the drawing room.

Muncaster is also famous for its gardens and, in particular, the rhododendrons, azaleas, and camellias which are best viewed between March and June. The woodland gardens themselves cover some 77 acres and, as well as the beauty of the vegetation, there are some splendid views over the Lakeland fells. These extensive grounds also contain a fascinating Owl Centre which is home to more than 180 birds of 50 different species. Here, visitors can meet the birds daily at 14.30 (late March to early November) when a talk is given on the work of the centre and, weather permitting, the owls display their flying skills. Other attractions include a very well-equipped children's play area with an aerial runway, scramble net and fireman's pole; a nature trail and orienteering course, plant centre, gift shop and licensed café. The gardens and owl centre are open daily throughout the year; the castle is open each afternoon from the end of March to the end of October (closed Saturday).

soldiers. Little remains of Glannaventra except for the impressively preserved walls of the Bath House. Almost 12ft high, these walls are believed to be the highest Roman remains in the country.

In the 18th century Ravenglass was a base for smugglers bringing contraband in from coastal ships - tobacco and French brandy. Today, the estuary has silted up but there are still scores of small boats and the village is a charming resort, full of atmosphere. The layout has changed little since the 16th century; the main street is paved with sea pebbles and leads up from a shingle beach. Once, iron-ore was brought to the estuary by narrow gauge railway from the mines near Boot, in Eskdale, about eight miles away.

One of the town's major attractions is the 15" narrow gauge **Ravenglass and Eskdale Railway** which runs for seven miles up the lovely Mite and Esk River valleys. Better known as "La'al Ratty", it was built in 1875 to transport ore and quarried stone from the Eskdale Valley and opened the following year for passenger traffic. Since then the railway has survived several threats of extinction. The most serious occurred at the end of the 1950s when the closure of the Eskdale granite quarries wiped out the railway's freight traffic at a stroke. However, at the auction for the railway in 1960 a band of enthusiasts outbid the scrap dealers and formed a company to keep the little railway running.

Today, the company operates 12 locomotives, both steam and diesel, and 300,000 people a year come from all over the world to ride on what has been described as "the most beautiful train journey in England". The La'al Ratty is still the best way to explore Miterdale and Eskdale and enchants both young and old alike. There are several stops along the journey and at both termini there is a café and a souvenir shop. At the Ravenglass

station there is also the Railway Museum which brings to life the history of this remarkable line and the important part it has played in the life of Eskdale.

A mile or so east of Ravenglass stands **Muncaster Castle**. Apart from the many treasures (including tapestry, silver, and porcelain collections), the stunning Great Hall, Salvin's octagonal library and the barrel ceiling in the drawing room, **Muncaster** is also famous for its gardens. The grounds contain a fascinating Owl Centre, well-equipped children's play area, a nature trail and orienteering course, plant centre, gift shop and licensed café (see panel opposite).

Originally part of the Muncaster Castle Estate, **Muncaster Water Mill** can be traced back to 1455 though it is thought that this site may be Roman. The situation is certainly idyllic, with the mill race still turning the huge wooden water wheel and the Ravenglass and Eskdale Railway running alongside. In November 1996, Pam and Ernie Priestley came to the mill and Ernie put his years of engineering experience to use as the miller. The mill is open every day from Easter to the end of October, working just as it has done for hundreds of years. Visitors can see the machinery in action, and also enjoy some delicious refreshments in the 17th century byre tea rooms. Naturally, the organic flour ground here is used in all the cakes, breads, and scones, and the flour is also on sale.

AROUND RAVENGLASS

WABERTHWAITE
4 miles S of Ravenglass on the A595

No visit to west Cumbria is complete without the inclusion of a trip to RG Woodall's shop. Found in the heart of

BROWN COW INN

Waberthwaite, Millom, Cumbria LA19 5YJ
Tel: 01229 717243 Fax: 01229 717295
e-mail: browncow@westlakes.co.uk
website: www.westlakes.co.uk/browncow.htm

Conveniently located on the A595 about 3 miles south of Ravenglass, the **Brown Cow Inn** is a delightful traditional hostelry with a well-deserved reputation for its excellent food. Not only is the food good, it is available throughout the day, every day, from 9am until 11pm (last orders, 10pm). You can start the day with a full English or Continental Breakfast, have a break for morning coffee or tea, return for Afternoon or High Tea, and of course enjoy lunch and dinner here as well!

Mine hosts at the Brown Cow are Keith and Freda Hitchen, with Keith the chef. His menu includes local delicacies such as Waberthwaite Ham, and Cumberland Gammon or Sausage, as well as fish dishes, a vegetarian special and a good choice of meals for children. Keith is generous with his servings

but if you don't have a large appetite you can order smaller portions at £1 less than the menu price. Meals are served in the non-smoking dining room, in the bar or in the snug with its blazing open fire. On Thursday evenings, Keith excels himself with a selection of Indian dishes, (up to 7 courses if you wish), and at Sunday lunchtime a choice of 2 roasts is available from noon right through the day. The inn also provides a takeaway service and if you are looking for somewhere to stay in this lovely area, the Brown Cow has a self-catering flat available which sleeps up to 4 people - children are welcome.

THE SHIP INN

57 Main Street, Millom, Cumbria LA18 4BL
Tel: 01229 773079

The oldest pub in Millom, **The Ship Inn** is an authentic traditional pub just 5 minutes walk from the centre of the town. Inside, it's full of character, with real fires, lots of atmosphere and, always a good sign, lots of local people. Mine host, Anthony Cook-Harvey, only took over here in the autumn of 2000 but he has had many years experience in the hospitality business. The Ship is open all day, every day, and good pub grub is served all day between 11am and 9pm. (Please note, cash or cheques only accepted).

The inn always has two real ales on tap, Hartley's XB and a rotating guest ale, along with 3 Shires Mild, Guinness, Carling lager and Strongbow cider on draught. If the weather is friendly, customers

can enjoy their refreshments in the pleasant beer garden at the rear of the inn. This lively pub has regular entertainment on Thursday, Friday and Saturday nights, usually in the form of discos with a DJ. If you are thinking of staying in this peaceful corner of the county, The Ship has 3 comfortable guest bedrooms available, (1 family and 2 twins), for bed & breakfast guests. If desired, evening meals can also be provided by arrangement.

this village, Richard Woodall is world famous for his sausages, in particular for the Waberthwaite Cumberland Sausage, and is the proud possessor of a Royal Warrant from the Queen.

BOOTLE
7 miles S of Ravenglass on the A595

This ancient village is particularly picturesque and quaint. The river Annas flows beside the main road and then dives under the village on its way to the sea. High up on Bootle Fell, to the southeast of the village, lies one of the best stone circles in Cumbria. Over the years, many of the 51 stones that make up the **Swinside Stone Circle** have fallen over. When it was originally constructed and all the stones were upright, it is likely, as they were also close together, that the circle was used as an enclosure.

Silecroft Beach

SILECROFT
10 miles S of Ravenglass off the A595

Perhaps of all the villages in this coastal region of the National Park, Silecroft is the perfect example. Just a short walk from the heart of the village is the beach which extends as far as the eye can see. On the horizon lies the distant outline of the Isle of Man. There is also an area of Special Scientific Interest close by, a tract of coastal scrubland which provides the perfect habitat for the rare Natterjack toad.

MILLOM
13 miles S of Ravenglass on the A5093

This small and peaceful town stands at the mouth of the River Duddon with the imposing Black Combe Fell providing a dramatic backdrop. Originally called Holborn Hill, the present day name was taken from nearby Millom Castle which is now a private, working farm. Like many neighbouring towns and villages in Furness, Millom was a small fishing village before it too grew with the development of the local iron industry. **Millom Folk Museum** tells the story of the town's growth and there is also a permanent memorial here to Norman Nicholson (1914-1987) who is generally regarded as the best writer on Lakeland life and customs since Wordsworth himself. Nicholson's book *Provincial Pleasures* records his affectionate memories of Millom, the town where he spent all his life.

HOLMROOK
2 miles N of Ravenglass on the A595

Situated on the banks of the River Irt, where it is possible to fish for both salmon and sea trout, this small village also lies on the Ravenglass and Eskdale Railway line. Though the village Church of St Paul is not of particular note, inside there is not only a 9th century cross of Irish style but also memorials to the Lutwidges, the family of Lewis Carroll.

DRIGG
2 miles N of Ravenglass on the B5343

The main attractions here are the sand dunes and the fine views across to the Lakeland mountains and fells. There is also an important nature reserve, **Drigg Dunes**, on the salt marshes that border the River Irt but - take note, adders are common here.

SANTON BRIDGE
3 miles NE of Ravenglass off the A595

The churchyard of **Irton Church**, reached from Santon Bridge via an unclassified road, offers the visitor not only superb views of the Lakeland fells to the west but also the opportunity to see a beautiful Anglican Cross, in excellent condition, that is certainly 1,000 years old. Though the original runic inscription has been eroded away over time, the fine, intricate carving can still be seen. The Bridge Inn here plays host each November to the "World's Biggest Liar" competition, (see Gosforth below).

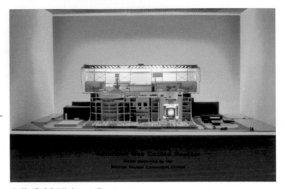

Sellafield Visitors Centre

SEASCALE
4 miles N of Ravenglass on the B5343

One of the most popular seaside villages in Cumbria, Seascale enhanced its resort status in 2000 by restoring the Victorian wooden jetty to mark Millennium Year. Stretching out into the Irish Sea, it is the focal point for fishing, beach casting, wind surfing and water-skiing, and also provides the starting point for many walks, including the Cumbrian Coastal Way which passes along the foreshore. This fine sandy beach enjoys views over to the Isle of Man and the Galloway Mountains of Scotland while, behind the village, the entire length of the western Lakeland hills presents an impressive panorama.

Two Victorian buildings stand out: the **Water Tower**, medieval in style and with a conical roof, and the old **Engine Shed** which is now a multi-purpose Sports Hall.

A couple of miles north of the village is Cumbria's most controversial visitor attraction - and also one of its most popular. **The Sellafield Visitors Centre** (free) is designed to present "the acceptable face of nuclear power" by means of hands-on interactive

Sellafield Visitors Centre

scientific experiments, impressive demonstrations and dazzling displays of technology. In 10 different zones, visitors can experience the sensation of being in the heart of a reactor, take their place at a workstation, look forward into the year 2050AD in Atomopolis and much more. The Centre is open all year and the complex also includes a gift shop and restaurant.

GOSFORTH
5 miles N of Ravenglass on the A595

On the edge of this picturesque village, in the graveyard of St Mary's Church, stands the tallest ancient cross in England. Fifteen feet high, the **Viking Cross** towers above the huddled gravestones in the peaceful churchyard. Carved from red sandstone and clearly influenced by both Christian and pagan traditions, the cross depicts the crucifixion, the deeds of Norse gods and Yggdrasil, the World Ash Tree

that Norsemen believed supported the universe. The interior of the church also contains some interesting features. There's a **Chinese Bell**, finely decorated with Oriental imagery, which was captured in 1841 at Anunkry, a fort on the River Canton, some delightful carved faces on the chancel arch and a collection of ancient stones the most notable of which dates from Saxon times and depicts the Lamb of God trampling on the serpents of pagan faith.

A major attraction in this appealing village is the **Gosforth Pottery** (see panel below).

To the east of Gosforth runs Wasdale, the wildest of the Lake District valleys but easily accessible by road. The road leads to **Wast Water** which is just 3 miles long but the deepest lake in England. The southern shores are dominated by huge screes some 2000ft high that plunge abruptly into the lake and they provide an awesome

GOSFORTH POTTERY

Gosforth, nr Seascale, Cumbria CA20 1AH
Tel/Fax: 019467 25296   e-mail: gospot@potterycourses.co.uk
website: www.potterycourses.co.uk

Gosforth Pottery has been established here for more than 15 years and is now well-known for the beautifully crafted work on sale. Dick and Barbara Wright's experience goes back even further, some 25 years in fact. Dick throws the pots on a wheel, Barbara decorates and glazes the pieces, and then Dick takes care of the firing. The resulting earthenware and stoneware pots are eminently collectable, so too are the other pieces on display. These have been created by more than 20 other British potters and they present an extraordinary range of decorative and practical items.

Dick and Barbara give pottery lessons and hold residential courses throughout the year for anyone interested in pottery. Dick teaches how to throw a pot, while Barbara runs Raku and Smoking kilns and also demonstrates decorative techniques. For people on holiday there are 'Pots and Pizza' evenings.

You could also combine your pottery instruction with a lakeland holiday because, from the summer of 2001, a self-catering flat above the pottery will be available. Aptly named The Potter's Barn, the flat can sleep up to 6 people and the rental is all-inclusive apart from fuel. During the season, the apartment is let by the week, but at other times can be booked for a minimum of 2 nights.

THE WHEATSHEAF INN

The Square, Gosforth, Cumbria CA20 1AL
Tel: 019467 25821

Just a few yards off the main west coast road, the A595, **The Wheatsheaf Inn** is a charming old hostelry which dates back to the early 1800s. Its black and white frontage looks very inviting and the interior is just as attractive with its ancient beams, open fire and traditional dark wood furniture. Pauline and Dougie took over here in the late summer of 2000 and while maintaining the inn's olde worlde atmosphere have plans to extend its amenities. By the time you read this, the beer garden will be completed and operational and they also intend to lay on regular entertainment. Meanwhile, visitors will find an excellent and varied choice of quality food served every lunchtime and evening, (except Sunday evenings), with the regular menu supplemented by daily specials.

The inn is open all day, every day, and the wide selection of beverages on offer includes Theakstons Best, Ruddles and John Smith's Smooth along with two draught lagers, two draught ciders and Guinness. Gosforth village itself is of course best known for its extraordinary 15ft high Viking Cross which towers above the huddled gravestones in the peaceful churchyard. Carved from red sandstone, the cross depicts the Crucifixion, the deeds of Norse gods and Yggdrasil, the World Ash Tree that Norsemen believed supported the universe.

GOSFORTH HALL COUNTRY HOTEL & RESTAURANT

Gosforth Village, Cumbria CA20 1AZ
Tel: 019467 25322 Fax: 019467 25992
e-mail: gosforthhall@aol.com

Located on the quiet western edge of the Lake District National Park, **Gosforth Hall Country Hotel & Restaurant** is close to the deepest lake in England, Wastwater, and to the country's highest mountain, Scafell Pike (3210ft). Built in Jacobean times, some 350 years ago, the hotel stands next to St Mary's Church and its famous 15ft high Viking Cross. Many of the building's original features have been retained and, as a rare example of its type, the structure enjoys a Grade 2* listed building status.

The Hall is run by its owners, Jill and Andrew, a friendly and welcoming couple who do their best to make sure their visitors have a memorable stay and are always available should you need any assistance. They also take great pride in the food on offer: all home cooked and based on fresh local produce. If you have any special dietary needs, just let them know and they will do their best to help. The restaurant is open every lunchtime and evening, except on Sunday and Monday evenings. The fully licensed restaurant seats 40, but booking ahead for Friday and Saturday evenings is strongly recommended.

The hotel has 10 guest bedrooms, eight of which are en suite. One of them, the Excelsior Suite, has a 4-poster bed and en suite giant bath and must be seen to be believed! Guests can stay on either a dinner, bed & breakfast, or bed & breakfast basis, and credit cards are accepted.

Wast Water Lake

and it is hidden away amidst a tiny copse of evergreen trees. Local legend suggests that the roof beams came from a Viking ship and it is certainly true that until late Victorian times, the church had only an earth floor and few seats.

As well as the deepest lake and the smallest church, Wasdale also boasts the highest mountain, **Sca Fell Pike** (3,205ft) - and the world's biggest liars. This latter claim goes back to the mid-1800s when Will Ritson, "a reet good fibber", was the publican at the inn. Will enthralled his patrons with tall stories of how he had crossed foxes with eagles to produce flying foxes and had grown turnips so large he could hollow them out to make a comfortable residence. In the same spirit, the "Biggest Liar in the World" competition takes place every November, usually at the Bridge Inn at Santon Bridge,

backdrop to this tranquil stretch of water. A lake less like Windermere would be hard to find as there are no motorboats ploughing their way up and down the lake; this is very much the country of walkers and climbers and from here there are many footpaths up to some of the best fells in Cumbria.

Wasdale Head, just to the north of the lake, is a small, close-knit community with a far-famed Inn that has provided a welcome refuge for walkers and climbers since the mid-1800s. who have been out discovering Wasdale and the lake. The village church is claimed to be the smallest in England - although this title is hotly disputed by Culbone in Somerset and Dale Abbey in Derbyshire. Wasdale's church was built in the 14th century

Scafell Pike

THE ROYAL OAK INN

Beckermet, Cumbria CA21 2XB
Tel/Fax: 01946 841551

According to archaeologists, the little village of Beckermet stands on the site of a Stone Age village, one of the oldest settlements in Cumbria. Today, **The Royal Oak Inn** stands at the heart of the village. It's a typical Lake District hostelry with its black and white frontage but what is not so typical is the excellent food served in the restaurant here.

At lunchtime, the extensive menu, (also available in the bar), offers a choice of tapas, Italian, Chinese and Indian dishes, as well as old favourites such as Steak, Mushroom & Ale Pie, Grilled Gammon or Fish & Chips. Also available are salad platters, "bulging jackets", filled bagels and freshly made sandwiches. In the evenings, the elegant 65-seater restaurant is supplemented by the non-smoking Chez Marianne

Brasserie, which seats 26. Diners have the choice of a table d'hôte menu, which changes every month, or an à la carte selection which includes steaks, grills, chicken or fish dishes, all accompanied by fresh seasonal vegetables or side salad. Complement your meal with one of the 3 real ales on tap, or with a selection from the wine list.

As well as superb food, the Royal Oak also offers quality accommodation in 8 guest bedrooms, some of which are on the ground floor. All the rooms are en suite and well-equipped with lots of little extras. Children are welcome and the inn offers special weekend rates at very reasonable prices.

THE BLACKBECK INN

nr Egremont, Cumbria CA22 2NY
Tel: 01946 841661 Fax: 01946 841007
website: www.blackbeck.co.uk

Its whitewashed walls gleaming in the sunlight and decked with rows of colourful hanging baskets, **The Blackbeck Inn** looks very inviting indeed. To the rear flows the small brook of the same name; at the front is a pleasant courtyard with a water feature next to the bar. In summer, the courtyard is a virtual sun trap and ideal for barbecues.

Originally a small country farmhouse, its owners began serving afternoon teas here in 1960. Over the years, the house has been extended stage by stage without losing its original character. Today, the inn is well known for its excellent food, served every lunchtime and evening. The very extensive

menu ranges from traditional favourites such as Cumberland Sausage or Steaks, through fish and poultry dishes, flans and pies as well as light meals and sandwiches.

Open all year round, the inn has 21 en suite bedrooms, 6 of which are on the ground floor. The rooms are exceptionally well-equipped with a telephone compatible for the Internet, TV with selected satellite stations, hair dryer, trouser press, complimentary beverage facilities and full room service. There's a spacious residents' lounge and the Blackbeck's function room is ideal for wedding receptions as well as business meetings and presentations - an overhead projector and screen is available along with wide screen TV and video.

when contestants from all over the country vie in telling the most enormous porkies.

CALDER BRIDGE
7 miles N of Ravenglass on the A595

From this small, grey, 19th century settlement there is an attractive footpath to **Calder Abbey**. It was founded by monks of Savigny in 1134 but amalgamated with the Cistercians of Furness Abbey when it was ransacked by the Scots a few years later. After the Dissolution the monastery buildings lapsed slowly into the present-day romantic ruin. Part of the tower and west doorway remain, with some of the chancel and transept, but sadly these are unsafe and have to be viewed from the road. To the northeast of the village, the River Calder rises on Caw Fell. **Monk's Bridge**, the oldest packhorse bridge in Cumbria, was built across it for the monks of Calder Abbey.

EGREMONT
12 miles N of Ravenglass on the A595

This pretty town is dominated by **Egremont Castle** with walls 20ft high and an 80ft tower. It stands high above the town, overlooking the lovely River Ehen to the south and the market place to the north. The castle was built between 1130 and 1140 by William de Meschines on the site of a former Danish fortification. The most complete part still standing is a Norman arch that once guarded the drawbridge entrance. Nearby is an unusual four-sided sundial and the stump of the old market cross dating from the early 13th century.

A legend concerning the castle is related in Wordsworth's poem, *The Horn of Egremont*. Apparently, a great horn hanging in the castle could only be blown by the rightful lord. In the early 1200s,

the rightful lord, Eustace de Lucy was on a Crusade to the Holy Land, together with his brother Hubert. The dastardly Hubert arranged with local hit men to have Eustace drowned in the Jordan. Hubert returned to Egremont but during the celebration feast to mark his inheritance a mighty blast on the horn was heard. The hit men had reneged on the deal: Eustace was still alive. Hubert prudently retired to a monastery.

Egremont's prosperity was based on the good quality of its local red iron ore and jewellery made from it can be bought at the nearby **Florence Mine Heritage Centre**. Visitors to the mine, the last deep working iron ore mine in Europe, can join an underground tour (by prior arrangement) and discover why the miners became known as the "Red Men of Cumbria". The museum here also tells story of the mine which was worked by the ancient Britons and there is a recreation of the conditions that the miners endured at the turn of the 20th century.

In September every year the town celebrates its **Crab Fair**. Held each year on the third Saturday in September, the Fair dates back more than seven centuries - to 1267 in fact, when Henry III granted a Royal Charter for a three-day fair to be held on *"the even, the day and the morrow after the Nativity of St. Mary the Virgin"*. The celebrations include the "Parade of the Apple Cart" when a wagon loaded with apples is driven along Main Street with men on the back throwing fruit into the crowds. Originally, the throng was pelted with crab apples - hence the name Crab Fair - but these are considered too tart for modern taste so nowadays more palatable varieties are used. The festivities also feature a "greasy pole" competition, (with a pole 30ft high), a pipe-smoking contest, wrestling and hound-trailing. The highlight, however, is the **World Gurning Championship** in which contestants place their head through a braffin, or horse collar, and vie to produce the most grotesque expression. If you're toothless, you start with a great advantage!

WHITEHAVEN

The first impression is of a handsome Georgian town but Whitehaven was already well-established in the 12th century as a harbour for use by the monks of nearby St Bees Priory. This was a small-scale operation - most of the town was developed in the 17th century by the Lowther family to service their nearby mines. Whitehaven's growth in those years was astonishing by the standards of the time - it mushroomed from a hamlet of just 9 thatched cottages in 1633 to a sizeable, planned, town with a population of more than 2000 by 1693. Its "gridiron" pattern of streets, unusual in Cumbria, will be familiar to American visitors and the town boasts some 250 listed buildings. By the mid-1700s, Whitehaven had become the third largest port in Britain, its trade based on coal and other cargo business, including importing tobacco from Virginia, exporting coal to Ireland, and transporting emigrants to the New World. When the large iron-steamships arrived however, the harbour's shallow draught halted expansion and the port declined in favour of Liverpool and Southampton. For that reason much of the attractive harbour area - now full of pleasure craft and fishing smacks - and older parts of the town remain largely unchanged.

The harbour and its environs have been declared a Conservation Area and it's here you'll find **The Beacon** where, through a series of innovative displays, the history

THE DISTRESSED SAILOR

Egremont Road, Hensingham, Whitehaven,
Cumbria CA28 8NH
Tel: 01946 692426 Fax: 01946 694522

The only pub of this name in the country, **The Distressed Sailor** makes a clear reference to the ever-present perils for mariners along the nearby stretch of the rugged Cumbrian coast. Built in the late 1700s, it's an attractive whitewashed building with lots of hanging baskets of flowers making a colourful impression throughout the summer. Inside, wood panelled walls, wooden floors and local memorabilia around the walls all add to the traditional atmosphere.

Mine hosts, Lee and Stephanie, a young and enthusiastic couple who have been here since 1997, are both accomplished cooks and they have made The Distressed Sailor one of the top eating places in the county - 90% of their business is food. Their

extensive menu has something for everyone: steaks, chicken dishes, Italian and Mexican choices, fish choices (including a Fresh Catch of the Day), vegetarian options and a "Kiddies Corner". All the dishes are prepared from the freshest ingredients and are cooked to order. Food is served every lunchtime and evening, except on Mondays (unless it's a Bank Holiday). The pub also serves a good choice of well-maintained ales, amongst them Youngers Scotch, Theakston's Best and John Smith's, plus Beamish Black, 3 draught lagers and a draught cider.

Whitehaven Harbour

navigational instruments, miners' lamps, and surveying equipment. The Beilby "Slavery" Goblet, part of the museum's collection, is one of the masterpieces of English glass-making and is probably the finest example of its kind in existence.

As well as the elegant Georgian buildings that give the town its air of distinction, there are two fine parish churches that are worth a visit. Dating from 1753, **St James' Church** has Italian ceiling designs and a beautiful Memorial Chapel (dedicated to those who lost their lives in the two World Wars and also the local people who were killed in mining accidents) whilst the younger St Begh's Church, which was built in the 1860s, is striking with its white sandstone walls dressed with red.

Whitehaven is interesting in other ways. It still has a grid pattern of streets dating back to the 17th century, a layout that substantiates its claim to be the first planned town in Britain. Many of the fine Georgian buildings in the centre have been restored and **Lowther Street** is a particularly impressive thoroughfare. Also of note is the harbour pier built by canal engineer, John Rennie, and considered to be one of the finest in Britain. There is a fascinating walk and a Nature Trail around **Tom Hurd Rock**, above the town.

The town has a curious literary association with Dean Swift, the poet, satirist, journalist and author of *Gulliver's Travels*. As a sickly infant in a poverty-stricken Dublin home, Swift was wet-nursed by a young girl from Whitehaven named Sarah. She was suddenly called to the deathbed of a relative in Cumbria

of the town and its harbour are brought to life. Visitors can also monitor, forecast and broadcast the weather in the Met. Office Weather Gallery, learn about the "American Connection" and John Paul Jones' attack on the town in 1772, or settle down in the cinema to watch vintage footage of Whitehaven in times past.

There's more history at **The Rum Story** which opened in early 2000 and tells the story of the town's connections with the Caribbean. The display is housed in Jefferson's, the oldest surviving UK family of rum traders.

Whitehaven's **Museum and Art Gallery** is particularly interesting. The museum deals with the history of the whole of Copeland (the district of Cumbria in which Whitehaven lies) with special emphasis on its mining and maritime past. The displays reflect the many aspects of this harbour borough with a collection that includes paintings, locally made pottery, ship models,

MANOR HOUSE HOTEL & COAST TO COAST BAR

Main Street, St Bees, Cumbria CA27 0DE
Tel: 01946 822425 Fax: 01946 824949

One of the oldest buildings in this small village, **Manor House Hotel** dates back to 1720. Right next door, the Coast to Coast Bar occupies the former Royal Oak Inn which has an even longer history that goes back to 1697.

Very traditional in character, both establishments are run by Danny and Carolyn Hilferty who arrived here in 1999 and offer both locals and visitors a very sincere and warm welcome. They also serve appetising food every lunchtime and evening, either in lounge bar or the in the 36-seater restaurant with its crisp linen tablecloths and flowers on each table. Customers can choose from either the regular menu or the specials board and there's a wide choice of keg ales, draught lagers and cider, and other beverages to complement the meal.

St Bees is well known to walkers of course as the western starting point of Wainwright's Coast to Coast walk, a 190-mile long path that wends its way across the neck of England to Robin Hood's Bay on the North Yorkshire coast. The village also makes a good base for exploring the unspoilt western lakes and fells. Manor House offers quality accommodation in 8 recently refurbished guest rooms, (7 double/twin rooms, 1 single), all of which are en suite and beautifully furnished and decorated.

THE ODDFELLOWS ARMS

Main Street, St Bees, Cumbria CA27 0AD
Tel: 01946 822317

With its traditional lakeland black and white frontage, set off by colourful hanging baskets, **The Oddfellows Arms** looks very inviting indeed and mine hosts, Margaret Thomson and her daughters Lisa and Helen, make sure that visitors feel very welcome. The inn dates back to the early 1800s and the interior reflects that period with both the bar area and the cosy dining room retaining many of the original features. Glinting brass and copper items, along with local memorabilia decorating the walls add to the appeal.

During the season, an appetising choice of meals is available every day from noon until 7pm - make your selection either from the regular menu or from the specials board. (The home made pies are especially in demand). Out of season, food is served from 4pm until 7pm, with an extension to 9pm on the popular Steak Nights. At any time of the year, booking for Sunday lunch is strongly recommended. The Oddfellows always has two real ales on tap, (both from the Jennings brewery), along with an extensive range of beers, lagers, and other beverages. Children are welcome and the pub is ideally placed, close to the sea, for providing refreshment to those on a seaside visit.

from whom she expected a legacy. By now Sarah was so attached to the child she could not bear a separation and carried him off with her to Whitehaven. Later, guilt-stricken, she wrote to Mrs Swift admitting what she had done and received an answer asking her to continue looking after Jonathan, Mrs Swift being concerned about the effect on the boy's delicate health of another sea crossing. Swift stayed with the girl for 3 years and was clearly well looked after in every way - by the time he returned to Dublin he was in robust health and "could read any chapter in the Bible".

AROUND WHITEHAVEN

ST BEES
3 miles S of Whitehaven on the B5343

St Bees Head, a red sandstone bluff, forms one of the most dramatic natural features along the entire coast of northwest England. Some four miles long and 300ft high, these towering, precipitous cliffs are formed of St Bees sandstone, the red rock which is so characteristic of Cumbria. Far out to sea, on the horizon, can be seen the grey shadow of the Isle of Man and, on a clear day, the shimmering outline of the Irish coast. From here the 190-mile **Coast to Coast Walk** starts on its long journey across the Pennines to Robin Hood's Bay in North Yorkshire.

Long before the first lighthouse was built in 1822, there was a beacon on the headland to warn and guide passing ships away from the rocks. The present 99ft high lighthouse dates from 1866-7, built after an earlier one was destroyed by fire. St Bees Head is now an important Nature

Reserve and the cliffs are crowded with guillemots, razorbills, kittiwakes, gulls, gannets, and skuas. Bird watchers are well-provided for with observation and information points all along the headland. There is a superb walk of about eight miles along the coastal footpath around the headland from St Bees to Whitehaven.

St Bees itself, a short walk from the headland, is a small village which lies huddled in a deep, slanting bowl in the cliffs, fringed by a shingle beach. The village is a delightful place to explore, with its main street winding up the hillside between old farms and cottages. It derives its name from St Bega, daughter of an Irish king who, on the day she was meant to marry a Norse prince, was miraculously transported by an angel to the Cumbrian coast.

According to legend, on Midsummer Night's Eve, St Bega asked the pagan Lord Egremont for some land on which to found a nunnery. Cunningly, he promised her only as much land as was covered by snow the following morning. But on Midsummer's Day, three square miles of land were blanketed white with snow and here she founded her priory. (Incidentally, this "miracle" snowfall is a not uncommon feature of a Cumbrian summer on the high fells).

St Bees Head

THE SHEPHERD'S ARMS HOTEL

Ennerdale Bridge, Cumbria CA23 3AR
Tel/Fax: 01946 861249
e-mail: enquiries@shepherdsarmshotel.co.uk   www: shepherdsarmshotel.co.uk

The picturesque little village of Ennerdale Bridge is well known to walkers on Wainwright's Coast-to-Coast path since the route west of here is generally regarded as the most scenic part of the 190-mile walk from St Bees to Robin's Hood Bay. Standing in the heart of the village, **The Shepherd's Arms Hotel** is a small and friendly hostelry which has been owned and run by Norman Stanfield since 1997. The building itself dates back to 1604 and the interior, with its open fires and old beams, has a wonderfully traditional atmosphere. The 5 real ales on tap here earned the inn an entry in the CAMRA Good Pub Guide and the food here also enjoys an excellent reputation.

There's an extensive bar menu which includes daily specials and a wide selection of vegetarian dishes. Game in season is a speciality. During the autumn and winter months, the bar is a popular venue for local folk and jazz groups.

The Shepherd's Arms is an ideal base from which to explore this unspoilt area and there are 8 guest bedrooms, 6 of them en suite, the other two with their own private bathrooms. All the bedrooms are non-smoking and guests can stay on either a bed & breakfast, or dinner, bed & breakfast basis.

THE STORK HOTEL

Rowrah Road, Rowrah, Frizington, Cumbria CA26 3XJ
Tel: 01946 861213
e-mail: storkhotel@hotels.activebookinguk.com

Conveniently located on the A5086 Egremont to Cockermouth road, **The Stork Hotel** is also close to the Coast to Coast cycle way and within easy reach of the spectacular western lakes and fells.

Built in 1860 to serve travellers on the railway which has sadly long disappeared, this inviting hostelry with its black and white frontage, real fires and lots of atmosphere has been owned and run by the Heydon family for more than 25 years. And for the whole of that time it has featured in the *Good Beer Guide*. A Free House, The Stork offers customers a choice of 2 permanent real ales along with a guest ale, as well as 2 draught lagers, draught cider and Guinness.

Tasty home cooked food is available every lunchtime and evening during the summer, evenings only out of season. Choose from the regular menu or from the daily specials board. Children are welcome and credit cards accepted. If you are planning to stay in this scenic area of the county, The Stork has 5 comfortable guest bedrooms, (1 family, 4 twins), which are available all year round. There are special rates for longer stays.

The Priory at St Bees grew in size and importance until it was destroyed by the Danes in the 10th century: the Benedictines later re-established the priory in 1129. **The Priory Church of St Mary and St Bega** is all that is now left and although it has been substantially altered there is still a magnificent Norman arch and a pre-Conquest, carved Beowulf Stone on a lintel between the church and the vicarage, showing St Michael killing a dragon.

Close by the church are the charming Abbey Cottages and **St Bees School** with its handsome clock-tower. The school was founded in 1583 by Edmund Grindal, Archbishop of Canterbury under Elizabeth I, and the son of a local farmer. The original red sandstone quadrangle bears his coat-of-arms and the bridge he gave to the village is still in use. Amongst the school's most famous alumni is the illustrious "Mr Bean", the comic actor Rowan Atkinson.

An anonymous resident of St Bees has also achieved fame of a kind. In 1981, archaeologists excavating a ruined chapel discovered one of the best preserved medieval bodies in England. It was the corpse of a local lord who had been buried in the 1300s in a dry airless vault. One of his shrouds, and hair found with the body, are now on display in the Whitehaven Museum, together with pictures of the body and the setting in which it was found.

CLEATOR MOOR
3 miles SE of Whitehaven on the B5295

The name of this once-industrial town derives from the Norse words for cliff and hill pasture. Cleator developed rapidly in the 19th century because of the insatiable demand during the Industrial Revolution

HUNTING HOW FARMHOUSE

at Adam Gill Farm, Moresby,
Whitehaven,
Cumbria CA28 6SF
Tel: 01946 693662

Enjoying grand views across the Solway Firth to the Scottish mainland, **Hunting How Farmhouse** provides quality self-catering accommodation in a wonderfully peaceful and unspoilt setting. It is surrounded by the 320 acres of John and Jean Messenger's working livestock farm, located only a mile from the Georgian fishing port of Whitehaven and with the Lake District National Park just a few miles to the east. There are some delightful coastal walks nearby and the recently opened Whitehaven Golf Course is a mere half a mile away. For more information about the area, just ask John who has lived here since 1932.

The farmhouse itself dates back to the 17th century but is fully equipped with all modern amenities, including an oil-fired Aga cooker, microwave, dishwasher, fridge, automatic washer, colour TV and pay phone. The ground floor comprises kitchen, sitting room, dining room and games room, while upstairs there are 4 bedrooms, (2 doubles, 1 twin & 1 single), and a bathroom with 3 piece suite and a shower over the bath. A free bag of coal is provided for the open fires but there's also oil-fired central heating throughout. The elevated garden with its superb sea views is provided with garden furniture and a barbecue area. The house is available from Easter to the end of October but please note that it is non-smoking and pets are not allowed.

for coal and iron ore. As the Cumbrian poet Norman Nicholson wrote:

From one shaft at Cleator Moor
They mined for coal and iron ore.
This harvest below ground could show
Black and red currants on one tree.

Cleator is surrounded by delightful countryside and little evidence of the town's industrial past is visible. But there is a thriving business nearby - the Kangol Factory Shop in Cleator village which stocks a huge range of hats, scarves, bags, caps and golf wear.

ENNERDALE BRIDGE
7 miles E of Whitehaven off the A5086

Ennerdale Water

Wordsworth described Ennerdale's church as *"girt round with a bare ring of mossy wall"* - and it still is. The bridge here crosses the River Ehen which, a couple of miles upstream runs out from **Ennerdale Water**, one of the most secluded and inaccessible of all the Cumbrian lakes. However, the walks around this tranquil lake and through the quiet woodlands amply repay the slight effort of leaving your car at a distance. The Coast to Coast Walk runs the whole length of Ennerdale and there's a general consensus that this section is by far the most beautiful.

5 The North Cumbrian Coast

The North Cumbrian coast, from Workington to the Solway Firth, is one of the least known parts of this beautiful county but it certainly has a lot to offer. It is an area rich in heritage with a network of quiet country lanes, small villages, old ports, and seaside resorts. The coast's largest town, Workington, founded by the Romans, was once a large port, exporting coal and iron from the surrounding area. Though its importance has declined, it is still the country's largest producer of railway lines. Further up the coast is Maryport, again a port originally built by the Romans.

However, Maryport has not gone down the industrial route to the extent of its neighbour and, as well as being a quaint and picturesque place, it is also home to a fascinating museum dedicated to the town's maritime past.

Wordsworths Birthplace, Cockermouth

Inland lies Cockermouth on the edge of the National Park, a pretty market town with some elegant Georgian buildings. However, most visitors will be more interested to see and hear about the town's most famous son, William Wordsworth, who was born here in 1770.

The northernmost stretch of coastline, around the Solway Firth, is an area of tiny villages with fortified towers standing as mute witness to the border struggles of long ago. These villages were the haunt of smugglers, wildfowlers, and half-net fishermen. What is particularly special about this coastline is its rich birdlife. The north Cumbrian coast was also the setting for Walter Scott's novel, *Redgauntlet,* and the fortified farmhouse by the roadside beyond Port Carlisle is said to be the *"White Ladies"* of *the novel.*

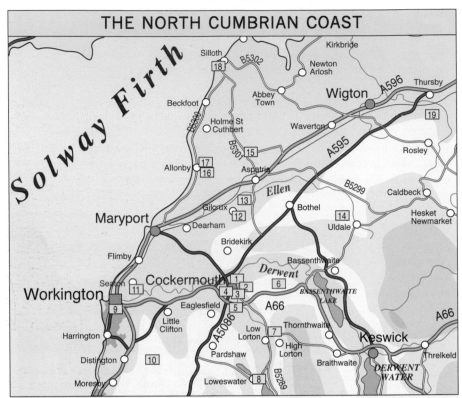

THE NORTH CUMBRIAN COAST

© MAPS IN MINUTES ™ (1999)

PLACES TO STAY, EAT, DRINK AND SHOP

COCKERMOUTH

No wonder Cockermouth is one of the 51 towns in Great Britain to be designated a "gem town" and recommended for preservation by the Department of the Environment. A market town since 1226, Cockermouth has been fortunate in keeping unspoilt its broad main street, lined with trees and handsome Georgian houses, and dominated by a statue to the Earl of Mayo. The Earl was Cockermouth's M.P. for ten years from 1858 before being appointed Viceroy of India. His brilliant career was brutally cut short when he was stabbed to death by a convict at a prison settlement he was inspecting on the Andaman Islands.

But Cockermouth boasts two far more famous sons. Did they ever meet, one wonders, those two young lads growing up in Cockermouth in the 1770s, both of them destined to become celebrated for very different reasons? The elder boy was Fletcher Christian who would later lead the mutiny on the *Bounty*; the younger lad was William Wordsworth, born here in 1770 at Lowther House on Main Street, an imposing Georgian house now maintained by the National Trust. Now known as **Wordsworth House**, it was built in 1745 for the Sheriff of Cumberland and then purchased by the Earl of Lowther who let it to his land agent, John Wordsworth, William's father. All five Wordsworth children were born here: William on 7th April 1770. Many of the building's original features survive, amongst them the staircase, fireplace, and fine plaster ceilings. A few of the poet's personal effects are still here and the delightful walled garden by the River Cocker has been returned to its Georgian splendour.

Wordsworth was only eight years old when his mother died and he was sent to

Wordsworth House

school at Hawkshead, but later he fondly recalled walking at Cockermouth with his sister Dorothy, along the banks of the rivers Cocker and Derwent to the ruined castle on the hill. Built in 1134 by the Earl of Dunbar, **Cockermouth Castle** saw plenty of action against Scottish raiders, (Robert the Bruce himself gave it a mauling in 1315), again during the Wars of the Roses and in the course of the Civil War it was occupied by both sides in turn. Mary, Queen of Scots, took refuge at the castle in 1568 after her defeat at the Battle of Langside. Her fortunes were so low that she was grateful for the gift of 16 ells (about 20 yards) of rich crimson velvet from a wealthy merchant. Part of the castle is still lived in by the Egremont family; the remainder is usually only open to the public during the Cockermouth Festival in August.

THE BUSH HOTEL

Main Street, Cockermouth,
Cumbria CA13 9JS
Tel: 01900 822064

Noted for its top quality local brews, Jennings Ales, **The Bush Hotel** is an appealing former coaching inn with a striking black and white frontage, and with the arched entrance to the courtyard for the old stage coaches still in place. The interior has also retained its wonderful olde worlde atmosphere with lots of character and charm and the friendly staff, led by mine host Maureen Williamson, make this a very welcoming hostelry.

As well as serving the popular local brews, (Jennings Best Bitter, Cock-A-Hoop and Cumberland Ale), there's also a wide selection of other beers, lagers, cider and Guinness, including a choice of rotating guest ales. The food at The Bush is also highly recommended. Maureen is a gifted cook and an excellent range of appetising dishes is available from noon until 2pm daily. Choose from the regular menu or from the varied specials boards. On Sunday afternoons, between 2.30pm and 6pm, the inn also serves her famous home-made soups along with a good choice of sandwiches. (Please note that evening meals are not available). Children are welcome and most major credit cards are accepted.

A lively place at any time, The Bush is especially animated on Tuesday nights when the Quiz Night begins at 9.30pm. Visitors are definitely encouraged to join in!

THE CASTLEGATE GUEST HOUSE

6 Castlegate, Cockermouth, Cumbria CA13 9EU
Tel: 01900 826749
e-mail: vince@vjfernandez.fsnet.co.uk website: www.smoothhound.co.uk/hotels/castlegate.html

Located just a short walk from the town centre, **The Castlegate Guest House** is a dignified Grade II Listed Georgian town house with an impressive pillared and porticoed entrance. Dating back to around 1730, the interior is equally gracious, with a fine staircase and elegant items of period furniture. This outstanding guest house has been owned and run since the early 1980s by Winifred Adams and her family who make visitors instantly feel at home.

There are 6 guest bedrooms, 3 of which are en suite, the other 3 sharing 2 bathrooms. All the rooms are attractively decorated and furnished and equipped with colour TV, tea/coffee making facilities and hand basins. A full English breakfast is included in the tariff and special diets can be catered for. Breakfast is served in the handsome dining room where a whole dresser is lined with a striking collection of teapots of all shapes, colours and sizes.

The Castlegate is only a few hundred yards from the town's cultural focus, the Kirkgate Centre, and about the same distance from Jenning's Brewery with its popular brewery tours. Cyclists are well served - both the Reivers' and the C2C routes pass by the door, and for golfers a short 5-mile drive will bring them to the Cockermouth Golf Course.

Opposite the Castle entrance, **Castlegate House** is a fine Georgian house, built in 1739, which hosts a changing programme of monthly exhibitions of the work of Northern and Scottish artists - paintings, sculptures, ceramics and glass. The works are for sale and interest free credit is usually available through the Northern Arts Purchase Plan. To the rear of the house is a charming walled garden which is open from time to time during the summer.

Just around the corner from Castlegate House is **The Toy & Model Museum** which exhibits mainly British toys from around 1900 to the present. There are many visitor operated displays including 0 and 00 gauge vintage tinplate trains, Scalextric cars, Lego models and even a helicopter to fly.

Almost next door, **Jennings Brewery** offers visitors a 90-minute tour which ends with the option of sampling some of their ales - Cumberland Ale, Cocker Hoop or the intriguingly named Sneck Lifter. The last independent brewing company in Cumbria, Jennings have been brewing traditional beers since the 1820s and today there are more than 100 Jennings' pubs across the north of England. In addition to the tours, Jennings has a shop selling gifts and leisure wear, the latter boldly emblazoned with the names of its various brews.

A short walk from the Brewery brings you to the **Kirkgate Centre** which is housed in a converted Victorian primary school. Run by volunteers, the Centre offers a wide range of events and activities including live music, amateur and professional drama, films, dance, workshops, exhibitions of art and local history.

Two more visitor attractions stand either side of Wordsworth House in the Main Street. **The Printing House**

TITHE BARN HOTEL

41 Station Street, Cockermouth,
Cumbria CA13 9QW
Tel: 01900 822179 Fax: 01900 821361

Built just over a century ago, **The Tithe Barn** is a fine example of a late-Victorian public house, constructed in the days when buildings were designed to last and to provide ample space. It stands in the heart of the town and since 1997 has been run by Bill and Carol McKenzie, a warm and friendly couple who are both Cumbrian born and bred. Between them, they have more than 20 years experience in the hospitality business and know how to make their customers feel genuinely welcome.

They also serve excellent food in the eye-catching bar every lunchtime and evening, with a menu featuring wholesome home-made food and supplemented by daily specials listed on the blackboard. Sunday lunch at the Tithe Barn is very much in demand so that's when the upstairs restaurant, seating 40, is also used. Even so, booking ahead is strongly recommended.

Popular with locals and visitors alike, the Tithe Barn is open all day, every day for ale. An excellent range of Jennings ales is available, along with 2 draught lagers, a draught cider and Guinness.

SIMONSCALES MILL

Simonscales Lane, Cockermouth, Cumbria CA13 9TG
Tel: 01900 822594
e-mail:ericlowes@simonscales.fsnet.co.uk

In times past, **Simonscales Mill** functioned as both a flax and bobbin mill, indeed the old mill race can still be seen. It enjoys a lovely setting on the banks of the River Cocker and lies within its owners, Mr and Mrs Lowes' five acre smallholding.

The old mill has been tastefully converted to a delightful self-catering cottage which is especially suitable for wheelchair users - it has an ETB Category 2 Accessible rating. The cottage's private patio, amply provided with garden furniture and with a barbecue area, overlooks the river which is teeming with wild life - salmon and trout splashing upstream in late summer and autumn; herons, dippers, waterhens, an occasional kingfisher and a host of mallards and goosanders. The cottage can sleep 4/5 persons in the two bedrooms, each of which has its own en suite bathroom. On the ground floor, there's a tastefully furnished studio style lounge/dining room and well-equipped kitchen. Children are welcome, with a cot and high chair available on request and, outside, a play area for the under 5s and an adventure climbing frame with swings and slides for the over 5s'. Pets too are welcome as long as they don't chase the Lowes' sheep, lambs, hen, donkey or Shetland pony. (The Lowes also have two dogs and a cat).

Also within the smallholding is a well-equipped static caravan, which is also set beside the river. The caravan can accommodate up to 5 people and, like the cottage, is available all year round.

SOUTHWAITE FARM

Cockermouth, Cumbria CA13 0RF
Tel/Fax: 01900 822370

Just a short drive south of Cockermouth, **Southwaite Farm** occupies a marvellously peaceful and unspoilt location alongside the River Cocker, a perfect spot to stay for bed & breakfast or for a self-catering holiday. The river, noted for its salmon and sea trout, runs for a mile through this 300-acre working sheep farm which owns the fishing rights. Visitors are welcome to fish here during the season from July to October.

Bed & breakfast guests stay in handsome old farmhouse which dates back to 1714. There are 3 guest bedrooms, one of which is en suite. Children are welcome and evening meals are available by arrangement. Adjacent to the farmhouse, the old stable and hayloft have been imaginatively converted into a luxury self-contained dwelling, Orchard Cottage. Downstairs, there's a spacious lounge with a

dining area, and a well-appointed kitchen with cooker, microwave, fridge freezer, dishwasher and washing machine. The two bedrooms are upstairs, one with a double 4-poster bed, the other with a double and a single bed. All bedding is provided, there's ample parking for several cars and the cottage is available all year round. Living up to its name, the cottage stands beside an orchard where there's a large play area for children. There are lovely riverside walks and the enchanting northern lakes of Derwent Water, Crummock Water, Buttermere and Loweswater are all within easy reach.

Museum occupies a building dating back to the 16th century and has on display a wide range of historical presses and printing equipment, the earliest being a Cogger Press dated 1820. Visitors are offered the opportunity to gain hands-on experience by using some of the presses to produce cards or keepsakes.

On the other side is the **Mining Museum** which incorporates the Creighton Mineral Museum, based on the collection amassed by William Shaw. Mining for minerals in the area goes back to Roman times with Shap granite, garnet, andesite and the Cumberland Green Slate which is such a distinctive feature of many Lakeland houses. Also on display are miners' lamps, tools, vintage photographs and a dazzling display of fluorescent minerals in "Aladdin's Cave". The Museum shop stocks minerals and fossils for sale, as well as jewellery, original paintings, photographs and crafts.

Located just south of the town, the **Lakeland Sheep & Wool Centre** (free) provides an introduction to life in the Cumbrian countryside with the help of a spectacular visual show, 19 different breeds of live sheep and a wide variety of exhibits. The Centre also hosts indoor sheepdog trials and sheep-shearing displays for which there is a small charge. Open all year round, the Centre has ample free parking, a shop selling woollen goods and gifts, a large café-restaurant and even en suite accommodation.

AROUND COCKERMOUTH

BRIDEKIRK
2 miles N of Cockermouth off the A595

The village church contains one of the finest pieces of Norman sculpture in the country, a carved font with a runic inscription and a mass of detailed embellishments. It dates from the 12th century and the runic inscription states that:

Richard he me wrought
And to this beauty eagerly me brought;

Richard himself is shown on one side with a chisel and mallet. Not only is this a superb example of early English craftsmanship but it is exceedingly rare to find a signed work. Ancient tombstones stand round the walls of this cruciform church and inside it has unusual reredos of fleur-de-lys patterned tiles.

HIGH & LOW LORTON
5 miles SE of Cockermouth on the B5289

There is a yew tree, pride of Lorton Vale....

wrote Wordsworth in his poem Yew Trees, and astonishingly it's still there behind the village hall of High Lorton. It was in the shade of its branches that the Quaker George Fox preached to a large gathering under the watchful eye of Cromwell's soldiers. In its sister village, Low Lorton, set beside the River Cocker, is Lorton Hall (private) which is reputed to be home to the ghost of a woman who carries a lighted candle. Less spectral guests in the past have included King Malcolm III of Scotland who stayed here with his queen whilst visiting the southern boundaries of his Kingdom of Strathclyde of which this area was a part.

LOWESWATER
7 miles S of Cockermouth off the B5289

Reached by narrow winding lanes, Loweswater is one of the smaller lakes, framed in an enchanting fellside and forest setting. The name, appropriately, means "leafy lake", and aeons ago it was just part of a vast body of water that

THE WHEATSHEAF INN

Embleton, Cockermouth, Cumbria CA13 9XP
Tel: 017687 76408

The Wheatsheaf Inn stands on the old coach road between Cockermouth and Keswick, a route now replaced by the A66. A former farmhouse, more than 200 years old, the inn is set on the hillside and enjoys panoramic views across the valley to Ling Fell. Inside, The Wheatsheaf is full of character with ancient beams and real fires all adding to the cosy, traditional atmosphere. Mine hosts are Kerry and Denise Thompson who arrived here in the autumn of 2000 and through their enthusiasm have given the old hostelry a new lease of life.

Wholesome home cooking is the speciality of the house and is available every lunchtime and evening during the week, and throughout the day from noon until 9pm on Saturdays and Sundays. Denise is a gifted cook and in addition to her regular menu, offers a choice of at least 3 or 4 main

courses on the specials board, and there's always a good selection of vegetarian options. At the time of writing, a separate dining area on the first floor is being prepared and this should be in full operation by the time you read this.

Quality Jennings Ales are served along with a wide range of draught lagers, cider, Guinness and other popular beverages.

NEW HOUSE FARM

Lorton, Cockermouth, Cumbria CA13 9UU
Tel/Fax: 01900 85404 e-mail: hazel@newhouse-farm.co.uk
website: www.newhouse-farm.co.uk

Occupying a superb position in Lortondale and standing in 17 acres of beautiful gardens and pastureland, **New House Farm** is a wonderful bed & breakfast establishment owned and run by Hazel Thompson. Dating back to the mid-17th century, this magnificent farmhouse is surrounded by fantastic countryside. Each of the three superb guest rooms enjoys an individual view of the three local landmarks of Swinside Mountain, Whiteside Mountain and Low Fell, and the rooms are named accordingly. Each bedroom has an en suite bathroom and each is individually decorated and furnished with guests' comfort in mind. Guests also have the use of two beautiful and stylish lounges, and there's also a separate dining room. Children over the age of 10 are welcome at this non-smoking establishment. Awarded 5 Diamonds by the AA, as well as numerous commendations from other tourism agencies, this is indeed "A Very Special Country Guest House". Right next door to the farmhouse is The Barn.

Built in the 1880s it is now a charming tea room serving a wide variety of meals and snacks every day between March and November. Especially popular are the home-made teas. From the Fireside Tea with a toasted tea cake, to the substantial Cumberland Tea with scone, gingerbread, biscuits and rum butter, there is always something on offer to satisfy the heartiest of appetites.

Loweswater

originator of the theory that all matter is composed of small indestructible particles called atoms. He was also the first to recognize the existence of colour blindness. He suffered from it himself and in medical circles it is known as Daltonism. A memorial to this remarkable man now marks the house where he lived in Eaglesfield.

included what is now **Crummock Water** and Buttermere. Because it is so shallow, never more than 60ft deep, Loweswater provides an ideal habitat for wildfowl which also benefit from the fact that this is perhaps the least visited lake in the whole of Cumbria. To the east of the lake lies the small village of the same name while to the north stretches one the quietest and least known parts of the National Park, a landscape of low fells through which there are few roads or even paths

EAGLESFIELD
2 miles SW of Cockermouth off the A5086

This small village was the birthplace of Robert Eaglesfield, who became confessor to Queen Philippa, Edward III's Queen. He was also the founder of Queen's College, Oxford where he was buried in 1349. Even more famous, however, is John Dalton who was born here in 1766. The son of Quaker parents, Dalton was teaching at the village school by the time he was 12. Despite having had no formal education himself, he became one of the most brilliant scientists, naturalists, and mathematicians of his age and was the

WORKINGTON

The largest town on the Cumbrian coast, Workington stands at the mouth of the River Derwent and on the site of the Roman fort of **Gabrosentum**. Its prosperity was founded on the three great Cumbrian industries - coal, iron and shipping. As early as 1650 coal was being mined here and, by the end of the 18th century, Workington was a major port exporting coal as well as smelting iron ore. Many of the underground coal seams extended far out to sea. In later years, Workington became famous for its fine quality steel, especially after Henry Bessemer developed his revolutionary steel making process in 1850. Workington is still the place in Britain where most railway lines are manufactured and also has a national reputation for the buses and lorries that are built just outside the town.

The seat of the Curwen family for over 600 years, **Workington Hall** has an interesting history. Originally built around a 14th century pele tower, the hall was developed over the years with

LOWESWATER HOLIDAY COTTAGES

Scale Hill, Loweswater, Cockermouth, Cumbria CA13 9UX
Tel: 01900 85232

Some 200 years ago, William Wordsworth stayed at the Scale Hill inn near Loweswater and recommended it as *"a roomy Inn with very good accommodation"*. A coaching inn dating back to 1620, Scale Hill continued to dispense hospitality to travellers through this spectacular corner of the Lake District until 1990 when its owners, the Thompson family, decided to change its rôle from a hotel to self-catering accommodation. They now live in the central part of the house while the wings have

been converted into 3 luxurious holiday cottages, each providing every possible convenience and comfort. Just across the cobbled yard from the main building, the former Coach House, built in the colourful local stone, has been imaginatively transformed into 4 beautifully furnished and decorated cottages. Two of them are on the ground floor with easy access for the disabled and all of them are well equipped with modern kitchens and colour TV. They sleep between 2 to 6 people and are available all year round. Scale Hill is ideally situated for exploring the peaceful western side of the Lake District. Walkers and anglers will be in their element here, so too will those who prefer just to "laze". Also available nearby are facilities for squash, tennis, sailing, paragliding and mountain biking, and there's also a trekking centre some 6 miles away and various golf courses of which the nearest is at Silloth, just 8 miles distant.

THE CUMBERLAND HOTEL

Western Lakes, Workington,
Cumbria CA14 2XQ
Tel: 01900 64401
Fax: 01900 872400
e-mail: cumberlandhotel@aol.com
website: www.workington.com/
cumberland hotel

Although only a short distance from the town centre, **The Cumberland Hotel** provides all the atmosphere and amenities of a country hotel. It was built more than a century ago to serve travellers arriving at the railway station just across the road and, in accordance with the standards of the time, the hotel was built on a grand scale. A number of the bathrooms, for example, could easily contain the bedroom space of some modern hotels. Comprehensively renovated in the mid-60s, and now owned and run by Anne McTear and her daughter Judith Banks, The Cumberland is now probably the best value quality hotel in West Cumbria.

The delightful Garden Restaurant serves a fine selection of local and continental dishes, excellent pastas and succulent steaks, complemented by a wide choice of European and New World wines. There are 30 guest bedrooms, all of them en suite (bath & shower, plus WC) and with the additional comforts of direct dial telephone, remote control colour TV, trouser press, hair dryer and complimentary tea and coffee bar. There are lifts with wheelchair access to all floors, no step access to all public rooms, and free car parking with 24 hour CCTV security. As well as providing an ideal base for exploring the western lakes, The Cumberland is also fully equipped to cater for parties and business conferences. There's a function suite that can accommodate up to 175 people, a dance floor and up-to-date audio-visual equipment.

extensive alterations being made in the 18th century by the then lord of the manor, John Christian Curwen. Now a stabilised ruin, there are commemorative plaques which give a taste of the hall's history. The most famous visitor was Mary, Queen of Scots who sought refuge here when she fled from Scotland in 1558. She stayed for a few days during which time she wrote the famous letter to her cousin Elizabeth I bemoaning her fate, *"for I am in a pitiable condition....having nothing in the world but the clothes in which I escaped"*, and asking the Queen *"to have compassion on my great misfortunes"*. The letter is now in the British Museum.

The Helena Thompson Museum, situated on Park End Road, is a fascinating place to visit with its displays telling the story of Workington's coal mining, ship-building, and iron and steel industries for which the town became internationally renowned. The Georgian Room gives an insight into the variety of decorative styles which were popular between 1714 and 1830, with displays of beautiful cut-glass tableware, porcelain from China, and period pieces of furniture. Bequeathed to the town by the local philanthropist Miss Helena Thompson, MBE, JP, the museum was opened in 1949 and contains some of her own family heirlooms. One particularly interesting exhibit is the Clifton Dish, a locally produced 18th century piece of slipware pottery, while further displays demonstrate the links between this local industry and the famous Staffordshire pottery families. Fashion fiends will be interested in the display of women's and children's dresses from the 1700s to the early 1900s, together with accessories and jewellery.

THE GREYHOUND INN

Pica, Workington, Cumbria CA14 4QG
Tel/Fax: 01946 830379

With the traditional black and white frontage of Cumbrian hostelries, **The Greyhound Inn** stands about a mile outside the small village of Pica. Apparently, when this early 19th century farmhouse became an alehouse, the village belonged to the Quaker owners of the nearby mine. Their faith would not permit licensed premises on their land so the inn stood just beyond their boundaries. The Greyhound has been owned and run since 1995 by Ann and Derick Banks, both of whom are Cumbrian born and bred. Indeed, Derick owned an adjacent farm for 18 years before becoming a publican.

Ann is the cook and her excellent cooking has made this hidden-away country inn a popular resort for anyone who appreciates fine cuisine. Virtually everything on both the bar and restaurant

menus is home cooked and the extensive choice includes old favourites such as Roast Beef & Yorkshire Pudding, as well as fish and vegetarian dishes, salads, omelettes, jacket potatoes, baguettes and sandwiches. Food is available every Friday, Saturday and Sunday lunchtimes and evenings but please note that the inn is closed on Tuesdays.

Currently, the inn has 2 guest bedrooms, both en suite doubles, with more rooms becoming available during the lifetime of this book. An adjacent field has stands for touring caravans, with showers and toilets on site.

THE COACHMAN

43 High Seaton, Seaton, Workington,
Cumbria CA14 1LJ
Tel: 01900 603976

Standing on the outskirts of the village, **The Coachman** is a delightful old 18th century inn which began life as a farmhouse, opened later as licensed premises under the name "The Weary Traveller" and ever since has been the lively social centre of Seaton. There are records of dancing classes being held in the attic here in 1886, and today Saturday evening customers are treated to live entertainment from 8.45pm.

Ian and Susan Bell took over here in the summer of 2000 and while Ian, a Cumbrian born and bred, still works locally, Susan is always here as a charming "mine host". The food here is strongly recommended and available every lunchtime and evening. Choose from an extensive menu that offers 13 main courses, 4 fish dishes, 7 vegetarian options, and much more. Specialities of the house

include tasty home-made pies but everything on the menu is home-cooked and based on fresh local produce. Children are especially well-served with their own menu which contains no fewer than 11 choices. Such is the popularity of the food here that booking is strongly recommended, especially at weekends.

Ales on offer include Theakston's Bitter and Mild, John Smith's Extra Smooth, Fosters and Becks lagers, Strongbow cider and Guinness. There's a pleasant beer garden to the rear, good access for the disabled and ample off road car parking.

NORTH AND EAST OF WORKINGTON

MARYPORT

6 miles NE of Workington on the A596

Dramatically located on the Solway Firth, Maryport is a charming Cumbrian coastal town rich in interest and maritime history. The old part is full of narrow streets and neoclassical, Georgian architecture which contrast with sudden, surprising views of the sea. Some of the first visitors to Maryport were the Romans who built a clifftop fort here, **Alauna**, which is now part of the Hadrian's Wall World Heritage Site. The award-winning **Senhouse Roman Museum** tells the story of life in this outpost of the empire. Housed in the striking Naval Reserve Battery, built in the 1880s, the museum

holds the largest collection of Roman altars from a single site in Britain.

Modern Maryport dates from the 18th century when Humphrey Senhouse, a local landowner, developed the harbour at what was then called Ellenport to export coal from his mines, and named the new port after his wife, Mary. Over the next century it became a busy port as well as a ship-building centre; boats having to be launched broadside because of the narrowness of the harbour channel. The town declined, along with the mining industry, from the 1930s onwards. It nevertheless attracted the artist L.S. Lowry who was a frequent visitor and loved painting the harbour. Today, Maryport is enjoying a well-earned revival, with newly restored Georgian quaysides, steep cobbled streets, clifftop paths, sandy beaches and a Marina full of fishing boats and colourful pleasure craft.

Maryport Harbour

steamships: the *Flying Buzzard*, a tug from the River Clyde, and the Vic96, a World War II supply ship.

Maryport's other attractions include a fresh fish shop, appropriately named The Catch, an indoor Karting Centre, and a factory shop where the world famous New Balance athletic footwear, clothing and bags are on sale at competitive prices.

The town's extensive maritime history is preserved in the vast array of objects, pictures and models on display at the **Maritime Museum** (free), overlooking the harbour. Housed in another of Maryport's more interesting and historic buildings, the former Queen's Head public house, the museum tells of the rise and fall of the harbour and docks. Other exhibits explore the town's connections with the ill-fated liner, the *Titanic*, and with Fletcher Christian, instigator of the mutiny on the Bounty. The Tourist Information Centre is also located here.

Close by is the **Lake District Coast Aquarium** where a series of spectacular living habitat recreations introduce visitors to the profusion of marine life found in the Solway Firth - thornback rays (which can be touched), some small sharks, spider crabs and the comically ugly tompot blenny amongst them. Open all year, the Aquarium also has a gift shop and a Quayside Café which enjoys superb views of the harbour and the Solway.

Just down the road from the Aquarium, at Elizabeth Dock, is the **Steamship Museum** which is home to two restored

DEARHAM
7 miles NE of Workington off the A594

Though this is not a pretty village, it has a very beautiful church with open countryside on three sides. The chancel is 13th century and there is a fortress tower built for the protection of men and beasts during the Border raids. There are also some interesting relics within the church including the Adam Stone, dating from 900, which depicts the fall of man with Adam and Eve hand in hand above a serpent, an ancient font carved with mythological beasts, a Kenneth Cross showing the legend of the 6th century hermit brought up by seagulls, and a magnificent wheel-head cross carved with Yggdrasil, the Norse Tree of the Universe.

GILCRUX
10 miles NE of Workington off the A596

From this village there are particularly good views across the Solway Firth to Scotland and it is well worth visiting for the 12th century **Church of St Mary** which is believed to be the oldest building in the district. Standing on a walled

The Masons Arms

Gilcrux, Wigton, Cumbria CA7 2QX
Tel: 016973 20765

Once a busy little coal mining village, Gilcrux stands on the hillside overlooking the Ellen valley and enjoying grand views across the Solway Firth to Scotland. When the mines were still working, the village managed to support no fewer than 7 licensed premises: today, only **The Masons Arms** survives. It's a charming old hostelry, with old beams and an open fire helping to create a wonderfully traditional atmosphere.

Esther and Paul Bowness, both of them local people, took over here late in 1999 and quickly established a reputation for good food, fine ales and genuinely welcoming hospitality. Food is served every evening and also at Sunday lunchtime (when booking is strongly recommended). Esther's menu offers a wide choice of dishes, ranging from a 16oz T-Bone Steak to a vegetarian Leek and Mushroom Crumble. Pizzas, jacket potatoes and sandwiches are also available, and there's a separate menu for children. Some scrumptious desserts are listed on the blackboard.

This family-friendly inn has a games room for the younger ones, with sweets and other goodies on sale, and to the rear there's a spacious beer garden. And if you happen to be visiting on the first Saturday of the month, you'll find that Esther and Paul have laid on live music for your entertainment!

The Grey Goat Inn

Baggrow, Aspatria, Cumbria CA5 3QH
Tel: 016973 21380

The tiny hamlet of Baggrow sits close to the River Ellen, about 3 miles east of Aspatria. It's well worth seeking out in order to visit **The Grey Goat Inn**, a characteristic Cumbrian hostelry with a black and white frontage set off in summer by a colourful display of hanging baskets.

The inn is owned and run by Glenn Stamper who took over here in the autumn of 2000. A friendly and outgoing host, he very quickly established the Grey Goat's reputation for warm hospitality, good food and well maintained beers. The inn dates back to the late 1700s and inside there's lots of exposed stone and a stone-tiled floor. At the time of writing, food is only available at weekends but during the course of 2001 Glenn will be extending this to every evening. Meals can be enjoyed either in the spacious lounge bar or, in good weather, in the attractive beer garden to the rear. Ales on offer include one real ale, Jennings Bitter, Jennings Old Smoothy and Bass Mild along with a wide range of other popular beverages. Glenn has also introduced occasional evening entertainments of all kinds - just phone for details.

This peaceful little village makes an ideal base for exploring north Cumbria and the Grey Goat has one guest bedroom, a twin en suite, available all year around and located in the adjacent annexe. The inn also has a space at the rear for one touring caravan; during 2001 this will be increased to standings for 3 caravans.

mound and with a buttressed exterior, it has a thick-walled chancel. The village is remarkable for the number of its springs, at least five of which have never failed even in the driest summers.

pagan swastika engraving. Like many other churches in the area, the churchyard contains a holy well in which it is said St Kentigern baptised his converts.

ASPATRIA
14 miles NE of Workington on the A596

Lying above the shallow Ellen Valley, Aspatria's main interest for most visitors lies in the elaborate memorial fountain to "Watery Wilfred", Sir Wilfred Lawson MP (1829-1906), a lifelong crusader for the Temperance Movement and International Peace. According to one writer, *"No man in his day made more people laugh at Temperance meetings"*. Also worth a visit is the much restored Norman church that is entered through a fine avenue of yew trees. Inside are several ancient relics including a 12th century font with intricate carvings, a Viking hogback tombstone, and a grave cover with a

ALLONBY
11 miles N of Workington on the B5300

This traditional Solway village is backed by the Lake District fells and looks out across the Solway Firth to the Scottish hills. Popular with wind-surfers, the village has an attractive shingle and sand beach which received a Seaside Award in 1998. Allonby is well known for its ponies which roam freely on the greens and if you fancy a foreshore ride there's a riding school located close to the beach. The **Allerdale Way** and the **Cumbrian Cycle Way** both pass close by, and the village is also on the Smuggler's Route trail. Smuggling seems to have been a profitable occupation around here - a Government

ART OF AFRICA GALLERY IN CUMBRIA

Holly Lodge, Arkleby, Aspatria, Cumbria CA5 2BT
Tel: 016973 23533 Fax: 0845 127 4502
e-mail: gallery@artofafrica.cumbria.com
website: www.artofafrica.cumbria.com

Hidden away in the tiny hamlet of Arkleby, the **Art of Africa Gallery in Cumbria** offers the unusual combination of an outstanding collection of African arts and crafts and also 2 self-catering cottages to let. This unique enterprise is the brainchild of Brian and Di Dawes who after living in South Africa for many years moved to their delightful 200-year-old

home in 1986. At that time, their hobby was collecting contemporary art from Africa, especially South Africa. The collection grew to such an extent that they decided to open their home as a gallery back in October 1999. They now fund a project in South Africa which enables village women to produce art through their embroidery and felting skills. Other craftspeople create their own artefacts through recycling.

The Gallery display covers a huge range of eminently collectable items - paintings, ceramics, functional art, jewellery, basket ware, carvings, sculptures, pots, wire art, textiles and much more. The Gallery is open Saturdays, Sundays and Bank Holidays from 11am to 6pm, and at other times by arrangement.

To the rear of the property, the old coach house and a former stable have been transformed into 2 attractive self-catering cottages. Each sleeps up to 4 people and are available all year round, with shorter breaks accepted out of season. Children and dogs are welcome.

THE SWAN INN

Westnewton, nr Wigton, Cumbria CA7 3PQ
Tel: 016973 20627

Arriving at **The Swan Inn** in the summer of 2000, Alan and Suzanne Benson have worked hard to restore this traditional Cumbrian inn, dating back to the 18th century, to its original character. Located in the heart of this pretty village, the inn was built as a simple alehouse but today offers excellent home-cooked food, quality ales and comfortable accommodation.

During the season, The Swan is open all day and throughout the year food is served every evening, from 6.30pm to 9pm, and on Sundays from noon until 9pm in

the dining room(re-decorated since the photo was taken!). There are two real ales always on tap, Jennings Bitter, brewed in nearby Cockermouth, and Yates Bitter, brewed in the village, as well as a wide range of all the popular beverages.

Alan and Suzanne have completely refurbished the inn's 3 guest bedrooms. They are all twin rooms, with two of them provided with en suite facilities. Children are welcome and a hearty breakfast is included in the tariff.

SPRING LEA CARAVAN & LEISURE CENTRE

Allonby, Cumbria CA15 6QR
Tel: 01900 881331 Fax: 01900 881209
website: www.springlea.co.uk

Occupying a prime position on the Solway Coast, **Spring Lea Caravan and Leisure Centre** has been providing visitors with top quality accommodation and a wide range of amenities for almost half a century. John Williamson's father established the business and he now runs it with the aid of his sons Shaun and Nick.

One of the premier parks for family holidays in Cumbria, Spring Lea has excellent facilities for touring caravans and campers - clean, regularly maintained toilets, hot showers, shaving points, laundry room, electric hook-ups and easy parking close to the vans. Also on site are 3 static caravans which are available to rent. Never more than 2 years old, the caravans can sleep up to 6 people. Just a short walk away, are 3 modern cottages, luxuriously appointed and with accommodation for up to 6 people. All

visitors to Spring Lea enjoy free membership of the Leisure Centre which has a 50ft swimming pool, a small children's pool with a Dolphin slide, a sauna and jacuzzi. There's also a well-equipped games room with video games, table tennis and pool tables. Younger children have their own soft play area.

Upstairs, the bar/restaurant offers a good selection of drinks and a choice of delicious home-made meals. In high season, the Centre also hosts live shows every Saturday, a Sunday quiz night for all ages, and a karaoke evening on Fridays.

enquiry into contraband trade reported in 1730 that "the Solway people were the first working-class folk to drink tea regularly in Britain".

In the early 1800s, Allonby was a popular sea-bathing resort and the former seawater baths, built in 1835 and now Grade II listed buildings, still stand in the old **Market Square**. In those days, the upper floor was in popular use as a ballroom for the local nobility. Allonby still keeps much of its Georgian and early Victorian charm with cobbled lanes, alleyways, and some interesting old houses. It was also an important centre for herring fishing and some of the old kippering houses can still be seen.

HOLME ST CUTHBERT
14 miles N of Workington off the B5300

This inland hamlet is also known as Rowks because, in the Middle Ages, there was a chapel here dedicated to St Roche.

The present church dates from 1845 but it contains an interesting torso of a medieval knight wearing chain mail. Found by schoolboys on a nearby farm, the hollowed-out centre of the torso was being used as a trough. It seems to be a 14th century piece and could be a representation of Robert the Bruce's father who died at Holm Cultram Abbey.

Northeast of the hamlet, and enveloped among low hills, is a lovely 30-acre lake known as **Tarns Dub** which is a haven for birdlife. A couple of miles to the southwest, the headland of **Dubmill Point** is popular with sea anglers. When the tide is high and driven by a fresh westerly wind, the sea covers the road with lashing waves.

BECKFOOT
16 miles N of Workington on the B5300

At certain times and tides, the remains of a prehistoric forest can be seen on the

THE WESTWINDS HOTEL

Allonby, Cumbria CA15 6PE
Tel: 01900 881345 Fax: 01900 881160

Built in 1907, **The Westwinds Hotel** is an impressive Edwardian building, originally a Vicarage, which enjoys panoramic views across the Solway Firth. Nearby, stretches a vast expanse of sands along the length of Allonby Bay, walkers can follow the Allerdale Ramble and for cyclists, there's the Cumbrian Cycle Way.

The Westwinds is very much a family business, owned and run by the Hingleys - Clive and his brother David who is the chef, and Clive's daughters Karen and Kirsty who look after the bar. David's menu offers an extensive choice and is available every lunchtime and evening in the summer, evenings only during the winter. Meals are served in the non-smoking restaurant where the regular menu is supplemented by daily specials. To complement your meal, there's a good selection of real ales and draught bitters, lagers and cider. If you are planning to eat here at weekends, it's definitely a good idea to book ahead. Children are welcome and credit cards accepted.

The Westwinds has 6 spacious guest bedrooms, all doubles and available all year round - come on a dinner, bed & breakfast, or bed & breakfast basis. The hotel also has a well-appointed function room with seating for 50 people and ideal for office parties, small weddings, christenings, birthdays, funeral teas and other special occasions.

GOLF HOTEL

Silloth-on-Solway, Wigton, Cumbria CA7 4AB
Tel: 016973 31438 Fax: 016973 32582

Overlooking the village green and Solway Firth, the **Golf Hotel** is an attractive building dating back to 1847 and sympathetically extended over the years. For the past quarter of a century, the hotel has been owned and run by Christine and Fausto Previtali, a welcoming couple who have established a well-merited reputation for providing quality food, drink and accommodation.

Food is served every lunchtime and evening in both the lounge bar and the elegant 40-seater restaurant. Choose from the comprehensive menu or from the selection of daily specials. Children are welcome and credit cards accepted. In addition to the wine list, there's a choice of real ales available,

including some from the local Derwent Brewery at Silloth. As well as the lounge bar, guests have the use of a snooker room and games room and, as the hotel's name suggests, the championship Silloth-on-Solway Golf Course is only 200yards away. Open all year round, the Golf Hotel has 22 comfortably furnished rooms, all of them en suite and including some family rooms and a room with a 4-poster bed.

Silloth itself is well known for its mild but invigorating climate, its relaxed and peaceful atmosphere and, perhaps best of all, its wonderful sea views and sunsets which inspired the great painter JMW Turner almost 200 years ago.

JEWELLERY BY MICHAEL KING

Todd Close, Curthwaite, Wigton,
Cumbria CA7 8BE
Tel/Fax: 01228 710756
e-mail: ASKing969@aol.com

From a workshop housed within a traditional 18th century long-house, **Jewellery by Michael King** produces beautiful pieces, exclusively designed and shaped from precious metals - gold, silver and platinum. Michael had a formal training in precious metals, art and design at the Kent Institute in Rochester, and then worked in London as a manufacturing jeweller. He then spent nearly ten years with the internationally acclaimed silversmith Christopher Lawrence before moving to Cumbria in 1982.

His work is strongly influenced by Celtic art - an appropriate source of inspiration since Cumbria was once part of the ancient Celtic kingdom of Rheged. Visitors to Michael's workshop, (which is open Monday to Saturday from 9.30am to 5.30pm, but closed on Bank Holidays), will find a dazzling display of exquisitely crafted pieces. There's a wide range of personal jewellery - rings, bangles, chains, necklaces, bracelets, cufflinks and more, as well as animal sculptures, chess sets, paper knives, and miniature silverware.

Michael is happy to accept commissions - earlier work commissioned from him includes a sterling silver crucifix, copied from an ancient relic found in the grounds of Carlisle Cathedral, and presented to the Queen; a ceremonial ring and cross for the Bishop of Penrith; and the jewellery and metalwork featured in the film *The Lost Kingdom*, most notably Arthur's sword Excalibur and the Raven Talisman worn by King Urien.

sand beds here and, to the south of the village, is the site of a 2ⁿᵈ century Roman fort known as Bibra. According to an inscribed stone found here, it was once occupied by an Auxiliary Cohort of 500 Pannonians (Spaniards) and surrounded by a large civilian settlement. The small stream flowing into the sea was used in World War I as a fresh water supply by intrepid German U-boats.

SILLOTH
18 miles N of Workington on the B5300

This charming old port and Victorian seaside resort is well worth exploring and its two-mile-long promenade provides wonderful views of the Solway Firth and the coast of Scotland. With the coming of the railways in the 1850s, Silloth developed as a port and railhead for Carlisle. The Railway Company helped to develop the town and had grey granite shipped over in its own vessels from Ireland to build the handsome church which is such a prominent landmark.

The region's bracing air and low rainfall helped to make Silloth a popular seaside resort. Visitors today will appreciate the invigorating but mild climate, the leisurely atmosphere, and the glorious sunsets over the sea that inspired Turner

to record them for posterity. The town remains a delightful place to stroll, to admire the sunken rose garden and the pinewoods and two miles of promenades. Silloth's 18-hole golf course was the "home course" where Miss Cecil Leitch (1891-1978), the most celebrated woman golfer of her day, used to play. Another keen woman golfer was the great contralto, Kathleen Ferrier, who stayed in the town for part of her tragically short life. The house on Eden Street where she lived is now a bank but a plaque on the wall records her stay here between 1936 and 1941.

WIGTON

The pleasant market town of Wigton has adopted the title "The Throstle Nest of all England" - throstle being the northern term for a thrush. The story is that a Wigton man returning home from the trenches of the Great War crested the hill and on seeing the familiar cluster of houses, churches, farms and the maze of streets, yards and alleys, exclaimed "Awa' lads, it's the throstle's nest of England".

For centuries, Wigton has been the centre of the business and social life of the Solway coast and plain, its prosperity being based on the weaving of cotton and linen. It has enjoyed the benefits of a Royal Charter since 1262 and the market is still held on Tuesdays. Today, most of the old town is a Conservation Area and, particularly along the **Main Street**, the upper storeys of the houses have survived in an almost unaltered state. On street corners, metal guards to prevent heavy horse-drawn

Silloth

wagons damaging the walls, can also still be seen.

One feature of the town that should not be missed is the magnificent **Memorial Fountain** in the Market Place. Its gilded, floriate panels are set against Shap granite and surmounted with a golden cross. It was erected in 1872 by the philanthropist George Moore in memory of his wife, Eliza Flint Ray, with whom he fell in love when he was a penniless apprentice. Bronze reliefs show four of her favourite charities - giving clothes to the naked, feeding the hungry, instructing the ignorant, and sheltering the homeless. The bronzes were created by Thomas Woolner, the pre-Raphaelite sculptor.

Wigton boasts a couple of interesting literary connections. Charles Dickens and Wilkie Collins stayed at The King's Arms Hotel in 1857, during the trip described in *The Lazy Tour of Two Idle Apprentices*, and the author and broadcaster Melvyn Bragg was born here. The town, often disguised as "Thurston", features in several of his novels, and sequences for A Time to Dance were set and filmed in Wigton.

AROUND WIGTON

SKINBURNESS
11 miles W of Wigton off the B5302

A lively market town, in the Middle Ages, Skinburness was used by Edward I in 1299 as a base for his navy when attacking the Scots. A few years later a terrible storm destroyed the town and what survived became a small fishing hamlet.

From nearby **Grune Point**, the start of the **Allerdale Ramble**, there are some tremendous views over the Solway Firth and the beautiful, desolate expanse of marshland and sandbank. Grune Point once contained a long vanished Roman fort, but now forms part of a designated Site of Special Scientific Interest notable for the variety of its birdlife and marsh plants.

ABBEYTOWN
5 miles W of Wigton on the B5302

As its name suggests, Abbeytown grew up around the 12th century **Abbey of Holm Cultram** on the River Waver and many of the town's buildings are constructed of stone taken from the abbey when it fell into ruins. Founded by Cistercians in 1150, the abbey bore the brunt of the constant feuds between the English and the Scots. In times of peace the community prospered and soon became one of the largest suppliers of wool in the North. Edward I stayed here in 1300 and again, in 1307, when he made Abbot Robert De Keldsik a member of his Council. After Edward's death the Scots returned with a vengeance and in 1319 Robert the Bruce sacked the abbey, even though his own father, the Earl of Carrick, had been buried there 15 years earlier.

The final blow came in 1536 when Abbot Carter joined the Pilgrimage of Grace, the ill-fated rebellion against Henry VIII's seizure of Church lands and property. The rebellion was put down with ruthless brutality and the red sandstone **Church of St Mary** only survived because local people pointed out that the building was necessary to provide protection against Scottish raiders. It is still the parish church and was restored in 1883, a strange yet impressive building with the original nave shorn of its tower, transepts and chancel. The east and west walls are heavily buttressed and a porch with a new roof protects the original Norman arch of the west door. Within the church buildings is a room, opened by Princess Margaret in 1973, which contains the gravestones of Robert the Bruce's father and that of Mathias and Juliana De Keldsik, relations of Abbot Robert. Nearby, there are some lovely walks along the River Waver which is especially rich in wildlife.

NEWTON ARLOSH
5 miles NW of Wigton on the B5307

Situated on the **Solway marshes**, the village was first established by the monks of Holm Cultram Abbey in 1307 after the old port at Skinburness had been destroyed by the sea. The village's name means "the new town on the marsh". Work on the church did not begin until 1393, but the result is one of the most delightful examples of a Cumbrian fortified church. In the Middle Ages, there was no castle nearby to protect the local population from the border raids and so a pele tower was added to the church. As an additional defensive measure, the builders created what is believed to be narrowest church doorway in the country, barely 2ft 7in across and a little over 5ft high. The 12in arrow-slot, east window is also the smallest in England. After the Reformation, the church became derelict but was finally restored in the 19th century. Inside, there is a particularly fine eagle lectern carved out of bog oak.

6 Keswick and the Northern Lakes

The northern Lakes is, for many enthusiasts, classic Lakeland, the scenery dominated by the rounded, heather-clad slopes of the Skiddaw range to the north of Keswick, and the wild, craggy mountains of

Borrowdale, to the south. Yet, despite this area's popularity, there are many hidden places to discover that are off the beaten track.

The major town, Keswick, on the shores of Derwent Water, is a pleasant Lakeland town that has much to offer the visitor. The lake too, is interesting as, not only is it in a near perfect setting, but

Dockray Church

it is unusual in having some islands - in this case four. It was the view over the lake, from Friar's Crag, that formed one of John Ruskin's early childhood memories.

However, there is much more to this part of Cumbria. The area is rich in history, as well as there being significant evidence of Roman occupation. In addition Castlerigg Stone Circle can be found here. Many of the villages relied on coal mining and mineral extraction for their livelihood.

But it is the wonderful, dramatic scenery that makes this area of the Lake District so special. Not only are there

Watendlath, Borrowdale

several charming and isolated lakes within easy reach of Keswick, but Buttermere, considered by connoisseurs to be the best of all, lies only a few miles away. Not all the lakes, however, are what they first appear to be: Thirlmere is a 19th century reservoir constructed to supply Manchester's growing thirst.

KESWICK AND THE NORTHERN LAKES

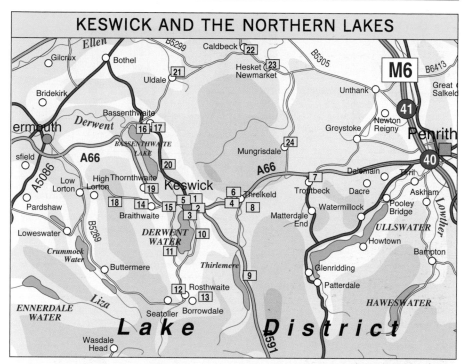

© MAPS IN MINUTES ™ (1999)

PLACES TO STAY, EAT, DRINK AND SHOP

THE OLD KESWICKIAN
RESTAURANT

7 Market Square, Keswick,
Cumbria CA12 5BD
Tel: 017687 73861

Between them, the Taylor family can supply most of your eating requirements in Keswick. Since 1987, Michael Taylor has been providing some of the best fish and chips to be found in Lakeland at his **Old Keswickian Restaurant** in the Market Square. He serves beautifully cooked fresh skinless fish in his spotlessly clean 70-seater restaurant every day from 11.15am to around 9.30pm in summer, 6.30pm in winter. There are both smoking and non-smoking areas. The restaurant's take away service continues until about 11.15pm all year round except over Christmas and for 3 weeks in January when the premises close for refurbishment.

Right next door to the Old Keswickian, Michael's daughter, Lisa, runs the Keswickian Tea Room where customers can enjoy a variety of light snacks in air-conditioned surroundings. The menu includes tea-cakes, scones and toasted sandwiches, home-made soup, cappuccino and cafetière coffees, speciality teas and soft drinks. Some 90% of the fare on offer is home-made and home-cooked on the premises.

If you are looking for a more substantial meal, then make your way to The Kingfisher Restaurant in Main Street which is run by Michael's son-in-law Alan Simpson and offers a wide choice of wholesome and appetising dishes.

BANK TAVERN

47 Main Street, Keswick, Cumbria CA12 5DS
Tel: 017687 72663 Fax: 017687 75168

Located in the main street of this popular tourist centre, the **Bank Tavern** is believed to be one of the oldest of Keswick's hostelries, dating back to the late 1700s. The interior has lots of atmosphere and olde worlde charm, a relaxing setting in which to enjoy the excellent food and drink on offer. The extensive menu, available every lunchtime and evening, includes a good choice of traditional fare along with curries, vegetarian dishes, salads, jacket potatoes and, at lunchtimes only, sandwiches and hot filled baguettes. Daily specials might include a 20oz steak, Green Thai Pork or Cajun Chicken. A full range of Jennings bitters is available and in good weather customers can enjoy their refreshments outside at the rear of the tavern. The Bank Tavern is open all day, every day, children are welcome and major credit cards are accepted. Housed in the old eaves are 5 guest bedrooms, all very cosy and full of character and with a shared bathroom nearby.

The Bank Tavern is a family run business with Pat and Ian Dixon, together with their son Stephen, as your welcoming mine hosts. They also run the **Four in Hand** pub in Lake Road which offers a similarly wide-ranging menu that includes some more unusual dishes, several of them accompanied by some interesting sauces. Whichever hostelry you visit,, you'll find the same friendly welcome and Dixon family hospitality!

KESWICK

"Above it rises Skiddaw, majestic and famous, and at its door is Derwentwater, the lake beyond compare". For generations, visitors to Keswick have been impressed

Blake Beck Bar Farm, Keswick

by the town's stunningly beautiful setting, surrounded by the great fells of Saddleback, Helvellyn and Grisedale Pike.

Tourism, now the town's major industry, actually began in the mid-1700s and was given a huge boost by the Lakeland Poets in the early 1800s. The arrival of the railway in 1865 firmly established Keswick as the undisputed "capital" of the Lake District with most of the area's notable attractions within easy reach.

The grandeur of the lakeland scenery is of course the greatest draw but, amongst the man-made features, one not to be missed is the well-preserved **Castlerigg Stone Circle**. About a mile to the east of the town, the 38 standing stones, some of them 8ft high, form a

circle 100ft in diameter. They are believed to have been put in place some 4,000 years ago and occupy a hauntingly beautiful position.

Keswick old town developed along the banks of the broad River Greta, with a wide main street leading up to the attractive **Moot Hall**. Built in 1813, the Hall has been at various times a buttermarket, courthouse and prison, Town Hall and now houses the Tourist Information Centre. A little further south, in St John's Street, the church of that name was built in the very same year as the Moot Hall and its elegant spire provides a point of reference from all around the town. In the churchyard is the grave of Sir Hugh Walpole whose once hugely popular series of novels, *The Herries Chronicle (1930-3)*, are set in this part of the Lake District.

In the riverside Fitz Park is the town's **Museum & Art Gallery** which is well worth a visit not just to see original manuscripts by Wordsworth and other lakeland poets but also for the astonishing

Castlerigg Stone Circle

HAZELDENE HOTEL

The Heads, Keswick on Derwentwater, Cumbria CA12 5ER
Tel: 01768772106 Fax: 01768775435
e-mail: helen8@supanet.com
website: hazeldene hotel.co.uk

Located only 200 yards from the town centre, the **Hazeldene Hotel** is also just a leisurely 7 minutes walk from the tranquil shores of Derwentwater and the spectacular scenery of Borrowdale. An impressive Victorian mansion built in 1892, the hotel has only had three different owners during its lifetime. Sisters Helen and Gill, who own and run the hotel today together with Helen's husband Howard, were actually born in the house. Between them, they have created a wonderfully relaxed and informal atmosphere.

Guests can relax in one of the attractive south-facing lounges or if they are feeling more energetic, pool and table tennis are available in the conservatory. Meals are served in the comfortable (and licensed) dining room overlooking the beautifully maintained grounds. The hotel's 20 spacious bedrooms are all comfortably furnished and provided with an en suite shower and toilet, colour television, hairdryer, drinks cabinet, direct dial telephone and tea-making facilities.

As well as the glorious walks through stunning countryside, the hotel is close to many other amenities - water sports, horse riding, golf, tennis, squash and bowls are all within easy reach, so too are Keswick's acclaimed theatre, museums and the mysterious 3000 year old Castlerigg Stone Circle, a remarkable cluster of 38 stones which commands some astounding views of the surrounding fells.

SALUTATION INN

Threlkeld, Keswick, Cumbria CA12 4SQ
Tel: 017687 79614

Located on the main street of this picturesque little village, the **Salutation Inn** has been welcoming visitors to this lovely part of Lakeland since at least the 1600s. Inside, gnarled old beams reflect the inn's antiquity, while horse brasses, local memorabilia and an open fire all add to the charm. The Salutation is well-known locally for its excellent food, available every lunchtime and evening. Everything is home made and freshly prepared and the menu includes a wide choice of steaks, grills, fish and poultry dishes, basket meals (one of which, a Jumbo Cumberland Sausage is billed "as not for the faint-hearted"!), salads and desserts. At lunchtime, this choice is supplemented by a range of sandwiches, hoagies (filled French sticks), and Jacket Potatoes. A children's menu is available at both lunchtimes and in the evening. To accompany your meal, there's a good selection of real ales plus mild, stout, lagers and cider. (Please note that the Salutation does not accept credit cards). Children and dogs are welcome at the inn and there's a separate family room upstairs. For additional entertainment there's a pool table and mine hosts Marian and Ian Leonard arrange a Quiz Night every other Sunday. If you are planning to stay in this spectacular corner of the Lake District, the inn has accommodation available.

"Rock, Bell and Steel Band" created by Joseph Richardson of Skiddaw in the 19th century. It's a kind of xylophone made of sixty stones - some a yard long -, sixty steel bars and forty bells. Four "musicians" are required to play this extraordinary instrument.

Surrounded by a loop of the River Greta to the northwest of the town is the surprisingly fascinating **Cumberland Pencil Museum** which, incidentally, boasts the six feet long "Largest Pencil in the World". The "lead" used in pencils (not lead at all but actually an *"allotrope of carbon"*) was accidentally discovered by a Borrowdale shepherd in the 16th century and Keswick eventually became the world centre for the manufacture of lead pencils. The pencil mill here, established in 1832, is still operating here although the "wadd", or lead, is now imported.

Other attractions in the town centre include the **Cars of the Stars Museum**, ideal for movie buffs since it contains such gems as Laurel and Hardy's Model T Ford, James Bond's Aston Martin, Batman's Batmobile and Mr Bean's Mini (see panel below), and **The Teapottery** which makes and sells a bizarre range of practical teapots in the shape of anything from an upright piano to an Aga stove.

A short walk from the town centre, along Lake Road, leads visitors to the popular **Theatre by the Lake** which hosts a year-round programme of plays, concerts, exhibitions, readings and talks. Close by is the pier from which there are regular departures for cruises around Derwentwater and ferries across the lake to Nichol End where you can hire just about every kind of water craft, including your own private cruise boat.

Another short walk will bring you to **Friar's Crag**. This famous view of Derwent Water and its islands, now National Trust property, formed one of John Ruskin's early childhood memories, inspiring in him *"intense joy, mingled with awe"*. The Crag is dedicated to the memory of Canon Rawnsley, the local vicar, who was one of the founder members of the Trust which he helped to set up in 1895.

AROUND KESWICK

THRELKELD
3 miles E of Keswick off the A66

From Keswick there's a delightful walk along the track bed of the old railway line to the charming village of Threlkeld, set in a plain at the foot of mighty **Blencathra**. The village is the ideal starting point for a number of mountain walks, including an ascent of Blencathra

CARS OF THE STARS MUSEUM

Standish Street, Town Centre, Keswick, Cumbria
Tel: 017687 73757

Located in the town centre, the **Cars of the Stars Museum** is definitely not to be missed by either movie buffs or devotees of vintage cars. This fascinating collection contains such gems as Laurel and Hardy's Model T Ford, James Bond's Aston Martin, Batman's Batmobile and Mr Bean's Mini. There are film set displays and vehicles from series such as The Saint, The Prisoner, Bergerac, The Avengers, Noddy, Postman Pat and the A Team. Even Del Boy's shabby 3-wheeler Reliant van from Only Fools and Horses is here. This unique museum is open from 10am to 5pm, daily between Easter and the New Year, weekends in December, and during the February half term.

THE BUNGALOWS

Sunnyside, Threlkeld, Keswick,
Cumbria CA12 4SD
Tel: 017687 79679
e-mail: paulsunley@msn.com
www: the bungalows.co.uk

This little village is well-known to
walkers as the ideal starting point for a
number of mountain walks, including
an ascent of Blencathra, one of the most
exciting of all the Lakeland mountains.
Set on the lower slopes of the Blencathra
range, **The Bungalows** offers visitors
excellent unobstructed views over the
peaceful village toward the Vale of St
Johns and the northern end of the
Helvellyn range - and also the choice of comfortable bed & breakfast or self-catering accommodation.
Available all year round, the two modern bungalows can each sleep up to 6 guests, plus a cot, and are
both fully furnished with well-equipped kitchens with cooker, microwave, fridge and washing machine.

Each bungalow is fully heated by off peak electric and electric fires - all electricity and linen is
included in the rental. For those who prefer bed & breakfast, the owners Paul and Val Sunley have 3
guest bedrooms, all of them with en suite facilities, colour television and tea/coffee-making equipment.
Rooms are available all year round and the Sunleys are justifiably proud of their international reputation
for service and northern hospitality. Threlkeld village itself has two inns and a golf course, and there
are facilities for fishing and pony trekking nearby. The Bungalows are within easy reach of all the
main Lakeland attractions, while to the east is the beautiful Eden Valley with its picturesque villages
and, a few miles to the north, Gretna Green provides a romantic gateway to Scotland.

GILL HEAD

Troutbeck, Penrith, Cumbria CA11 0ST
Tel: 017687 79652
website: www.gillheadfarm.co.uk

Set against the spectacular backdrop of
Blencathra and the northern fells, **Gill Head** is a
family run hill farm of some 350 acres where
visitors will find a wide choice of
accommodation. Bed & breakfast guests stay in
the charming 17th century farmhouse where
Amanda Steele and her parents, William and
Janice, have been welcoming visitors for more than 30 years. Available all year round, the 5 guest
bedrooms (3 doubles and 2 twins) are all non-smoking and provided with full en suite facilities,
colour TV, hospitality tray and toiletries. Children are welcome. Guests have the use of a cosy, oak-
beamed sitting room and also a residents' kitchen. The Steeles are noted for their delicious farmhouse
cooking - a hearty breakfast is included in the tariff and evening meals are available by arrangement.

For those who prefer self-catering, a beautifully furnished
ground floor apartment overlooking the garden is
available, also all year round. A twin-bedded room and
a double sofa bed can sleep up to 4 guests and the
accommodation also comprises a fully fitted kitchen,
bathroom and dining/lounge. Finally, for campers and
caravanners, a level sheltered site with panoramic views,
is available from Easter to the end of October. This
attractive site has electric hook-ups, modern well-
maintained shower, toilet and laundry facilities, and a
small shop for general provisions.

which is one of the most exciting of all the Lake District mountains. Also known as Saddleback and a smaller sister of Skiddaw to the west, the steep sides ensure that it looks every inch a mountain. Threlkeld is famous for its annual sheepdog trials though its economy was built up on the several mines in the area and the granite quarry to the south. At **Threlkeld Quarry & Mining Museum** visitors can browse through the collection of mining artefacts, wander through the locomotive shed and machine shop, or join the 40-minute tour through a recreated mine (see panel below).

MATTERDALE END
8 miles E of Keswick on the A5091

This tiny hamlet lies at one end of Matterdale, a valley that an essential stop on any Wordsworth trail for it was here, on April 15th 1802, that he and his sister

saw that immortal:
> *"host of golden daffodils,*
> *Beside the lake,*
> *beneath the trees,*
> *Fluttering and dancing in the breeze".*

THIRLMERE
4 miles S of Keswick off the A591

This attractive, tree-lined lake, one of the few in the Lakes that can be driven around as well as walked around, was created in the 1890s by the Manchester Corporation. More than a hundred miles of pipes and tunnels still supply the city with water from Thirlmere. At first, there was no public access to the lakeshore but today these are being opened up for recreational use with car parks, walking trails and picnic places.

The creation of this huge reservoir, five miles long, flooded the two hamlets of Armboth and Wythburn and all that

---

THRELKELD MINING MUSEUM

Threlkeld Quarry, Keswick, Cumbria CA12 4TT
Tel: 017687 79747 / 01228 561883
e-mail: coppermaid@aol.com website: www.golakes.co.uk

Entranced by the spectacular scenery of the Lake District, visitors are often unaware that in the past this was also a significant mining area. This industrial heritage is brought vividly to life at the **Threlkeld Quarry & Mining Museum** where visitors can browse through the collection of mining artefacts, wander through the locomotive shed and machine shop, or join the 40-minute tour through a recreated mine. At Threlkeld Quarry, men were employed from the 1870s until 1982 quarrying granite for railway ballast and road making, as well as producing granite setts and masonry stone. Several of the original buildings remain, including the locomotive shed which now houses various industrial diesel locomotives which can be seen out on the track from time to time. A new acquisition to the museum is the steam locomotive Sir Thomas Callender which should be in use from June 2001. On display in the Museum is probably the finest collection of small mining and quarrying artefacts in the North - everything from wedges, chisels and drills to candles,

clogs and kibbles (large iron buckets used for conveying the ore and spoil to the surface). There's also an excellent mineral collection and in the Geology Room a fascinating table top relief map of the Lake District, enhanced by rock specimens. The Museum Shop stocks the largest selection of mining, geology and mineralogy books in the north of England, (including a second-hand section), beautiful minerals from around the world, along with gemstone jewellery and a complete range of mine exploration and caving gear.

DALE HEAD HALL LAKESIDE HOTEL

Lake Thirlmere, Cumbria CA12 4TN
Tel: 017687 72478 Fax: 017687 71070
e-mail: enquiry@dale-head-hall.co.uk   website: www.dale-head-hall.co.uk

At **Dale Head Hall Lakeside Hotel** visitors will find a noble old hall dating back to Elizabethan times and occupying a glorious lakeside setting. The Leathes family lived here for 300 years until 1877 when the property was acquired by Manchester Corporation. The lake provided the city with clean drinking water; the house served successive Lord Mayors as an idyllic country retreat. Today, the mellow old house is a delightful, family run hotel offering quality cuisine and accommodation as well as self-catering apartments in the attractively converted Victorian coach house. Shirley and Alan Lowe bought the property

in 1990 and are now assisted by their daughter Caroline and son-in-law Hans. Caroline is a gifted cook who offers a different menu every day of the year, all of them based on prime ingredients accompanied by fresh vegetables and herbs from the hall's walled garden. Guests have the use of an enchanting residents' lounge, a relaxing place with a crackling log fire and overlooking the tranquil lake and gardens. The 12 guest rooms all have private bath and shower rooms and most enjoy lake views. Some are oak panelled and beamed, and two of them are on the ground floor. For those who prefer self-catering, the 4 luxury suites in the old stable house nestling at the foot of Helvellyn are ideal. They are all beautifully decorated with solid oak and retain original features such as the king post-beams, circular stone window frames and a flower-laden cobbled yard. Available all year round, the apartments each sleep 2 guests.

THE LEATHES HEAD

Borrowdale, Keswick, Cumbria CA12 5UY
Tel: 017687 77247 Fax: 017687 77363
website: www.leatheshead.co.uk

Set back from the B5289, about 3 miles from Keswick, **The Leathes Head Hotel** occupies a superb position, set in 3 acres of its own grounds and commanding glorious panoramic views over Derwent Water. Constructed in the attractive local grey stone, the hotel dates back to 1908 when it was built as a private house.

Thanks to its chef, David Jackson, the hotel enjoys a well-deserved reputation for outstanding food. A local man, David presents a daily changing menu featuring dishes based on the very best of fresh, local produce. His wonderful desserts are justly famous! Diners can savour his appetising cuisine in the elegant dining room with its spectacular views of the fells. (The 26-seater licensed restaurant is also open to non-residents, but booking is advisable). The Leathes has no fewer than 3 residents' lounges and a well-stocked bar.

There are 11 guest bedrooms, all of them spacious, en suite and with 2 on the ground floor which are suitable for the disabled. Four of the rooms are *extra* large with additional features and tremendous views.

Guests at The Leathes stay on a dinner, bed & breakfast basis but if you prefer self-catering, the hotel's owners, Janice and Ray Smith, can also offer 11 self-catering apartments in nearby Portinscale. Housed within a former converted hotel, the apartments sleep from 2 to 6 people.

remains of these places today is Wythburn chapel towards the southern end. Overlooking the narrow lake is **Helvellyn**, Wordsworth's favourite mountain and one that is also very popular with walkers and climbers today. At 3,116 feet, it is one of the four Lakeland fells over 3,000 feet high and the walk to the summit should not be undertaken lightly but those reaching the summit will find some spectacular views. The eastern aspect of the mountain is markedly different from the western as it was here that the Ice Age glaciers were sheltered from the mild, west winds.

BORROWDALE
Runs S from Keswick via the B5289

"The Mountains of Borrowdale are perhaps as fine as anything we have seen" wrote John Keats in 1818. Only 6 miles long, this brooding, mysterious valley, steep and narrow with towering crags and deep woods is generally regarded as the most scenic in the Lake District. Just to the south of Derwent Water are the Lodore Falls, where the Watendlath Beck drops some 120ft before reaching the lake. Further along the dale, in woodland owned by the National Trust, lies the extraordinary Bowder Stone which provides an irresistible photo-opportunity for most visitors. A massive 50ft square and weighing almost 2000 tons, it stands precariously on one corner apparently defying gravity. A wooden staircase on one side provides easy access to the top. South of Grange village, the valley narrows into the "Jaws of Borrowdale". Castle Crag, the western mandible of the Jaws, has on its summit the remains of the defensive ditches of a Romano-British fort.

Just south of Rosthwaite the road turns westwards to the village of Seatoller where there's a National Park Information

MANESTY HOLIDAY COTTAGES

Youdale Knot, Manesty, Keswick, Cumbria CA12 5UG
Tel: 017687 77216 Fax: 017687 77384
e-mail: alan.t.leyland@talk21.com
website: www.borrowdale.com/manesty

The Leyland family settled in this lovely corner of the Lake District some 150 years ago but still consider themselves to be relative newcomers for Manesty's history reaches back to the 12th century. Alan and Cheryl are the sixth generation to live here and it is they who will welcome you to their delightful **Manesty Holiday Cottages** which stand at the foot of Cat Bells and Maiden Moor, about 6 miles from Keswick.

There are 5 properties in all, the largest of which is "Manesty Band",(accommodating up to 7 people), which includes the original typical Lakeland barn which was imaginatively incorporated into the living quarters in the early 19th century. "Manesty", (for up to 6 guests), is the heart of the original farmhouse and its entrance hall, once the scullery, still has its original stone slab and bull's-eye window. "Manesty Dairy", the compact Edwardian dairy extension to the farmhouse, is suitable for 2 people, while "High Seat", a former farm building converted in the mid 20th century into a bungalow, has two bedrooms capable of accommodating up to 5 guests. "Cocklety How " is a more recent conversion of a 17th century barn and consists of 2 first floor self-contained apartments,"Cocklety How Stable Loft" (4 people) and "Cocklety How Studio" (2 people). There is an interconnecting door which offers the option of separate or combined occupation.

All these carefully maintained and well-equipped properties enjoy enchanting views of the Borrowdale.

Royal Oak Hotel

Rosthwaite, Borrowdale, Cumbria CA12 5XB
Tel/Fax: 017687 77214
website: www.royaloakhotel.co.uk

The Dowie family have owned and personally run the **Royal Oak Hotel** since 1970 but this traditional Cumbrian long house was already some 200 years old when they arrived. Built as a farmhouse, the hotel occupies a lovely position just beyond the "Jaws of Borrowdale", about 6 miles south of Keswick, and for more than a century has been welcoming visitors and walkers to this spectacular corner of the Lake District. Neil Dowie is himself a keen walker and climber, as well as being a member of the Mountain Rescue team, and is happy to advise guests on the best walking and climbing nearby.

Guests at the Royal Oak are accommodated on a dinner, bed and breakfast basis and the hotel has a well-deserved reputation for serving "set you up for the day" breakfasts, and appetising home cooked table d'hôte dinners. Guests are accommodated either in the main house, where there are 8 en suite and 3 standard guest bedrooms, each one quite different from the others, or across the courtyard in the recently converted barn annex, "Merrybreeches", which provides a further 4 spacious en suite rooms, all of which enjoy peaceful riverside views across Stonethwaite Beck.

Please note that this outstanding hotel is closed for 3 weeks in December and for 2 weeks in January - closed over Christmas but open for the New Year period.

The Langstrath Country Inn

Stonethwaite, Borrowdale, Keswick,
Cumbria CA12 5XG
Tel: 017687 77239

Stonethwaite is indeed a Hidden Place, a tiny hamlet at the end of a half-mile lane off the B5289 road southwards from Keswick through Borrowdale. But this picturesque cluster of whitewashed stone cottages is well-known to serious walkers since both the Cumbrian Way and the Coast to Coast footpath pass through here. Stonethwaite is also well worth seeking out in order to visit the **Langstrath Country Inn**, an attractive old building whose oldest parts date back to 1590. Despite its venerable age, the inn only acquired a licence in 1991, having been a private hotel for many years before that. Today it's a popular venue not just for walkers but for locals and visitors alike.

The owners, Donna and Gary MacRae, are a young and enthusiastic couple who have created a very friendly and relaxed atmosphere. Quality food is available every lunchtime from noon until 2pm, and in the evenings from 5.30pm to 8.30pm. A good range of real ales is on tap, including Black Sheep and Jennings. Children are welcome during the day but are not allowed in the bar in the evening. Whether you are walking or touring, the Langstrath makes an excellent base and its 10 guest bedrooms, about half of which have en suite facilities, are available all year round. Incidentally, the inn features in Ian McEwan's Booker prize-winning novel *Amsterdam* which also provides some memorable descriptions of the area.

Centre and a minor road turns off to **Seathwaite** which enjoys the unenviable reputation of being the wettest place in England with an average of 131 inches a year. Seathwaite is also the starting point for many fell walks and climbing expeditions particularly to the **Scafells** and **Great Gable**.

From Seatoller, the B5289 slices through the spectacular **Honister Pass**, overlooked by dramatic 1000ft high Honister Crag. At the top of the pass, the 18th century **Honister Slate Mine** has been re-opened and is once again producing the beautiful green slate that adorns so many Lakeland houses and is famous throughout the world. A fully guided tour of the mine is available which shows the current working of the mine and how a mixture of modern and traditional methods is still extracting the slate which was formed here some 400

Grange in Borrowdale

million years ago. After the tour, complimentary tea or coffee is served in the Bait Cabin beside a warm fire, and the complex also has an informative Visitor Centre and a gift shop selling the ornamental green slate.

BUTTERMERE
8 miles SW of Keswick on the B5289

Half the size of its neighbour, Crummock Water, Buttermere is a beautiful lake set in a dramatic landscape. To many connoisseurs of the Lake District landscape, this is the most splendid of them all. The walk around Buttermere gives superb views of the eastern towers of Fleetwith Pike and the great fell wall made up of High Crag, High Stile, and Red Pike.

In the early 1800s the village became involved in one of the great scandals of the age. Mary Robinson, the daughter of a local innkeeper, had been described as a maiden of surpassing beauty in J Budworth's book *A Fortnight's Ramble in the Lakes*. She became something of a local attraction

Borrowdale Valley

THE OLD FARMHOUSE

Braithwaite, Keswick,
Cumbria CA12 5SY
Tel/Fax: 01751 417379
e-mail: p.galloway@talk21.com

The charming village of Braithwaite, a frequent winner of the "Best Kept Village Award", sits along the banks of Coledale Beck, with the great mass of Grisedale Pyke (2593ft) forming a spectacular backdrop. **The Old Farmhouse** is located in the heart of the village, just across the road from Coledale Beck

Within its grounds, former farm buildings have been imaginatively converted to provide a good choice of self-catering accommodation. Built in stone and slate, the cottages have retained their traditional Lakeland character and enjoy a peaceful setting in the heart of the village, well away from busy roads. There are 7 cottages in all, facing onto the flower-bedecked farmhouse courtyard and with accommodation ranging from 1-2 people up to 2-4. Each cottage is fully furnished with fitted carpet, easy chairs, dining suite, colour TV and is well supplied with electric heaters. There's a very well-equipped kitchen and a WC/shower room with washbasin and shaver point.

Also available, in a separate 2-storey building overlooking the Old Farmhouse's rear courtyard, are two flats, one on the ground floor, the other on the upper floor, both of which can accommodate 2-4 guests. They are equipped to the same high standards as the cottages but are more spacious. Children are welcome, (cots and high chairs are available on request), and one well-behaved dog per cottage/flat is allowed on request. Available all year round, the properties provide a perfect base for exploring the scenic splendours of the area.

RICKERBY GRANGE COUNTRY HOUSE HOTEL

Portinscale, Keswick, Cumbria CA12 5RH
Tel: 017687 72344 Fax: 017687 75588
e-mail: val@ricor.demon.co.uk
website: www.ricor.demon.co.uk

Located only a few hundred yards from the north-western tip of Derwent Water, **Rickerby Grange Country House Hotel** enjoys all the advantages of a peaceful countryside setting as well as being little more than a mile from the centre of Keswick.

Surrounded by its own gardens and overlooked by Skiddaw, Cat Bells and Causey Pike, Rickerby Grange was built around 1900 by a local farmer for his daughter. As the name implies, it was built as The Grange to Rickerby House which stands close by in the village. The hotel has wonderfully relaxed and informal atmosphere thanks to the friendly and welcoming owners, Val and Tony. Guests stay on a dinner, bed & breakfast basis, with a traditional, freshly-prepared 5-course dinner, served in the elegant dining room, included in the tariff. Tony is an accomplished chef and his appetising dishes are one of the reasons that guests return here again and again.

The Grange has 14 attractively furnished and decorated guest bedrooms, all but two of which have en suite facilities. Three of them are on the ground floor and all are fully equipped with central heating, colour television, direct dial telephone and hospitality tray. Children over 5 are welcome, so too are properly trained dogs but these are not allowed in the public rooms.

with people flocking to the inn to admire her beauty, amongst them Wordsworth and Coleridge. Another was a smooth-tongued gentleman who introduced himself as Alexander Augustus Colonel Hope, MP, brother of the Earl of Hopetoun. Mary fell for his charms and married him, only to discover that her husband was really John Hatfield, a bankrupt impostor and a bigamist to boot. Hatfield was tried at Carlisle for fraud, a capital offence in those days, and Coleridge supplemented his meagre income by reporting the sensational trial for the Morning Post. Hatfield was found guilty and hanged at Carlisle gaol in 1802: Mary later married a local farmer and went on to live a normal and happy life. The author, broadcaster, and great supporter of Cumbria, Melvyn Bragg, tells her story in his novel, *The Maid of Buttermere*.

Crummock Water

CRUMMOCK WATER
9 miles SW of Keswick on the B5289

Fed by both Buttermere and Loweswater, this is by far the larger of the three lakes. In this less frequented part of western Cumbria, where there are few roads, the attraction of Crummock Water can usually be enjoyed in solitude. Best seen from the top of Rannerdale Knotts, to the east, the lake has a footpath running around it though, in places, the going gets a little strenuous.

BRAITHWAITE
3 miles W of Keswick on the B5292

This small village lies at the foot of the **Whinlatter Pass**, another of Cumbria's dramatic routes. The summit of this steep road, the B5292, is some 1,043ft above sea level and, on the westerly descent, there are magnificent views over Bassenthwaite Lake. The road runs through the **Whinlatter Forest Park** which has a Visitor Centre, trails and walks for all ages and abilities, an orienteering course, adventure playground, viewpoints, gift shop and a tearoom with a terrace

Buttermere

MELBECKS COTTAGES

Melbecks, Bassenthwaite, Keswick,
Cumbria CA12 4QX
Tel/Fax: 017687 76451

The four properties known as **Melbecks Cottages** occupy a superb position enjoying spectacular panoramic views of Bassenthwaite Lake and the surrounding fells, and with Skiddaw and Ullock Pike providing an impressive backdrop. Imaginatively converted from a large listed barn and fitted and furnished to a very high standard, the self-catering cottages stand in the heart of excellent walking country.

Many good walks are right on the doorstep and you can follow a mapped ascent of Skiddaw as described in Wainwright's *Northern Fells*. Three of the cottages, "Skiddaw", "Dodd" and "Dash" can sleep up to 4 guests; the fourth, "Randel", sleeps 2. All the properties have well-equipped kitchens, colour TV, video recorder (with more than 140 videos available), and everything is included in the tariff apart from electricity which is charged by a meter reading. The cottages share a large garden, a games room with table tennis and pool table, there's plenty of space for children to play and also ample parking. As we go to press, a fifth cottage, "Uldale", which will sleep up to 6 guests, is being prepared and should be available by the time you read this. The cottages enjoy a wonderfully peaceful and secluded setting but the village pub is just a short walk away, scenic Dash Falls only a little further, there are forest trails in Dodd Wood, about 3 miles distant, and the popular town of Keswick with its many visitor attractions is only a 7-mile drive.

CHAPEL FARM

Bassenthwaite, Keswick, Cumbria CA12 4QH
Tel: 01768 776495

Within easy walking distance of Bassenthwaite lake, **Chapel Farm** enjoys a magnificent position at the foot of Skiddaw. This working sheep and beef farm of 130 acres is the home of Vera and Wilson Fell who have lived here for some 30 years and for most of that time have been welcoming bed and breakfast guests to their charming home.

Anyone who has stayed here will heartily recommend Vera's cooking. A full Cumbrian breakfast is included in the tariff and, although evening meals are optional, you'd be well-advised to book one! A sample meal mighty include home made Mushroom Soup, with Roast Lamb and all the trimmings as the main course, followed by a home made Strawberry Pavlova or Chocolate Gateau, coffee and

mints. Vegetarian and special diets can also be catered for with prior arrangement and packed lunches are also available. Guests have the use of the comfortable sitting room with its real fire, television and an interesting collection of Border Fine Art ornaments.

Chapel Farm has 2 guest bedrooms - 1 double-bedded room which can also be a twin room, and a family room with 1 double bed and up to two further single beds. (A cot is available if required). Other amenities include drying facilities for wet clothing and boots, and ample car parking. Dogs are welcome by arrangement.

overlooking the woodlands and valley (see panel below).

BASSENTHWAITE LAKE
4 miles NW of Keswick on the A66

Here's one for the Pub Quiz: Which is the only lake in the Lake District? Answer: Bassenthwaite, because all the others are either Waters or Meres. Only 70ft deep and with borders rich in vegetation, Bassenthwaite provides an ideal habitat for birds - more than 70 species have been recorded around the lake. Successful breeding is encouraged by the fact that no power boats are allowed on the lake and some areas are off limits to boats of any kind. Also, most of the shoreline is privately owned with public access restricted mostly to the eastern shore where the Allerdale Ramble follows the lakeside for a couple of miles or so.

At the northern end of the lake, **Trotters & Friends Animal** Farm is home to many hundreds of animals - rare breeds, traditional farm favourites, endangered species, birds of prey and reptiles. Visitors to the 25-acre site can handle the animals, (including snakes and lizards, large and small), take a tractor trailer ride, watch the birds of prey demonstrations, find a quiet picnic spot or sample the fare on offer in Trotters Tea Room.

Rising grandly above Bassenthwaite's eastern shore is **Skiddaw** which, ever since the Lake District was opened up to tourists by the arrival of the railway in the 19th century, has been one of the most popular peaks to climb. Although it rises to some 3,054ft, the climb is both safe and manageable, if a little unattractive lower down, and takes around two hours. From the summit, on a clear day, there are spectacular views to Scotland in the north, the Isle of Man in the west, to the east are the Pennines, and the greater part

WHINLATTER FOREST PARK

Braithwaite, Keswick, Cumbria CA12 5TW
Tel: 017687 78469 Fax: 017687 78049 e-mail:
Rangers@whinlatter.demon.co.uk

The only Mountain Forest in England, **Whinlatter Forest Park** is also one of the Forestry Commission's oldest woodlands, providing a whole range of outdoor activities. The best place to start is at the Visitor Centre which has a wealth of information about the work of the Lakes Forest District and staff who will be happy to help you plan your day in the forest. Visitors can also book a forest classroom or a forest discovery

walk with the Rangers. There's a shop and tea room here, with a terrace overlooking the woodlands and valley, an adventure playground close by and the Centre is also the starting point for several trails suitable for the whole family. The trails are clearly waymarked to provide easily followed routes taking in some spectacular views across the fells and forests of North Lakeland. Cyclists will find many miles of forest roads with some routes offering off-road and technical sections for the enthusiastic mountain biker. And if you have never tried orienteering, Whinlatter's permanent orienteering course is the perfect place to start. For children, there are Rabbit Run and Fox Trot orienteering trails, both starting from the Visitor Centre, while for those who prefer easier terrain or are less mobile, Europe's first permanent trail orienteering course combines the navigational skills of traditional orienteering with an easy-going route along forest roads and paths.

of the Lake District lies to the south.

Also on the eastern shore is the secluded, originally Norman, **Church of St Bridget & St Bega** which Tennyson had in mind when, in his poem Morte d'Arthur, he describes Sir Bedivere carrying the dead King Arthur:

"to a chapel in the fields,

A broken chancel with a broken cross,

That stood on a dark strait of barren land".

This then would make Bassenthwaite

Lake the resting place of Excalibur but, as yet, no one has reported seeing a lady's arm, "clothed in white samite, mystic, wonderful", rising from the waters and holding aloft the legendary sword.

Set back from the lakeside, **Mirehouse** is a 17th century building which has been home to the Spedding family since 1688. Literary visitors to the house include Tennyson, Thomas Carlyle, and Edward Fitzgerald, the poet and translator of *The Rubaiyat of Omar Khayyam*. As well as

THWAITE HOWE COUNTRY HOUSE HOTEL

Thornthwaite, nr Keswick, Cumbria CA12 5SA
Tel: 017687 78281 Fax: 017687 78529
website: www.keswickhotels.itgo.com

Thwaite Howe Country House Hotel stands in its own lovely grounds of some 2 ½ acres and enjoys some glorious views across the Derwent Valley to the mountains of Skiddaw, Blencathra and Helvellyn. To the rear of the hotel stretches the expanse of Thornthwaite Forest with its many forest trails and walks, and an abundance of wild life - deer, red squirrels and many species of birds. The hotel is owned and run by Bill and Valerie Marshall, a friendly and welcoming couple who have created an informal and relaxed atmosphere in this outstanding hotel. They place great emphasis on offering value for money, especially with the delicious traditional home cooking which is prepared from the very best fresh local produce. Guests begin their day with a generous Cumbrian breakfast, packed lunches are available if required, and in the evening the appetising table d'hôte dinner is complemented by a choice of fine wines which includes some excellent house wines.

Residents have the use of a spacious lounge which, like the dining room, takes full advantage of the panoramic view. Both these rooms, like the rest of the hotel, are non-smoking - the only exception is the snug bar with its well-stocked shelves. The hotel has 8 guest bedrooms, all spacious and with an individual character. All of them have en suite bathrooms, colour television, radio, direct dial telephones, hair dryers, and tea /coffee-making facilities. Children over 12 are welcome; so too are well-behaved

dogs which, however, should be kept on a lead and not taken into the dining room or, if other guests object, the lounge.

Although Thwaite Howe and its surroundings are wonderfully peaceful, there are plenty of activities within easy reach. Boating on Bassenthwaite Lake is just a mile away, pony trekking facilities are nearby, and golf devotees are welcomed at Keswick and Penrith golf clubs. The appealing market towns of Keswick and Cockermouth are just 3 and 9 miles away respectively, and any part of the Lake District is easily accessible by car within a day trip.

Bassenthwaite Lake

afternoons during the season, and also on Friday afternoons during August.

ULDALE
11 miles N of Keswick off the A591

some manuscripts by these family friends, there is also a fine collection of furniture and visitors can wander around the wildflower meadow, the walled garden and the lakeside walk. The gardens are open daily from April to October but the house, because it is still a family home, is only open on Sunday and Wednesday

To the northeast of Bassenthwaite Lake stretches the area known locally as the "Land Back of Skidda", a crescent of fells and valleys constituting the most northerly part of the National Park. This peaceful region is well off the tourist track and offers visitors a delightful landscape of gently undulating bare-backed fells and valleys sheltering unspoilt villages such as Uldale. Horace Walpole featured Uldale and its moorland surroundings in two of his "Herries Chronicle" novels, *Judith Paris* and *The Fortress*. The village boasts a

MIRESIDE FARMHOUSE

c/o Parkergate, Bassenthwaite,
Keswick, Cumbria CA12 4QG
Tel: 017687 76962
Fax: 017687 76911
e-mail: sally@keswick.org.uk

Mireside Farmhouse presents an idyllic picture with its huge slate roof sloping down almost to the ground and the gnarled fells of Skiddaw rising in the background. Dating back to the 1600s, this solid stone house is a listed building and is also protected by rigorous National Park Authority regulations designed to maintain its traditional character. The interior was comprehensively restored in the spring of 1998 and provides a unique combination of rural tradition and modern comforts. The living area is open plan and together with the kitchen/dining area creates a lovely feeling of spaciousness. The focal point of the room is the original fire surround which now contains a functional woodburning stove. There's also a remote controlled television while a separate living room/children's room has a second TV, radio and games. At the top of the stone stairs, (beware the low beams!), there's a large double room, a large twin room, and 2

further twin rooms with grand views across to Skiddaw, Ullock Pike and the Keswick fells. A cot is available and fits easily into two of the 4 rooms. The upstairs bathroom has a shower and there's a second shower room plus toilet downstairs. Outside, the large lawn is dotted with fruit trees and bordered by a mountain stream. Garden furniture is provided, along with some rope swings. This outstanding property is available all year round, children and animals are welcome, and the value-for-money rental is all-inclusive - there are no hidden extras to worry about!

THE SNOOTY FOX COUNTRY INN

Uldale, Cumbria CA7 1HA
Tel: 016973 71479 Fax: 016973 71910
e-mail: snooty.fox@virginnet.co.uk

This pretty little village, "at back o' Skidda", lies in the heart of "John Peel Country" for it was with a farmer's daughter from Uldale that the famous huntsman eloped to Gretna Green and a marriage at the blacksmith's anvil. The appropriately named **Snooty Fox Country Inn** reflects the hunting traditions of the area and there's even a specially woven carpet in the restaurant patterned with images of a perky-looking fox. The inn itself dates back to before 1700 - an old document records that it was sold in 1735 for £7 8s.

Today, this popular hostelry is owned and run by Carol and Neil Tunstall who offer their customers an excellent choice of food, some fine ales and comfortable accommodation. Food is served every lunchtime and evening, either in the bar or in the separate non-smoking restaurant.

The regular menu offers a wide and varied choice of value for money dishes and is supplemented by daily specials listed on the blackboard. Real ale lovers will be delighted to find a choice of 3 real brews, one of which, Uld Ale, is especially brewed for the Snooty Fox by the local brewery at Hesket Newmarket. The inn hosts a quiz night on Sunday evenings and in the back bar there's a pool table.

If you are planning to stay in this wonderfully scenic corner of the National Park, the Snooty Fox has 3 attractive guest bedrooms, (1 double, 2 family), all of them en suite and with static prices throughout the year.

SWALEDALE WATCH

Whelpo, Caldbeck, Wigton, Cumbria CA7 8HQ
Tel/Fax: 016974 78409
e-mail: nan.savage@talk21.com

Set within the Lake District National Park and surrounded by glorious, unspoilt countryside, **Swaledale Watch** is a working sheep farm where Nan and Arnold Savage have been welcoming bed and breakfast guests since the early 1980s. Guests are free to wander around the 300-acre farm and, naturally, lambing time is a great favourite with visitors. Do bring your warm woollies and wellies!

Nan and Arnold will happily guide you to any

of the delightful walks nearby. One of them leads to the village of Caldbeck by way of The Howk, a limestone gorge with a beautiful waterfall. And should you be unlucky with the weather, just settle down in one of the lounges where, in front of an open fire, you can browse through a good selection of books, play board games or attempt one of the jigsaw puzzles.

Guests are accommodated either in the main house, where there are two rooms, or in the nearby annex, a beautifully converted old cowshed, where there are two more. All the rooms are very comfortable and tastefully decorated, and all have private facilities with both bath and shower. Other amenities include colour TV, clock radio, shoe cleaner and hospitality tray; clean towels are provided daily. Swaledale Watch is very conveniently situated, almost equidistant from Keswick, Cockermouth (Wordsworth's birthplace), Penrith, Carlisle and the Solway Coast.

friendly traditional pub, The Snooty Fox (see panel opposite), and a Victorian school which now houses the **Northern Fells Gallery** which stocks a wide range of work by Cumbrian artists - watercolours, jewellery, copperwork, ceramics, knitwear and woodcarvings, all available to buy. This tranquil village has one small claim to fame since it was the daughter of an Uldale farmer who eloped with and married the legendary huntsman John Peel.

John Peels Horn, Ireby

CALDBECK
13 miles N of Keswick on the B5299

Caldbeck is perhaps the best known village in the northern Lakes because of its associations with John Peel, the famous huntsman who died in 1854 and is buried in the churchyard here. His ornate tombstone is decorated with depictions of hunting horns and his favourite hound. Peel was Master of Hounds for over 50 years and was immortalised by his friend John Graves, who worked in a Caldbeck mill making the grey woollen cloth mentioned in the song, *"D'ye ken John Peel with his coat so grey?"* The tune itself is based on an old Cumbrian folk song adapted by William Metcalfe, a chorister at Carlisle Cathedral.

A few paces from Peel's tomb lies "The Fair Maid of Buttermere", mentioned earlier, whose grave bears her married name, Mary Harrison.

With its picturesque church, village green, cricket pitch, pond, and blacksmith's forge, Caldbeck has all the ingredients of a picture postcard village. There has been a church here since the 12th century, one of only eight in England to be dedicated to St Kentigern. The other seven are also to be found in the north of Cumbria, where Kentigern, a bishop in the Strathclyde area of Scotland who was also known as Mungo, spent his time in exile.

Some 200 years ago Caldbeck was an industrial village, with corn mills, woollen mills, and a paper mill all powered by the fast-flowing "cold stream" - the Caldbeck.

John Peels Grave

DENTON HOUSE

Hesket-Newmarket, Caldbeck,
Cumbria CA7 8JG
Tel: 016974 78415
e-mail: dentonhnm@aol.com

Once an important market town, Hesket-New-Market boasts a number of striking 17th and 18th century houses. One of them is **Denton House**, located in the heart of what is now an unspoilt, picturesque village. This friendly and welcoming guest house, is owned and run by Margaret and Stan Monkhouse, aided by their daughter, Susan Armstrong, and has been offering hospitality to visitors for more than 28 years.

Some 17 years ago, Margaret and Stan opened their popular restaurant which is open to non-residents although booking ahead is strongly recommended. Appetising home cooking is the order of the day and in addition to dinners and Sunday lunch the restaurant also serves Cream Teas during the season. Denton House has 7 guest rooms, 4 of them en suite, all of them attractively furnished and

decorated and provided with tea-making facilities. Children and pets are welcome with cots and high chairs available if required. Guests also have the use of a comfortable sitting room where there's a colour TV and video, and an inviting open fire. Outside, there's a pleasant garden and ample parking nearby and you can also visit the Old Crown next door for a taste of real ale which is brewee by the award-winning Hesket-Newmarket brewery.

Guests at Denton House can stay on either a dinner, bed & breakfast, or bed & breakfast basis, but please note that credit cards are not accepted.

NEAR HOWE

Mungrisedale, Penrith, Cumbria CA11 0SH
Tel/Fax: 017687 79678

Only a mile or so from the A66, **Near Howe** offers holiday-makers a choice of bed & breakfast or self-catering accommodation in wonderfully peaceful surroundings. Near Howe itself is a traditional, 200-year-old Cumbrian farmhouse surrounded by award-winning gardens and standing in 380 acres of rolling moorland in the heart of the Cumbrian fell country. It's the home of Christine and Gordon Weightman (and Ellie, their dog) who greet visitors with a warm, country welcome and will help in any way they can to make your stay as pleasant and comfortable as possible. Guests have the use of a comfortable residents' lounge with colour television, a games room, a smaller lounge with a well-stocked licensed bar and, for cooler evenings, there's a large open log fire. The farmhouse has 7 guest bedrooms, 5 of them en suite. All the rooms are non-smoking and provided with tea & coffee making facilities. The Weightmans are justifiably proud of their home cooking so do take advantage of staying on a dinner,

bed & breakfast basis. If you prefer self-catering, the Weightmans have two delightful properties, available all year round. Grisedale View sleeps 4 and is one of 3 cottages which have been beautifully converted from an old barn and enjoys marvellous views over the fells. Saddleback Barn, which sleeps 7, also commands spectacular views. Both properties have been furnished to a very high standard and have extremely well-equipped kitchens. Guests are welcome to enjoy Near Howe's large, well-tended garden, to dine at the farmhouse if they wish, and to take advantage of its bar.

Priest's Mill, built in 1702 by the Rector of Caldbeck, next to his church, was a stone grinding corn mill, powered by a waterwheel which has now been restored to working order. It is open to the public and has an accompanying Mining Museum and a collection of old rural implements. The mill buildings are also home to a gift shop and craft workshops.

About a quarter of a mile outside the village is the limestone gorge known as **The Howk**, a popular beauty spot where the Caldbeck rushes past the restored ruins of one of the old bobbin mills.

HESKET NEWMARKET
13 miles N of Keswick off the B5305

Set around a well-kept village green, this pleasing little village used to have its own market, as the name suggests, and much earlier there was probably also a racecourse here since that is what "Hesket" meant in Old Scandinavian. It could well be the reason why the village's main street is so wide. Although the market is no longer held, Hesket hosts two important agricultural events each year: an Agricultural Show and Sheep Dog Trials. There's also a vintage motor cycle rally in May. Charles Dickens and Wilkie Collins stayed at Hesket Newmarket in the 1850s and wrote about it in their *Lazy Tour of Two Idle Apprentices*.

MUNGRISDALE
7 miles NE of Keswick off the A66

The name of the village comes from Mungo, the name by which St Kentigern was known by those close to him, and the village church, not surprisingly, is dedicated to him. Grisedale comes from the Norse and means pig valley. Though **St Kentigern's Church** is believed to have been established here as early as AD552, the present building dates from 1756 and it contains a fine example of a 17th century triple-decker pulpit.

A memorial on the church wall reveals an intriguing connection with Wordsworth. The tablet commemorates Raisley Calvert whose son Raisley was "nursed by Wordsworth". The younger Raisley was a sculptor and friend of the poet but fell ill of "consumption" (tuberculosis). Wordsworth spent many hours by his bedside in Penrith hospital but Raisley passed away in 1795, leaving in his will the huge sum of £900 to his friend. The bequest was timely, (Wordsworth's finances were in a desperate state), and enabled the poet to complete with his friend Coleridge the seminal poems that were published in 1798 as the *Lyrical Ballads*.

7 In and around Penrith

Penrith is the most historic of Lakeland towns and was almost certainly settled long before the Romans arrived. They quickly appreciated its

Brothers Water

strategic position on the main west coast artery linking England and Scotland and built a fort nearby although nothing visible remains today. Most of the town's oldest buildings have also disappeared, victims of the incessant Border conflicts. But Penrith today is a busy place, its location close to the M6 and within easy reach not only of the Lakes but also the Border Country and the Yorkshire Dales making it a hub of this northwestern corner of England.

Only a few miles from the town, Ullswater, eight miles long and the second longest lake in Cumbria is also one of its most beautiful, indeed Wordsworth claimed that Ullswater provided "the happiest combination of beauty and grandeur which any of the Lakes affords". It was while he and his sister were walking near the lake that they came across the *"host of daffodils"* immortalised in his most famous poem.

Martindale

The area around Penrith has some interesting old buildings, notably Shap Abbey and Brougham Castle, as well as two outstanding stately homes, Hutton-in-the-Forest where the Inglewood family have lived since 1605, and Dalemain, a fine mixture of medieval, Tudor and Georgian architecture which has also been inhabited by the same family for more than 300 years. Sadly, Greystoke Castle, which according to Edgar Rice Burroughs was the ancestral home of Tarzan, is not open to the public.

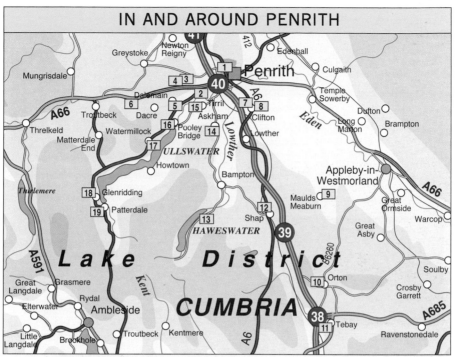

IN AND AROUND PENRITH

Mungrisdale
Greystoke
Newton Reigny
Edenhall
Culgaith
Penrith
40
Dalemain
Temple Sowerby
A66
Troutbeck
Dacre
Tirril
Askham
Clifton
Dufton
Long Marton
Brampton
Threlkeld
Watermillock
Pooley Bridge
Lowther
Matterdale End
ULLSWATER
Howtown
Bampton
Appleby-in-Westmorland
A66
Thirlemere
Glenridding
Maulds Meaburn
Great Ormside
Warcop
Patterdale
Shap
Great Asby
39
HAWESWATER
Lake District
Orton
Soulby
Great Langdale
Grasmere
Crosby Garrett
Elterwater
Rydal
CUMBRIA
A685
Ambleside
38
Tebay
Little Langdale
Brockhole
Troutbeck
Kentmere
Ravenstonedale

© MAPS IN MINUTES ™ (1999)

PLACES TO STAY, EAT, DRINK AND SHOP

WHITE HORSE

Great Dockray, Penrith, Cumbria CA11 7BL
Tel: 01768 890780

Located in the oldest part of this historic town, the **White Horse** is a handsome Georgian building dating back to the early 1700s. Today, it's very much a family-run business with mine hosts Jessie and Scott Millar assisted by their son Scott and daughter Karen. Since they took over here in 1999 they have established the White Horse as Penrith's most popular venue for good drink, entertainment and food - especially food! Not only is the menu very extensive, it's supplemented by a varied selection of daily specials and available from noon until 8pm. And since the Millars have a supper licence, you can still get something to eat until late at night. The inn's main menu is famous for the section headed "Really hungry? Try a giant platter" which lists dishes that would leave even Desperate Dan

more than satisfied. The Massive Mixed Grill, for example, contains six different kinds of meat items along with onion rings, grilled tomato, fried egg, mushrooms, hash browns and chips! For smaller appetites, there's a good choice of traditional pub favourites, vegetarian dishes, jacket potatoes, burgers, sandwiches and toasties, as well as a children's menu. To accompany your meal, there's a good selection of beers, lagers, ciders, Guinness and much more. It's not only the quality of the food and drink that keeps the White Horse busy. Six nights a week, after 8.30pm, the Millars lay on varied entertainments - a Music Quiz, karaoke, live bands and discos.

RHEGED DISCOVERY CENTRE

Redhills, Stainton, Penrith,
Cumbria CA11 0DX
Tel: 01539 441164

Penrith's latest and most spectacular visitor attraction, **Rheged Discovery Centre**, opened in Easter 2000 and dedicates itself to "a celebration of 2000 years of Cumbria's history, mystery and magic - as never seen before". Open

all year round, the Centre is housed in the largest earth-covered building in Britain, and is carefully designed to blend harmoniously with the surrounding fells. Although it is built on 7 levels, from the outside Rheged looks like just another Lakeland hill. Inside, babbling brooks and massive limestone crags replicate the Cumbrian landscape but the centrepiece is a 6-storey high, giant cinema screen, 60ft wide and 48ft high, on which is shown a specially commissioned film, *The Lost Kingdom*, which relates the story of the ancient Kingdom of Cumbria which once extended from Strathclyde in Scotland to Cheshire. Only a couple of minutes drive from Exit 40 of the M6, Rheged also offers visitors a retail shopping street, a useful information centre, special exhibitions, and restaurants and coffee shops which specialise in local delicacies and also provide panoramic mountain views.

PENRITH

In Saxon times Penrith was the capital of the Kingdom of Cumbria but after the Normans arrived the town seems to have been rather neglected - it was sacked several times by the Scots before **Penrith Castle** (free) was finally built in the 1390s.

The much-maligned Richard, Duke of Gloucester, (later Richard III), strengthened the castle's defences when he was Lord Warden of the Western Marches and responsible for keeping the peace along the border with Scotland. By the time of the Civil War, however, the castle was in a ruinous state. The Cromwellian General Lambert demolished much of what was left and the townspeople helped themselves to the fallen stones to build their own houses. Nevertheless, the ruins remain impressive, standing high above a steep-sided moat.

A short walk from the castle brings you to the centre of this lively town with its charming mixture of narrow streets and wide-open spaces, such as **Great Dockray** and **Sandgate**, into which cattle were herded during the raids. Later they became market places and a market is still held every Tuesday.

Penrith has a splendid Georgian church in a very attractive churchyard, surrounded by a number of interesting buildings. The oldest part of **St Andrew's Church** dates from Norman times but the most recent part, the nave, was rebuilt between 1719 and 1772, possibly to a design by Nicholas Hawksmoor. Of particular interest is the three-sided gallery and the two chandeliers which were a gift from the Duke of Portland in 1745 - a reward for the town's loyalty during the Jacobite Rising. A tablet on the wall records the deaths of 2,260 citizens of Penrith in the plague of 1597.

The church's most interesting feature however, is to be found in the churchyard, in the curious group of gravestones known as **Giant's Grave** - two ancient cross-shafts, each 11ft high, and four 10th century hogback tombstones which have arched tops and sharply sloping sides. They have clearly been deliberately arranged but their original purpose is no longer known. According to a local legend the stones mark the burial place of a 5th century King of Cumbria, Owen Caesarius. Also buried somewhere in the churchyard is Wordsworth's mother but her grave is not marked.

Overlooking the churchyard is a splendid Tudor house, bearing the date 1563, which is now a restaurant but was, at one time, Dame Birkett's School. The school's most illustrious pupils were William Wordsworth, his sister Dorothy, and his future wife, Mary Hutchinson. William is also commemorated by a plaque on the wall of the Robin Hood Inn stating that he was a guest here in 1794 and again in 1795.

Other notable buildings

Penrith Castle

STONEFOLD COTTAGES

Stonefold, Newbiggin, Stainton, Penrith,
Cumbria CA11 0HP
Tel/Fax: 01768 866383
website: www.northlakes.co.uk/stonefold

Enjoying a lovely position with grand panoramic views across the Eden Valley to the Pennines and the Lake District hills, **Stonefold Cottages** have been ingeniously converted from an 18th century stone barn. Available all year round, the three cottages are attractively furnished and decorated to give that country feel, and the beamed ceilings, latched pine doors, pine furnishing and soft print sofas all add to the charm and character. Each cottage has a comprehensively equipped kitchen, (with electric cooker, hob & fridge with ice box), colour television and shower over bath. "Curlew Cottage" sleeps 3, "Swallow Cottage" has one double bedroom, and "Robin's Nest" is ideal for that special honeymoon-type break with its splendid 4-poster bed. The owner of the cottages, Gill and Grahame Harrington, live in the main house nearby and are always happy to help visitors ensure that their holiday runs smoothly. They have also arranged for guests at Stonefold Cottages to enjoy free use of the leisure facilities at the nearby North Lakes Hotel. The cottages are ideally placed for exploring the varied attractions of the area and for those who like visiting the local country pubs, there are several within walking or easy travelling distance. In addition to the 3 cottages at Stonefold, standing for up to 15 caravans is available from Easter to October, with electric hook-ups, showers and toilets all on site.

THE OLD POST OFFICE

c/o Prospect House, Newbiggin,
Stainton, Cumbria CA11 0HT
Tel/Fax: 017684 83634

The little village of Newbiggin is located about 3 miles north of Ullswater, surrounded by beautiful scenery and with some lovely walks nearby. It's a peaceful place for a holiday, and **The Old Post Office** provides comfortable self-catering accommodation for up to 5 guests plus a cot.

Formerly a farm worker's house, the building dates back to the 1700s and its low-beamed ceilings are just part of the old world charm. A spacious garden provides the perfect place to relax on sunny days. The house is owned by Kathy and Lindsay Whitehead who live just across the road in the main farmhouse and run the 420-acre dairy, beef and sheep farm.

The Old Post Office is fully equipped with modern amenities although guests are asked to bring their own towels. Otherwise the rental is all-inclusive, with no hidden extras to pay. Children and pets are welcome but please note that smoking is not permitted upstairs. There is parking for up to 3 cars and the house is available all year round. During the season, there's a minimum rental of one week but out of season short breaks of 2-3 nights are available. The location is ideal for touring and exploring, with the magnificent scenery of the Lake District National Park virtually on the doorstep, and the Yorkshire Dales also within easy reach.

Market Square, Penrith

in the town include the **Town Hall** which is the result of a 1905 conversion of two former Adam-style houses, one of which was known as Wordsworth House as it was the home of the poet's cousin, Captain John Wordsworth.

The town is dominated by **Beacon Hill Pike**, which stands amidst wooded slopes high above Penrith. The tower was built in 1719 and marks the place where, since 1296, beacons were lit to warn the townsfolk of an impending attack. The beacon was last lit during the Napoleonic wars in 1804 and was seen by the author Sir Walter Scott who was visiting Cumberland at the time. Seeing it prompted Scott to hasten home to rejoin his local volunteer regiment. It is well worth the climb from Beacon's Edge, along the footpath to the summit, to enjoy a magnificent view of the Lakeland fells. It was, however, also on top of this hill, in 1767, that Thomas Nicholson, a

murderer, was hanged. The gibbet was left on the summit and so was Nicholson's ghost, seen in the form of a skeleton hanging from the noose.

About a mile southeast of the town, the substantial and imposing remains of **Brougham Castle** (English Heritage) stand on the foundations of a Roman fort. The castle was inherited in the 1640s by the redoubtable and immensely rich Lady Anne Clifford whose patrimony as Countess of Pembroke, Dorset and Montgomery, also included another half dozen northern castles. She spent a fortune restoring them all in medieval style and when told that Cromwell had threatened to destroy them replied *"As often as he destroys them I will rebuild them while he leaves me a shilling in my pocket"*. Brougham was her favourite castle and she died here in 1676 at the age of 86. From the castle there's a delightful riverside walk to Eamont Bridge and the circular Mayburgh Earthwork, which dates from prehistoric times. On the huge embankment, more than 100 yards across, stands a single, large stone about 10ft high. Close to the village, on the banks of the River Eamont, is Giant's Cave, the supposed lair of a man-eating giant called Isir. This local tale is linked with the legend of Tarquin, a giant knight who imprisoned 64 men in his cave and was eventually killed by Sir Lancelot. Some people also claim that Uther Pendragon, King Arthur's father, lived here and that he too ate human flesh. A nearby prehistoric earthwork has been known as King Arthur's Round Table for many centuries.

Penrith's latest and most spectacular visitor attraction, **Rheged Discovery Centre**, opened in Easter 2000 and dedicates itself to "a celebration of 2000 years of Cumbria's history, mystery and magic - as never seen before" (see panel on page 142).

PARK HOUSE FARM

Dalemain, Penrith, Cumbria CA11 0HB
Tel/Fax: 017684 86212
e-mail: park.house@faxvia.net
website: www.eden-in-cumbria.co.uk/parkhouse

Visitors to **Park House Farm** will be treading in the footsteps of some very distinguished guests. In the early 1800s, William and Dorothy Wordsworth were frequent visitors to the farmhouse which was then the home of Tom Hutchinson, William's brother-in-law. Built in 1750, Park House stands in its own private valley surrounded by a 300-acre traditional sheep farm. Today, it's the home of Mary Milburn, a charming lady who has been welcoming bed & breakfast guests here for some 13 years. Arriving guests are greeted with a refreshing pot of tea and home baked treats, and the genuine Cumbrian hospitality includes a hearty farmhouse breakfast. There's an inviting and comfortable sitting room where guests can relax in front of an open fire with books to browse through and colour television to watch.

The house has just 2 guest rooms, capable of accommodating a maximum of 6 visitors, and although each is provided with its own en suite facilities there's also a separate guest bathroom. Both (non-smoking) rooms have tea and coffee making facilities and electric blankets are supplied for extra comfort. Guests also enjoy concessionary admission to nearby Dalemain House, a magnificent Tudor and early Georgian house that has been home to the same family since 1679. Dalemain's enchanting gardens are world-famous and the house itself provided authentic locations for many scenes in London Weekend Television's production of *Jane Eyre*. Also well worth visiting is the nearby village of Dacre with its 14th century castle, a mostly-Norman church and, in its churchyard, the mysterious medieval carvings of stone bears.

ARCOS HOLIDAY COTTAGES

Arcos, Hutton John, Penrith, Cumbria CA11 0LZ
Tel: 01768 483300
e-mail: ray-c@arcos-holidays.freeserve.co.uk website: www.arcos-holidays.freeserve.co.uk

Located on the edge of the Lake District National Park, only 2.5 miles from Ullswater, Hutton John is a wonderfully peaceful hamlet of just 8 houses nestling beside a stream. It's a perfect setting for a relaxing holiday and **Arcos Holiday Cottages** provides a choice of attractive self-catering properties in both Hutton John and in the nearby village of Penruddock.

Poplar House is a charming 17th century farmhouse with oak beams and an open fire, where the accommodation comprises 2 double and 1 single bedrooms, bathroom, kitchen/diner and separate lounge. Ivy Cottage nearby has 2 double bedrooms, bath & shower, lounge and dining room, small kitchen and pantry. There are two further properties in Penruddock - Pinetrees and Sycamore Lodge. Each of them is a modern bungalow enjoying panoramic views of the North Lakeland hills and with 3 double bedrooms, bath & shower, kitchen/diner, lounge and garage. Cots are available, bedding can be hired, and table linen and towels are also available. Because of the proximity of his sheep, the owner of Arcos Holiday Cottages, Raymond Cowperthwaite, can only accept pets by prior arrangement. Raymond is always happy to help visitors plan their holiday in this glorious corner of Lakeland. An enthusiastic walker and climber himself, he can guide you to the best walks and routes, as well as to other activities nearby - pony trekking, sailing, wind-surfing, golf and much more.

SOUTH AND WEST OF PENRITH

DALEMAIN
3 miles SW of Penrith off the A592

Dalemain House is one of the area's most popular attractions - an impressive house with a medieval and Tudor core fronted by an imposing Georgian façade. The house has been home to the same family since 1679 and over the years they have accumulated fine collections of china, furniture and family portraits. The grand drawing Rooms have fine oak panelling and 18th century Chinese wallpaper, and visitors also have access to the Nursery (furnished with toys from all ages) and Housekeeper's Room. The Norman pele tower houses the regimental collection of the Westmorland and Cumberland Yeomanry, while the 16th century Great Barn contains an interesting assortment of agricultural bygones and a Fell Pony Museum. The extensive grounds include a medieval herb garden, a knot garden with a fine early Roman fountain, a deer park, and woodland and riverside walks.

DACRE
4 miles SW of Penrith off the A66

There is much of historic interest in this village. The church occupies a site of a former monastery which was mentioned by the Venerable Bede in his accounts of Cumberland in the 8th century. A later reference shows that, in 926, the Peace of Dacre was signed between Athelstan of England and Constantine of Scotland.

Fragments of masonry are reputed to have come from the monastery and the four weather-beaten carvings of bears in the churchyard are probably of Anglo-Viking origin.

A 14th century pele tower, **Dacre Castle** (private) is a typical example of the fortified house or small castle that was common in northern England during the Middle Ages. This was the seat of the Dacre family, Catholic Earls of

Dacre Castle

Cumberland, and its turrets and battlements have walls which are 8ft thick. Leonard Dacre took part in the ill-fated Rising of the North in 1589 and, some time later, the estate passed to the Earls of Sussex who restored the castle in 1675 and whose coat of arms can still be seen.

GREYSTOKE
5 miles W of Penrith on the B5288

According to Edgar Rice Burroughs, Greystoke Castle (private) was the ancestral home of Tarzan, Lord of the Apes, a fiction which was perpetuated in the dismal 1984 film *Greystoke*, directed by Hugh Hudson. Tarzan's aristocratic credentials would have come as

GEORGE & DRAGON

Clifton, nr Penrith, Cumbria CA10 2ER
Tel: 01768 865381 Fax: 01768 865266

In the orchard at the rear of the **George & Dragon** stands the Rebel Oak, a venerable old tree from which Scotsmen defeated in the Battle of Clifton Moor were hanged. The battle, in December 1745, was the last to be fought in England: the 11 English dragoons who also perished in the conflict are buried in the local churchyard. The George & Dragon began life as a coaching inn and is today a warm and welcoming hostelry owned and run by Arthur and Veronica Bainbridge. Veronica is in charge of the kitchen and her appetising home made dishes, served in generous quantities, are available every lunchtime and evening.

The attractive restaurant area with its darkwood furniture can seat up to 70 diners but if you are planning to eat here at the weekend, booking ahead is strongly recommended. A free house, the George & Dragon offers a wide range of beverages which includes 2 real ales, Tetley's and Burton's, along with all the popular brands. Sample them in the bar with its wealth of horse brasses and other equine memorabilia. The inn has a separate games room and, if you are planning to stay in this pleasant corner of the county, there are 6 guest rooms available on a bed & breakfast basis all year round, except over the Christmas period. Please note that, although young people are welcome in the bar and restaurant, the bedrooms are not suitable for children.

WETHERIGGS COUNTRY POTTERY LTD

Clifton Dykes, Penrith, Cumbria CA10 2DH
Tel: 01768 892733 Fax: 01768 892722

One of Cumbria's most popular visitor attractions, **Wetheriggs Country Pottery Ltd.** provides a grand day out for all the family. Founded in 1855, Wetheriggs has been a working pottery ever since and is now the only steam-powered Country Pottery in Britain. The steam engine, *Josephine*, was fully restored by TV's celebrated engineer and steeplejack Fred Dibnah, and is in full flow on most Sundays during the season. At the heart of the complex is the "Pots of Fun" studio where experts provide demonstrations of throwing and pot decoration and visitors are encouraged to "have a go" at this slippery art themselves. You can create your own pieces - even make a complete dining set, as a wedding present perhaps, and once you have created it, the pottery will fire it for you, box it up and even gift wrap it if you wish.   The Pottery's long history is recalled in the Pottery Museum which displays early slipware designs, dinnerware and kitchenware from the 1800s and early 1900s, original tools and photographs. Naturally, the Pottery's extensive range of products is on sale, there's a Collectibles Shop, and the Country Gifts & Local Cumbrian Craft display includes some interesting and unusual items. Children are very well provided for. There are two play areas, specially designed for fun and creative play, and they can also Meet the Animals, watch the Birds of Prey display (Sundays during the season), and discover the Natural Newt Pond. The licensed Country Café, with outside seating for fine days, provides wholesome and appetising meals and snacks throughout the day. Open 6 days from Easter to the end of September 10.00-17.30 (closed Tuesdays). Open 5 days from October to Easter (closed Tuesdays and Wednesdays). Open 7 days throughout Cumbrian school holidays.

something of a surprise to the dignified Barons of Greystoke whose effigies are preserved in **St Andrew's Church**. As imposing and spacious as a cathedral, St Andrew's boasts a wonderful east window with much 13th century glass and, in the Lady Chapel, a figure of the Madonna and Child carved by a German prisoner-of-war.

About 100 yards from the church stands the **Plague Stone** where, during medieval times, coins were left in vinegar in exchange for food for the plague victims. An ancient **Sanctuary Stone**, now concealed behind a grille, marks the point beyond which fugitives could claim sanctuary.

Around the time of the American War of Independence, **Greystoke Castle** was bought by the 11th Duke of Norfolk, a staunch Whig who delighted in annoying his died-in-the-wool Tory neighbour, the Duke of Portland. Portland of course detested the American rebels so Norfolk built two curious castle/farmhouses close to Portland's estate, and named them Fort Putnam and Bunkers Hill after the two battles in which the British had been trounced. Norfolk displayed a similarly elegant disdain for one of his tenants, a religious bore who maintained that church buildings were an abomination. The Duke built a medieval-looking farmhouse for him and crowned it with a very ecclesiastical spire.

Greystoke village itself is a gem, its attractive houses grouped around a trimly-maintained village green. Nearby are the stables where Gordon Richards trained his two Grand National winners, *Lucius* and *Hello Dandy*.

CLIFTON
3 miles S of Penrith on the A6

One of the last battles to be fought on English soil took place at nearby **Clifton Moor** in December 1745. Bonnie Prince Charlie was in retreat and his exhausted troops were easily routed by the English forces. Eleven soldiers were killed and are buried in Clifton churchyard, but some of the wounded Highlanders were hanged from the Rebels' Tree on the outskirts of the village. The tree is a sorry sight nowadays with its gaunt, dead branches but it is still a place of pilgrimage for the Scots.

To the southeast of the village is **Wetheriggs Country Pottery** which was founded in 1855 (see panel opposite). Not only can visitors try their hand at the often messy business of throwing a pot, but tours of the steam-powered pottery are also available.

LOWTHER
4 miles S of Penrith off the A6

Lowther Castle, is now only a shell, most of it having been demolished in 1957, but is was clearly once a grand place; after one visit Queen Victoria is reputed to have said that she would not return to Lowther Castle as it was too grand for her.

The ancestral owners of the castle were the illustrious Earls of Lonsdale, a family of statesmen and sportsmen. The most famous is perhaps the 5th Earl (1857-1944), known as the Yellow Earl because of the colour of the livery used on his private carriage. He was the first President of the Automobile Association and permitted his family colours to be used by the motoring organisation. The earl was also a patron of amateur boxing and the Lonsdale Belt emerged from his interest. The yellow flag of the Lonsdales can be seen in Lowther Church.

Part of the castle grounds have been turned into the **Lowther Leisure & Wildlife Park**, with both open-air and wet-weather rides and amusements. Ideal for children, it makes a change from

TRAINLANDS

Maulds Meaburn, Penrith,
Cumbria CA10 3HX
Tel: 017683 51249
Fax: 017683 53983
e-mail: bousfield@trainlands.u-net.com

Trainlands is a delightful 17th and 18th century farmhouse located in the Lyvennet Valley above the village of Maulds Meaburn and well away from busy roads although Junction 38 of the M6 can be reached in a matter of minutes. Trainlands is the home of David and Carol Bousfield who welcome bed & breakfast guests to this working farm of around 350 acres which consists of 70 dairy cows, cattle and sheep.

David has farmed Trainlands for some 30 years and his son is set to carry on the tradition. The farmhouse has 3 guest bedrooms, (although only 2 are generally used), all of them enjoying a 3 Diamond ETB rating. None of them is en suite since the necessary extensions would have spoilt the appearance of the property. A hearty Cumbrian breakfast is included in the tariff and evening meals are available by arrangement. Carol makes her own jams, marmalades and preserves.

Trainlands is open to visitors from April to the end of November - children over 12 are welcome and all guests can enjoy a guided tour of the farm if they wish, just remember to bring your wellies! There are some excellent walks nearby and a short drive will take you to the charming little town of Appleby-in-Westmorland with its historic castle, railway station on the scenic Settle to Carlisle line, and its world famous annual Horse Fair.

THE GEORGE HOTEL

Orton, Penrith, Cumbria CA10 3RJ
Tel/Fax: 015396 24229
e-mail: peter@georgehotel.net
website: www.georgehotel.net

Located in the pleasant little village of Orton in the Lune Valley, **The George Hotel** seems miles away from the rush and bustle of modern life but is only about a 10-minute drive from the M6. It's a friendly, family run inn, owned by Peter and Val Graveson. Until a few years ago, Peter farmed locally but was happy to exchange the milking parlour for the George's welcoming bar! Val is an accomplished cook and her quality food is available every lunchtime and evening, except weekday lunchtimes during the winter. Her "across the board" menu has something for every palate but her curries and chilli dishes are particularly popular. Children are welcome - they have their own special menu, and there's a toy box for the younger ones to dip into. Beverages on offer at the George include 2 real ales, along with a wide selection of all the popular brands and a good choice of wines. Peter has been awarded a

Cask Marque for 2001 in recognition of the quality ales he serves. Built in Georgian times, the hotel has 5 guest bedrooms, (2 doubles, 2 twins, 1 family), all available at very reasonable prices. The tariff includes a full English breakfast which is served in the first floor dining room overlooking the village. The George provides an excellent starting point for motorists or walkers exploring the Lake District, the Pennines and the Yorkshire Dales. Other activities available locally include several golf courses within a few miles, and for a really memorable tour of the area Hot Air Balloon flights over the lakes and mountains are available.

sightseeing and, for those who enjoy peace and quiet, this can also be found by taking the picturesque walks around the park among the herds of red deer. The single entry charge includes access to more than 40 attractions and the site also offers picnic areas, a restaurant and café.

Lowther village itself was built in the 1680s by Sir John Lowther who moved his tenants here to improve the view from the new house he was building. He also built **St Michael's Church** where several generations of the Lowthers are buried in a series of magnificent tombs beginning with a medieval style alabaster monument to Sir Richard who died in 1608. One can then follow the fashions in funerary sculpture through the obligatory skull of the late-17th century to the grandiose representation of the 1st Viscount Lonsdale who sits nonchalantly nursing his viscount's coronet. Later monuments show a moustachioed Henry, Earl of Lonsdale, in military garb and a charming Pre-Raphaelite plaque to Emily, wife of the 3rd Earl, who is depicted with her favourite dog at her feet.

MAULDS MEABURN
11 miles SE of Penrith off the A6

This charming village in the Lyvennet Valley has a large green through which the river flows, crossed by footbridges and stepping stones. As well as a fine collection of 17th and 18th century cottages, there is also an early 17th century Hall.

ORTON
15 miles S of Penrith on the B6260

By far the best approach to Orton is along the B6290 from Appleby to Tebay. This scenic route climbs up onto the moors, passing **Thunder Stone**, some mighty limestone bluffs and the pavements of **Great Asby Scar**, the setting for BBC-TV's

The Tenant of Wildfell Hall. As you descend the side of Orton Scar, grand views open up of the Howgills and the Lune Gorge with the Shap Fells looming on the horizon.

A village now, (*"one of the prettiest in Westmorland"* according to one writer), for centuries Orton was a market town of some consequence with a charter granted in the 13th century by Edward I and a licence to hold fairs accorded by the puritan Oliver Cromwell. There are reminders of Orton's former importance in the noble church tower, completed in 1504; in the attractive proportions of Petty Hall, an Elizabethan house at the lower end of the village, (a private residence, incidentally); and the grandeur of Orton Hall, built in 1662 and now converted into holiday apartments.

Orton's most famous visitor was Bonnie Prince Charlie, on his way northwards after the crushing defeat of his troops at Derby. He was followed soon afterwards by the Duke of Cumberland, "Butcher" Cumberland, the victor of the Battle of Culloden. The Duke may have stayed in the village at an inn which was later re-named the Cumberland Hotel. The Inn, dating from 1632, still stands in the centre of the village although it is now a private house.

To the north there is some superb limestone scenery and the village stands below **Orton Scar**, on which a beacon was lit to warn people to seek safety from advancing Scottish raiders. The village church, in common with many in the Eden Valley, has a massive 16th century tower that was built for defensive purposes and, presumably, was one place that the villagers sought shelter. Orton, too, was the birthplace of George Whitehead (1636-1723) who, along with George Fox, was one of the founders of the Quaker Movement.

THE BARNABY RUDGE TAVERN

Tebay, Penrith, Cumbria CA10 3XG
Tel: 015396 24328
website: www.justfiveminutesaway.com

A unique feature of the **Barnaby Rudge Tavern** is its galleried dining room which overlooks the bar below. Also unusual is the inn's position, clinging to the hillside so that some rooms are at roadside level, others on the floor beneath. The tavern's history is also rather out of the ordinary since it was originally built, in 1880, as the local Co-operative store and only became an inn during the early 1970s. Today, it's run by Sandra and Jim, a friendly couple with a genuinely warm welcome for one and all. The inn is noted for its quality food, served every lunchtime between noon and 2pm, and in the evenings from 7pm until 9pm. Sandra does most of the cooking, which is based on traditional English cuisine, while Jim

is celebrated for his appetising home made soups. The regular menu is supplemented by at least 12 daily main course specials. Beverages on offer include real ales, draught lagers, cider and Murphy's. Children are welcome and the inn is also dog-friendly! The inn has 4 guest bedrooms although Sandra and Jim prefer to limit the number of visitors to 6 at any one time. A generous breakfast is included in the tariff, one that will certainly set you up for a day exploring the spectacularly scenic countryside all around or, perhaps, enjoying the superb trout and salmon fishing on the River Lune.

TEBAY
17 miles S of Penrith, by Exit 38 of the M6

At one time a sheep farming area and a railway settlement, this long rambling village now owes its importance to the arrival of the M6 motorway, Cumbria's main thoroughfare - the local services are the only privately owned and run motorway services in the country. While the motorway may not be a particularly attractive asset, its very central and easily accessible location makes this a convenient base for touring Cumbria and the surrounding scenery is just as beautiful as that found in more isolated places.

The village was the home of Mary Baynes, the Witch of Tebay, who died in 1811 at the age of 90. She is said to have foretold the coming of fiery horseless carriages speeding across Loups Fell where, today, the London to Glasgow railway line runs. Greatly feared by the

Shap Abbey

people of Tebay, she is said to have withered and died at the same time as some eggs on which she had put a curse were fried in boiling fat.

SHAP
10 miles S of Penrith on the A6

This small village on the once congested A6 enjoys some grand views of the hills. In coaching days Shap was an important staging post for the coaches before they tackled the daunting climb up **Shap Fell**

to its summit some 850ft above sea level. Much earlier, in medieval times, the village was even more significant because of nearby **Shap Abbey**, constructed in the local Shap granite which has been used in many well-known buildings, St Pancras Station and the Albert Memorial in London amongst them.

The Abbey stands about a mile to the west of the village, just inside the National Park, and it's well worth seeking it out to see the imposing remains of the

The Greyhound Hotel

Main Street, Shap, Penrith, Cumbria CA10 3PW
Tel: 01931 716474 Fax: 01931 716305
e-mail: postmaster@greyhoundshap.demon.uk

The Greyhound Hotel's long history of hospitality began in 1684 when newly-weds Richard and Ann Whinfel built it as a coaching inn. They also established Green Farm opposite to supply the inn with fresh produce. About 20 years later, the family extended the inn to its present size by adding the front elevation in 1703. Some 30 years later, Bonnie Prince Charlie stayed here overnight during his march south in 1745.

Today, this charming old hostelry enjoys an excellent reputation for its high quality meals and comfortable accommodation. The owners, Derrick Newsome and Keith Taylor, both spent more than 12 years teaching Hospitality and Catering at Further Education Colleges and before that had worked

for many years in top of the range eating establishments. Their extensive menu offers a wide selection of no-nonsense freshly prepared dishes, including a variety of interesting vegetarian choices. Wherever possible, all meals are based on locally bred or grown ingredients, dishes such as the pan-fried Medallions of Shap Abbey Lamb, for example. A wide range of carefully chosen wines, real ales, lagers and spirits are available to complement your meal which can be enjoyed either in the cosy bar with its open fireplace or in the 50-seater restaurant. Derrick and Keith are also happy to cater for parties and small functions, whether in

the restaurant, back bar or meeting room.

The Greyhound has 10 guest bedrooms, all attractively furnished and decorated and equipped with colour television and hospitality tray. For those looking for budget accommodation, the hotel also has bunk facilities for up to 10 people. Shap itself is an interesting spot to explore and the village provides an excellent base for exploring the North Pennine fells and valleys. It stands mid-way on the Coast to Coast Walk from St Bees to Robin Hood's Bay and the nearby M6 provides easy access not only to the Lake District "gateways" but also to the Yorkshire Dales and the Scottish Borders.

Haweswater Beck from Shap Abbey

the Abbey and local builders continued the depredations. But the mighty west tower and some of the walls remain, and they enjoy a lovely setting - secluded, tranquil and timeless.

From the Abbey there's a pleasant walk of well under a mile to Keld, a tiny village of just 17 houses. So quiet today, in medieval times Keld was a busy little place servicing the monks of Shap Abbey nearby. It was the monks of Shap Abbey who built the village's oldest building, the early-16th century **Keld Chapel** (NT). After the closure of the Abbey, the chapel fell on hard times and for two hundred years was used as a dwelling house. (That's when the incongruous chimney was added). In 1860 it was "serving as a cow-house" but was

only abbey founded in Westmorland; the only one in the Lake District mountains; the last abbey to be consecrated in England (around 1199) and the last to be dissolved, in 1540. Henry VIII's Commissioners seem to have been especially thorough in their demolition of

HAWESWATER HOTEL

Bampton, Penrith, Cumbria CA10 2RP
Tel: 01931 713235 Fax: 01931 713145

Occupying a unique position on the eastern bank of Haweswater and enjoying superb views of the great fells of Bampton Common, the **Haweswater Hotel** offers its guests peace and seclusion in elegant, comfortable surroundings, as well as outstanding cuisine and, of course, miles of stunning scenery. Built in 1937, the hotel makes the most of its wonderful setting with huge picture windows in the residents' lounge, the bar and the restaurant framing a view of the lake and mountains. In good weather, the same vista can be enjoyed from the terrace. Guests have the choice of either the Mardale Restaurant with its à la carte menu or the Mardale Bar which offers tea, coffee, bar meals, afternoon teas and packed lunches. When owners Ken Weller and Jane Tomkinson bought the hotel in 1997 it was virtually derelict. He has completely refurbished the whole property and there are now

16 centrally heated guest bedrooms, some of them en suite and most with a magnificent view of the lake and surrounding countryside. Three of the rooms have balconies. Since most visitors come to Haweswater for a complete break, there are no televisions in the rooms. Children are welcome and so too are dogs, providing guests bring sleeping baskets or bed covers. As Ken Weller says, "Mostly we specialize in 'Inactivity Breaks'" but Special Activity Breaks *are* available, featuring Aromatherapy, Bird Watching, Fishing, Orienteering, Painting, Tai Chi, Photography, Walking - indeed, just state your interest and the hotel will do its best to oblige!

Haweswater Beck

saved from this ignominious rôle in 1918 by the National Trust. A service is held in the chapel once a year in August; at other times, a notice on the chapel door tells you where you can obtain the key.

BAMPTON
8 miles S of Penrith off the A6

For several hundred years this small village was well-known for its Grammar School, two of whose pupils rose swiftly in the church hierarchy. One was Hugh Curwen who as a Protestant became Chaplain to Henry VIII, as a Catholic under Queen Mary was elevated to the Archbishopric of Dublin, and then prudently re-embraced Protestantism when Elizabeth succeeded to the throne. Another Bampton boy was less pliable. Edmund Gibson was baptised in the church here in 1669 and later became a fiery Bishop of London who repeatedly denounced the degenerate morals of the age with little apparent effect.

A couple of miles south of Bampton, **Haweswater** is the most easterly of the lakes. It is actually a reservoir, created in the late 1930s to supply the growing needs of industrial Manchester. Beneath the water lies the village of Mardale and several dairy farms for which Haweswater Valley was once famous. By 1940, the lake had reached its present extent of 4 miles and Manchester Corporation set about planting its shores with conifers and today the area is managed as a nature reserve. Walkers have a good chance of seeing woodpeckers and sparrow hawks, buzzards and peregrine falcons, and with luck may even catch sight of golden eagles gliding on the thermals rising above Wallow Crag.

Above Haweswater runs the **High Street**, actually a Roman road, which is now one of the most popular fell walks in the Lake District. It overlooks the remote and lovely Blea Tarn and the lonely valley of Martindale, a cul-de-sac valley to the

THE QUEENS HEAD INN

Askham, Penrith, Cumbria CA10 2PF
Tel: 01931 712225 Fax: 01931 712811
websites: www.infotel.co.uk or
www.smoothound.co.uk/hotels/thequeen.html

Set beside the sloping village green of this picturesque little village, **The Queens Head Inn** is a delightful traditional hostelry with a history stretching back to the 1600s. The interior has a wonderfully olde worlde atmosphere with lots of exposed beams, brass and copper memorabilia and local hunting prints. Open fires in the lounge and main bar add to the welcoming ambience. The inn enjoys an outstanding reputation for its home cooked food, served in either of the two restaurants, (one of which is non-smoking), with snacks and light meals also available in the bar. Dishes are based on local produce and recipes wherever possible, (traditional favourites such as "Derwentwater Duckling", for example), and the menu includes fresh fish as well as generous

portions of steak. The regular menu is supplemented by a daily-changing specials board. The excellent accommodation, all of it en suite, includes the Lowther Suite which boasts a hand-forged 4-poster bed created by the local blacksmith. The suite has a bathroom and a separate lounge which can be transformed into a twin or double room. If you are looking for an active holiday, the inn provides a superb base for fell walking, golfing and country pursuits, and there is also an open air swimming pool right next door. Ullswater is close by, as is Haweswater, home to England's only breeding pair of golden eagles.

QUEENS HEAD INN

Tirril, nr Penrith, Cumbria CA10 2JF
Tel: 01768 863219 Fax: 01768 863243
e-mail: bookings@queensheadinn.co.uk
website: www.queensheadinn.co.uk

A Grade II Listed Building, the **Queen's Head Inn** was built around 1719 and almost three centuries later is the epitome of an English country inn. There are no fewer than four open fireplaces, the largest of which still has in place the original hooks for smoking meats. Ancient beams, polished brassware and vintage memorabilia all add to the atmosphere and charm. One of the most interesting items on display is a sale document of 1836. In that year the Wordsworth family sold the inn to John Bewsher and the "Wordsworth Indenture", as it's known, carries the signatures of Christopher Wordsworth, Chancellor of Cambridge University, and his even more illustrious brother, the poet William Wordsworth. Today, this privately owned free house is owned

and run by Chris and Jo Tomlinson who offer their customers home cooked food of the highest standard, (the inn is one of only 3 in Cumbria to be recommended by the *Which? Good Food Guide*), and a choice of 4 real ales, three of which are brewed by Chris in the adjacent Tirril Brewery. The Queen's Head was one of the first pubs in the country to receive the Cask Marque for the outstanding quality of its ales. The inn is also an ideal base for exploring Lakeland and the Yorkshire Dales. It has 7 guest bedrooms, 4 of them en suite, and all comfortably furnished and provided with colour television and hospitality tray.

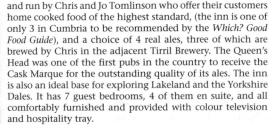

south of Ullswater, where England's last remaining herd of wild red deer can often be seen.

ASKHAM
3 miles S of Penrith off the A6

Located on the western bank of the River Lowther, across from the Lowther Leisure and Wildlife Park, Askham is a pleasant village set around two greens with Askham Fell rising to the west. The fellside is dotted with prehistoric monuments including one known as the Copt (or Cop) Stone which is said to mark the burial site of a Celtic chieftain. On the edge of the village is Askham Hall (private), now the home of the head of the Lonsdale family who abandoned Lowther Castle in 1936 and moved here.

Askam Church and Mausoleum

TIRRIL
2 miles S of Penrith on the B5320

Like its neighbour, Yanwith, Tirril has connections with the Quaker Movement. At Tirril there is an old **Quaker Meeting House** (now in private ownership), whilst Yanwath Hall, reputed to be the finest manorial hall in England, was the birthplace of the Quaker Thomas

Wilkinson. Modern Yanwath also boasts an interesting gallery, located in a cottage garden setting. Laburnum Ceramics is dedicated to contemporary ceramics and glass, and, small though it is, over the course of a year exhibits the work of some 80 different artists. In addition to the ceramics, there are displays of original paintings, prints, textiles and turned wood.

POOLEY BRIDGE
5 miles SW of Penrith on the B5320

In Wordsworth's opinion Ullswater provides *"the happiest combination of beauty and grandeur, which any of the Lakes affords"*, an opinion with which most visitors concur. The poet also noted the curious fact that the lake creates a sextuple echo, a natural phenomenon that the Duke of Portland exploited in the mid-1700s by keeping a boat on the lake equipped *"with brass guns, for the purpose of exciting echoes"*.

The charming village of Pooley Bridge stands at the northern tip of **Ullswater,** and there are regular cruise departures from here during the season, stopping at Glenridding and Howton. Rowing and powered boats are available for hire and since Ullswater is in effect a public highway, you can also launch your own boat. Do make sure though that you observe the 10mph speed limit which applies over the whole of the 8-mile-long serpentine lake. Also, the greater part of the shoreline is privately owned and landing is not permitted. Licences are

GRANNY DOWBEKINS

Pooley Bridge, Ullswater, Penrith, Cumbria CA10 2NP
Tel: 01768 486453

With its rear garden running down to the River Eamont, **Granny Dowbekins** enjoys a beautiful location in this popular village at the head of Ullswater. Dorothy and Jack Hindle bought this quality tea room in the summer of 2000 and, with the assistance of their son Colin and daughter-in-law Hazel, quickly established a reputation for serving excellent home made food. The generous Cream Teas and delicious home made cakes are especially popular but the menu also offers a wide choice of other options. The two cosy rooms, (both non-smoking), can seat up to 30 customers, and in good weather refreshments can be enjoyed in the attractive riverside garden. The tea room is open daily, all year round, from 10.30am until 5pm. Children are welcome.

THE QUIET SITE

Watermillock, Penrith, Cumbria CA11 0LS
Tel: 017684 86337 Fax: 017684 86610

Voted "Best Site in Britain" by the readers of *Camping* magazine, **The Quiet Site** occupies a quiet, secluded position in the heart of the National Park, only 1.5 miles from Ullswater. The 4-acre site is open from March 1 to the end of October for caravans, motor-homes and tents, and a 6-berth static caravan is also available to rent. The beautifully maintained site has a unique olde-worlde bar, a well-stocked shop, a large adventure playground, TV room and games room, excellent toilet facilities, laundry room and electric hook-up points.

GREYSTONES COFFEE HOUSE

Glenridding, Penrith, Cumbria CA11 0PA
Tel: 017684 82392 Fax: 017684 82122

Standing alongside the beck that tumbles through the centre of the village, **Greystones Coffee House** provides visitors to Glenridding, the most popular of the Ullswater's lakeside communities, with top quality home made cakes and breads, as well as a good range of light snacks and jacket potatoes.

Owned and run by Julian and Nicola, Greystones has a very cosy and welcoming atmosphere, with service that is courteous, friendly and efficient. The coffee house is non-smoking, children are welcome, so too are "small, dry dogs"! In good weather, customers can enjoy their refreshments in the attractive garden. Greystones is open every day from March to November, from 10am until around 6pm; from December to February, it is only at weekends, from 10am until dusk.

Julian also runs Sharmans Convenience Store, just a few yards away, which is one of those intriguing shops which seem to stock just about every conceivable commodity within its comparatively small space. Julian and Nicola also offer self-catering accommodation in a Victorian miner's house which stands high on the hillside above the village and enjoys some grand views along Ullswater. The house is available all year round and while bookings by the week only are accepted during the season, shorter breaks of a minimum of 3 nights are available out of season.

Ullswater

a wooded gorge and then into Ullswater. Known collectively by the name of the largest fall, the 70ft high **Aira Force**, they can easily be reached on foot through the woodlands of Gowbarrow Estate which is owned by the National Trust. This famous waterfall, which can be viewed from stone bridges at top and bottom, was the setting for the romantic and tragic story of Emma who fell in love with a renowned knight called Sir Eglamore. He had to leave her to follow the Crusades. As the months lengthened into years and he had not returned, Emma became so distraught that she started to sleepwalk to Aira Force where she eventually met her tragic death. On his return, the grief-stricken Sir Eglamore became a hermit and lived by the waterfall for the rest of his days.

required for fishing: these can be obtained from the tourist offices at Pooley Bridge and Glenridding.

The oldest building in Pooley Bridge is part of **Holly House** which dates back to 1691 whilst the "Bridge" of the village's name dates from 1763 when the elegant structure over the River Eamont was built at a cost of £400. At that time, a regular fresh fish market was held in the village square. Before Bridge was added, the name Pooley meant "pool by the hill" and was derived from the pond which existed behind Dunmallard, the cone-shaped hill on the other side of the River Eamont. Above the village, on the summit of Dunmallard, are the remains of an Iron Age fort and, of course, splendid views, southwards over Ullswater.

WATERMILLOCK
7 miles SW of Penrith on the A592

This small village, perfectly situated on the shores of Ullswater, is hidden amongst the woodland which occupies much of the lake's western shores. About 4 miles southwest of the village, there are a series of waterfalls which tumble down through

GLENRIDDING
14 miles SW of Penrith on the A592

A popular base for walkers about to tackle the daunting challenge of **Helvellyn** (3115ft), Glenridding is the largest and busiest of Ullswater's lakeside villages. Lake cruises depart from here, rowing boats are available for hire and there's plenty of room for waterside picnics.

PATTERDALE
15 miles SW of Penrith on the A592

Patterdale Village

Brothers Water

It is this village's magnificent setting that makes it such a popular tourist destination. Close to the head of Ullswater and with a series of fells framing the views, the splendid scenery is at odds with the rather unremarkable village. On the north side of the village is **St Patrick's Well**, which was thought to have healing properties, and the medieval chapel dedicated to the saint was rebuilt in the 1850s.

BROTHERSWATER INN

Patterdale, Penrith, Cumbria CA11 0NZ Tel: 017684 82239 Fax: 017684 82558
website: www.sykeside.co.uk

Located near the Kirkstone Pass and surrounded by breathtaking scenery, the **Brotherswater Inn** is a family-run business offering good food and drink, comfortable bed & breakfast accommodation, and a well-maintained site for campers and motorhomes. The inn itself is open all day, every day, offering a minimum of 3 real ales along with a wide selection of draught lagers, cider and other beverages, including around 130 different malt whiskies. Good, wholesome food is available throughout the day, starting with breakfast between 8am and 10am, and concluding with evening meals from 6pm until 9.30pm. Home made dishes are a speciality - Steak & Ale Pie, for example, made from top quality Cumbrian beef and Theakston's Ale. The inn has 7 guest bedrooms, one of which is en suite, all of them simply but tastefully furnished and equipped with colour television.

The nearby Sykeside Camping Park enjoys an idyllic setting, overlooked by Dove Crag, Hart Crag and Fairfield, and with tranquil Brotherswater close by. Site facilities include a spacious and well-equipped toilet block with a 24-hour supply of hot water; laundry, drying and ironing facilities; and a well-stocked shop where visitors can buy just about all the provisions they will need. Sykeside also boasts bunkhouse accommodation - centrally heated, carpeted rooms with between 2 and 6 beds. Each room is pleasantly appointed and furnished with tables, chairs and storage facilities as well as a toilet and wash basin.

8 The Eden Valley and East Cumbria

The River Eden is entirely Cumbrian and one of the few large rivers in England that flows northwards. In this chapter we follow the river from its source on the fells above Mallerstang, near the North Yorkshire border, to the outskirts of Carlisle where it turns sharply east and flows

Eden Valley

into the Solway Firth. For much of its course, the river is accompanied by the famous Settle to Carlisle Railway, a spectacularly scenic route saved from annihilation in the 1960s by the efforts of local enthusiasts. Carved through boulder clay and red sandstone and sandwiched between the Lakeland fells and the northern Pennines, the Eden Valley is green and fertile - in every sense another Eden. But the valley was vulnerable to Scottish raids in medieval times and the number of pele towers and castles in the area are testament to a turbulent and often violent past.

This, too, is farming country and many of the ancient towns and villages have a market place. Appleby-in-Westmorland, the old county town of Westmorland, not only had an important market but an annual horse fair which continues today and has gained a large following.

An attractive man-made feature of the valley is the collection of specially commissioned stone sculptures known as Eden Benchmarks dotted along its length. Each created by a different sculptor, they have been located beside public paths and, since they also function as seats, provide the perfect setting in which to enjoy the valley's unspoilt scenery. There are 10 of them in all, beginning with **Mary Bourne's Water Cut**, an intriguing limestone sculpture, shaped rather like a tombstone riven from top to bottom by a serpentine space representing the river. It stands on Lady Anne's Way, a public path along the eastern ridge of the Mellerstang Fells.

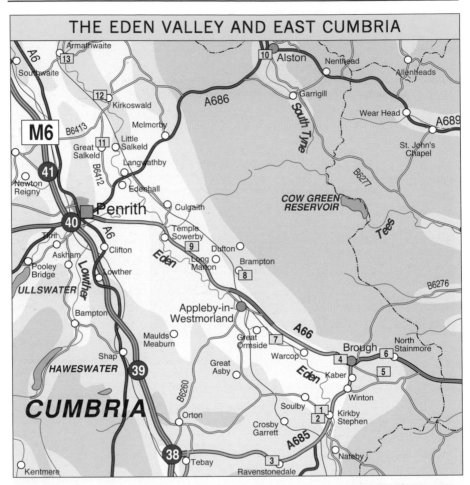

THE EDEN VALLEY AND EAST CUMBRIA

© MAPS IN MINUTES ™ (1999)

PLACES TO STAY, EAT, DRINK AND SHOP

KIRKBY STEPHEN

Surrounded by spectacular scenery, the old market town It was the Vikings who first established a village here and they named it "Kirke and bye", meaning churchtown. Although essentially part of the Eden Valley, Kirkby Stephen has a strong Yorkshire Dales feel about it. Indeed, the **Church of St Stephen**, with its long, elegant nave, has been called the Cathedral of the Dales.

Dating from 1220 and with a 16th century tower, St Stephen's Church is one of the finest in the eastern fells, dominating the northern end of the town from its elevated position. Until the last century the Trupp Stone in the churchyard received money from local people every Easter Monday in payment of church tithes and, at eight o'clock, the curfew is still sounded by the Taggy Bell,

Kirkby Stephen

THE PINK GERANIUM CAFÉ

40 Market Street, Kirkby Stephen, Cumbria CA17 4QW
Tel: 017683 71586

Located in the heart of this small Eden market town, **The Pink Geranium Café** is a tasteful eating place with an interior made colourful and interesting by the hand painted geraniums on the wall and the collection of tea cups hanging from the ceiling. Housed in an 18th century building, the café is owned and run by David and Diana - who took over here in December 1998.The couple have since built a solid reputation based on quality and value. The menu offers many home made dishes, including the now very popular steak and mushroom pie. Homemade soups are always freshly made and of unusual varieties. The toasted cheese scones are delicious and make for a welcome snack taken with a pot of

Twinings tea. Twinings teas feature throughout the menu including Darjeeling, Earl and Lady Grey - many fruit infusions are also on offer.

Customers are welcomed for a drink only, quick snack, light meal or a full three courses. A children's manu is available and a high chair if required. The Pink Geranium is open all year round apart from annual holidays. Daily from 9.00 am to 5pm-ish except Mondays (open Bank Holidays) and the occasional Friday during winter months.

once regarded by local children as a demon. Inside the church are a number of pre-Conquest stones, some of which show Norse influence. The most remarkable is the 10th century **Loki Stone**, one of only two such carvings in Europe to have survived. Loki was a Norse God and presumably Viking settlers brought their belief in Loki to Kirkby Stephen. The carving of Loki shows a figure resembling the Devil with sheep's horns, whose legs and arms are bound by heavy irons, an image symbolising the overpowering of paganism by Christian beliefs. For many years the stone lay undiscovered, reused as a building stone. The church also boasts some interesting memorials, amongst them the Elizabethan tomb of Thomas, Lord Wharton and his two wives, and the earlier memorial to Sir Richard de Musgrave of Hartley Castle who died in the early 1400s. Sir Richard was the man reputed to have killed that last boar upon Wild Boar Fell, and the story was given credence when, some years ago, the tomb was opened to reveal the bones of a man and woman alongside two tusks from a boar.

Between the church and the market place stand the cloisters which served for a long time as a butter market. The market, still held every Monday, has existed since 1351 and has always been a commercial focus for the surrounding countryside. In the 18th century knitting - mostly of stockings - was the most important product of the town and a restored spinning gallery reflects the importance of the woollen industry.

There are many delightful walks from the town, to **Croglam Earthworks** for example, a prehistoric fort, or to nearby **Stenkrith Park** where the second of the Eden Benchmarks can be found. Created by Laura White in Ancaster limestone and titled *Passage*, the sculpture is deceptively simple, suggesting perhaps the course of a

THE OLD FORGE RESTAURANT

39 North Road, Kirkby Stephen, Cumbria CA17 4RE
Tel/Fax: 017683 71832
e-mail: oldforgerestaurant@tinyonline.co.uk

The Old Forge Restaurant is housed in a former smithy which is now the home of Moira and Tom who established their outstanding eating-place in the summer of 1999. Moira is a gifted cook and offers an inviting menu that includes a good choice of traditional country fare along with some excellent vegetarian options. This regular menu of home made dishes changes depending on whether you are visiting in the summer or winter. Supplementing this menu, a selection of specials which changes every month, can be found set into the fireplace. The intimate restaurant with its interesting murals seats only 20 diners so it is essential to book at weekends and advisable at other times.

The restaurant is licensed so diners can enjoy a pre- or post-prandial drink either in Tom's Bar (where there's a fascinating collection of horseshoes), or in Moira's Snug. The Old Forge is open from

6.30pm until late every evening except Monday, (Monday & Tuesday from October to April) and although the restaurant is not normally open at lunchtime, Tom and Moira are happy to cater for pre-booked groups by arrangement. All major credit cards are accepted, apart from American Express. Kirkby Stephen itself is a charming little town well worth exploring for its magnificent medieval church whose greatest treasure is the Loki Stone. This 8th century Viking survival represents the Norse god Loki, a satanic figure depicted with his arms bound by heavy irons.

river bed. There are also some pleasant strolls along the riverside to a fine waterfall where the River Eden cascades into **Coop Karnel Hole**. Look out for the unusual shapes of the weathered limestone rock.

AROUND KIRKBY STEPHEN

OUTHGILL
5 miles S of Kirkby Stephen on the B6259

This remote village has close links with the Clifford family of Skipton Castle, North Yorkshire. The village **Church of St Mary**, first built in 1311, was repaired by Lady Anne Clifford who, from 1643 when she finally obtained possession of the Clifford estates, devoted her life to restoring her many properties and lived in each of them for varying periods of time. Her estates included 6 castles - Skipton and Barden in Yorkshire; Appleby, Brough, Brougham and Pendragon in Westmorland. Lady Anne's zeal for restoration didn't stop at castles: she also repaired the Roman road between Wensleydale and the Eden Valley, a route she often travelled (along with a huge retinue) between her castles and her birthplace at Skipton. The route is now known as Lady Anne's Way but in times past it was aptly called the High Way since it was a regular place of employment for highwaymen such as Dick Turpin and William "Swift" Nevison.

The landscape around Outhgill is remote and beautiful. To the south is **Wild Boar Fell**, a brooding, flat-topped peak where the last wild boar in England was reputedly killed, whilst tucked down in the valley are the romantic ruins of Lammerside and Pendragon Castles.

Pendragon Castle, about a mile north of the village, is shrouded in legend but

Wild Boar Fell

there are claims that it was the fortress of Uther Pendragon, father of King Arthur. If so, nothing remains of that 6th century wooden castle. The present structure dates from the 1100s and was built by Hugh de Morville, one of the four knights who murdered Thomas à Becket, to guard the narrow pass of Mallerstang. Twice it was burned by the Scots and twice restored, on the latter occasion by the formidable Lady Anne Clifford in 1660. Another mile or so downstream, **Lammerside Castle** dates from the 12th century but only the remains of the keep survive. They can be found along a bridle path between Pendragon and Wharton Hall.

RAVENSTONEDALE
5 miles SW of Kirkby Stephen on the A685

Known locally as Rissendale, this pretty village of stone-built cottages clustered along the banks of Scandal Beck lies on the edge of the **Howgill Fells**. The parish Church of St Oswald is especially interesting: built in 1738, it is one of the few Georgian churches in Cumbria. An earlier church, built on the same site, had a separate bell tower which rested on pillars and at its centre hung a refuge bell. Anyone guilty of a capital offence who managed to escaped to Ravenstonedale and sound the bell was free from arrest by the King's officials. This useful custom was finally abolished in the reign of James I.

The present church, surrounded by yew trees, is well worth a visit with its bow pews facing one another and its three-decker pulpit complete with a sounding board and, at the back of the third deck, a seat for the parson's wife. The window at the east end commemorates the last woman in England to be put to death for her Protestant faith. Elizabeth Gaunt was sentenced in 1685 by the notorious Judge Jefferies to be burnt at the stake for sheltering a fugitive rebel.

NATEBY
2 miles S of Kirkby Stephen on the B6269

Now a quiet hamlet of houses standing alongside a beck, for centuries Nateby was dominated by **Hartley Castle**. Believed to have been built in the 13th century, the castle was the home of Sir Andrew de Harcala, a renowned soldier during the reign of Edward II. Harcala was one of the first men to fight on a pony and he was made Earl of Carlisle in recognition of his service to the Crown. However, his failure to prevent Robert the Bruce invading the north of England led him to be accused of treason and he was executed in 1325. His castle was finally demolished by the Musgrave family who used the stone to build their manor house at Edenhall near Penrith.

The Black Swan at Ravenstonedale

Kirkby Stephen, Cumbria CA17 4NG
Tel: 015396 23204 Fax: 015396 23604
website: www.blackswanhotel.comm

Less than 10 minutes from Junction 38 of the M6 and easily accessible from the A66, The **Black Swan at Ravenstonedale** stands at the heart of this wonderfully sleepy little village. Time seems to have stood still here for half a century or more, making it a perfect retreat from the day-to-day pressures of the modern world.

Built of attractive lakeland stone in 1899, this spacious hotel enjoys an excellent reputation for its fine cuisine. A substantial breakfast is provided and much of the day is spent preparing for dinner which is based on local produce wherever possible, including Westmorland beef and lamb, local game and traditionally made cheeses. The wine list offers an interesting range of wines from around the world, all at sensible prices. The Black Swan's resident owners, Gordon and Norma Stuart, believe that a hotel should emulate a "home from home" and they make every effort to ensure that guests enjoy their stay and wish to visit them again. Guests have the use of a comfortable residents' sitting room with lots of magazines, books and an open fire. The quaint stonewalled bar is a popular meeting place and in summer everyone enjoys the delightful garden, bordered by the village beck. The hotel has 16 guest bedrooms, varying in size and aspect, with three at ground level and suitable for the disabled. All have private bathrooms and are equipped with television, direct dial telephone and lots of thoughtful little extras. For those who prefer self-catering, a newly refurbished annexe known as The Nick (because it used to be the village Police Station) provides comfortable accommodation for up to 8 people.

CROSBY GARRETT

4 miles W of Kirkby Stephen off the A685

Local legend has it that the Devil, seeing all the stones lying ready to build **Crosby Garrett Church**, carried them in his leather apron to the top of a nearby hill. He reasoned that, as people grew old, they would be unable to climb the hill and attend church and thus would come to him rather than go to Heaven.

Such tales apart, the church itself is said to be of Anglo-Saxon origin though the visible fabric is 12th century. Inside there are some superb carvings, particularly near the font. The church is also famous for its hagioscope, cut through the wall to allow people in the north aisle to see the altar. Near the church gates is a tithe barn, built in the 18th century to store farm produce given to the church as a religious tax. To the west of the village runs the Settle-Carlisle Railway whose splendid viaduct dominates Crosby Garrett.

WINTON

3 miles N of Kirkby Stephen off the A685

This a quiet and picturesque hamlet whose name, in old English, means pasture farmland. It is built on a spring line and, like many other Cumbrian villages of medieval origin, once followed the runrig, or two-field system of agriculture. The evidence is still visible in long, thin fields to the north of the village. These would have been individual strips in medieval times: the open fields were enclosed in the 17th and 18th centuries.

In the centre of the village is the manor house, built in 1726, and Winton's only three-storey building. It was formerly a boys' school where, apparently, the boys were treated like prisoners and not allowed to return home until the end of their education in case they told of their life at the school. The oldest building is

Winton Hall, built of stone and dated 1665, but its appearance suggests it to be older with its stone buttresses and mullioned windows with iron bars.

Those taking a walk on **Winton Fell** are likely to see red grouse lifting off from the large tracts of heather on the fellside. Indeed, the wildlife is much more prolific around this area where the limestone provides more plentiful food than on the fells around the lakes.

KABER

4 miles N of Kirkby Stephen off the A685

In 1663, this small village was the improbable focus of the Kaber Rigg Plot, a rebellion against Charles II led by Captain Robert Atkinson of Watergate Farm in Mallerstang. The rising failed and Atkinson was hanged, drawn, and quartered at Appleby; tragically, a messenger carrying his reprieve was delayed on Stainmore

APPLEBY-IN-WESTMORLAND

The old county town of Westmorland, Appleby is one of the most delightful small towns in England. It was originally built by the Norman, Ranulph de Meschines, who set it within a broad loop of the River Eden which protects it on three sides. The fourth side is guarded by Castle Hill. The town's uniquely attractive main street, Boroughgate, has been described as the finest in England. A broad, tree-lined avenue, it slopes down the hillside to the river, its sides lined with a pleasing variety of buildings, some dating back to the 17th century. At its foot stands the 16th century **Moot Hall**, (still used for council meetings and also housing the Tourist Information Centre); at its head rises the great Norman Keep of

THE CASTLE HOTEL

Main Street, Brough, Cumbria CA17 4AX
Tel: 017683 41252 / 42252 Fax: 017683 41775

Enjoying magnificent views of the Norman Castle and the surrounding Pennines, **The Castle Hotel** stands at the heart of this typical Westmorland village. Built in 1798 as a coaching inn, The Castle has been sympathetically refurbished to retain its traditional character along with all modern amenities.

Alwyn Robinson took over here in the summer of 2000, together with his business partner Helen Girvan. Tragically, Helen was killed in a car accident a few months later but Alwyn has continued to maintain the inn's reputation for quality food, drink and accommodation. The cooking is done by chef Scott Long, whose comprehensive à la carte menu based on the very best of Cumbrian produce is complemented by a select list of wines. Meals are served in the intimate Armoury Restaurant which is distinguished by its outstanding murals depicting the Age of Chivalry. Bar meals are also available in the comfortable

lounge bar while the public bar, as well as offering pool and darts, also has a good selection of real ales, beers, wines and spirits.

Conveniently located within easy reach of the Lake District, the Yorkshire Dales and the Scottish Borders, the Castle has 14 guest bedrooms, all attractively furnished and equipped with en suite bathroom, colour television with Sky satellite channel, direct dial phone and hospitality tray. Guests can stay on either a bed & breakfast or dinner, bed & breakfast basis. Children are welcome and credit cards accepted.

AUGILL CASTLE

Brough-in-Westmorland, Kirkby Stephen,
Cumbria CA17 4DE
Tel: 017683 41937 Fax: 017683 41936
e-mail: enquiries@augillcastle.co.uk
website: www.augillcastle.co.uk

A very special place in the very special Eden Valley, **Augill Castle** offers visitors historic surroundings, outstanding cuisine, sumptuous accommodation and a relaxing country house atmosphere. Described by the architectural guru Nikolaus Pevsner as *"A fine essay in early Victorian castle building"*, Augill was built in 1841 in a superb position with the dramatic North Pennines as a backdrop and with gardens opening out to views of the Yorkshire Dales and the Lakeland fells beyond. A flamboyant structure with its tower, turrets and castellations, the castle has had some equally colourful residents, not least Dr Abercrombie, surgeon to Queen Victoria and a prime suspect in the Jack the Ripper enquiries. In 1997, the now virtually derelict castle was bought by Simon and Wendy Bennett who have transformed the romantic old building into one of Cumbria's finest country houses.

Staying at Augill Castle provides some memorable experiences. Guests share breakfast and dinner around the 12ft table in the Gothic blue dining room where the food includes traditionally reared lamb, beef and pork from a neighbouring farm, locally grown fruit and vegetables, together with locally baked bread and free range eggs at breakfast time. Guests can relax in the huge lounge, surrounded by family antiques and paraphernalia, before retiring to one of the 6 guest bedrooms. All are en suite and individually designed by Simon and Wendy to reflect the castle's age and its history as a family home.

St Lawrence's Church, Appleby

Appleby Castle which is protected by one of the most impressive curtain walls in northern England. Attractions here include the dramatic view from the top of the 5-storey Keep; the stately Great Hall with its famous painting of Lady Anne Clifford and her family; and the attractive grounds which are home to a wide variety of animals and include a Rare Breeds Survival Centre.

During the mid-1600s, Appleby Castle was the home of Lady Anne Clifford, the remarkable woman who has already been mentioned several times and to whom Appleby has good cause to be grateful. The last of the Clifford line, the diminutive Lady Anne (she was just 4ft 10in tall) inherited vast wealth and estates, amongst them no fewer than six northern castles. She lavished her fortune on rebuilding or restoring them all. Churches and chapels in the area also benefitted from her munificence and at Appleby, in 1651, she also founded the almshouses known as the **Hospital of St Anne**, for "12 sisters and a Mother". Set around a cobbled square, the picturesque cottages and minuscule chapel still serve their original function, maintained by the trust endowed by Lady Anne: visitors are welcome.

Lady Anne died in 1676 in her 87th year and was buried with her mother in **St Lawrence's Church**. The church is well worth visiting to see their magnificent tombs and also the historic organ, purchased from Carlisle Cathedral in 1684, which is said to be oldest one still in use in Britain.

Just a few years after Lady Anne's death, James II granted the town the right to hold a Fair during the week following the second Wednesday in June. More than three hundred years later, the **Gypsy Horse Fair** is still thriving with hundreds of gypsies flooding into the little town (population: 1800) with their caravans and horse-drawn carts. The trade, principally in horses, and the trotting races provide a picturesque and colourful spectacle.

AROUND APPLEBY-IN-WESTMORLAND

BROUGH
8 miles SE of Appleby-in-Westmorland on the A66/A685

This small town, standing at the point where the Stainmore Pass opens into the Vale of Eden, is, in fact, two settlements: Church Brough and Market Brough. Church Brough is a group of neat houses and cottages clustered around a little market square in which a maypole stands

THE PUNCH BOWL INN

North Stainmore, Brough, Kirkby Stephen,
Cumbria CA17 4DY
Tel: 017683 41262

According to legend, **The Punch Bowl Inn** was one of the hideouts favoured by the notorious highwayman Dick Turpin - there is, reputedly, a 250 yard long escape tunnel leading from the basement. One wonders if the inn's amiable resident ghost is perhaps the spirit of the famous felon. The Punch Bowl was built in three different eras. The central part dates back to 1780, the wings were added exactly a century later, and the modern bar exactly a century after that. Today, this friendly hostelry is owned and run by Andy and Julie Beagle. Although they only took over in the summer of 2000, Julie had worked here for some 9 years before that. An accomplished cook, Julie offers an appetising menu of traditional pub food, starters, sandwiches and desserts, supplemented by

a choice of up to 10 daily specials. Most of the dishes are available in half portions for children and food is served every day from noon until 11pm. To accompany your meal there's an extensive selection of draught keg ales, stout, lagers, cider and a minimum of 2 real ales of which Black Sheep is the brew always on tap. The inn offers all the traditional pub amusements - pool, darts, cards, dominoes, and accommodation is also available, please phone for details. Located just a couple of minutes drive from the A66, the Punch Bowl provides an ideal base for touring the Lake District, the Yorkshire Dales and the Scottish Borders.

THE SANDFORD ARMS

Sandford, Appleby-in-Westmorland, Cumbria CA16 6NR
Tel: 017683 51121

Set beside the River Eden, just a few minutes drive from the A66, Sandford is a charming village of traditional stone dwellings. One of the most striking of these is **The Sandford Arms**, originally built in the 18th century as farm buildings and now a popular residential inn with a delightful lounge, restaurant and traditional tap room. Surrounded by a profusion of oak beams and some craftsmanly local stone work, customers can enjoy their real ales or a choice "malt" at the bar or by the open fire in winter.

Quality home-cooked food is available every lunchtime and evening, served either in the bar or in the separate non-smoking à la carte restaurant. The inn has a wonderfully relaxed and friendly atmosphere, due no doubt to the fact that it is a family-run business. The wholesome, appetising dishes are prepared by Carl and Craig, (Carl is a highly-trained chef), and their mum, Susan, and

Carl's fiancée are all involved in the running of this popular free house. The Sandford Arms also offers 5 comfortable, well-appointed guest bedrooms, all with an ETB 4 Diamond rating, all en suite and all enjoying stunning views across meadows to the Cumbrian fells. Each room is equipped with remote-controlled colour TV, direct dial telephone and tea/coffee-making facilities. An additional attraction for fishermen staying at the Sandford Arms during the trout season is that the inn has a daily allocation of four rods along a stretch of the beautiful River Eden, renowned for its "Brownies". Fishing is free to residents.

on the site of the former market cross. **Brough Castle** (English Heritage - free), built within the ramparts of the Roman camp of Verterae, was constructed to protect the Roman road over Stainmore Pass. The building of this Norman castle was begun by William Rufus in 1095 but it was largely destroyed in 1174 by William the Lion of Scotland. Many times Scottish raiders laid siege to Brough Castle and fierce battles were fought. An ancient ballad tells of the legendary bravery of one knight from the town who defended the tower alone after his comrades had fallen. He was finally vanquished when the Scottish army set fire to his hiding place but the incident was so dramatic that it became a part of local folklore and was remembered in the ballad of the *Valiant Knight of Brough*. Another fortification restored by the remarkable Lady Anne Clifford, the castle, with its tall keep 60ft high is well worth visiting, if only for the superb panorama of the surrounding fells seen from the battlements.

Market Brough is also an ancient settlement and was particularly important in the 18th and 19th centuries when it became a major coaching town on the stagecoach routes between England and Scotland. It was on the junction of several routes and boasted more than 10 inns. The width and breadth of its High Street also indicates its importance as a market town. Brough was granted a charter in 1330 enabling it to hold a weekly market as well as four cattle markets and an annual fair. One custom still celebrated in Brough is the **Twelfth Night Holly Burning**, a unique festival with pagan origins.

The distinctive, low hills that lie to the west of Brough are drumlins - heaps of material deposited by Ice Age glaciers. In this area many drumlins are marked by broad, grassy ridges, remains of ancient lynchets or ploughing strips.

NORTH STAINMORE
10 miles SE of Appleby-in-Westmorland on the A66

The village lies on the **Stainmore Pass** which carries the old Roman road, now the A66, through a remote area of the North Pennines which David Bellamy described as "England's last wilderness". Near Stainmore summit are the foundations of Maiden Castle, a Roman fort built to guard the pass against marauders. A few yards over the Cumbrian border, into County Durham, is the stump of the ancient **Rey Cross** which was erected before AD946 and which, until 1092, marked the boundary between England and Scotland. It is thought to be the site of the battle at which the last Viking King of York and North England, Eric Bloodaxe, was killed following his expulsion from the city.

WARCOP
5 miles SE of Appleby-in-Westmorland on the B6259

The largest village in this part of the Eden Valley, Warcop grew up as a crossing point of the river. The bridge, the oldest to cross the river, dates from the 16th century and the red sandstone buildings surrounding the village green, with its central maypole, make this a charming place to visit.

The **Church of St Columba** is built outside the village on the site of a Roman camp. An interesting building in its own right, it is particularly famous for the rush-bearing ceremony which takes place in late June each year. Warcop is surrounded by Ministry of Defence tank firing ranges from which the public is understandably excluded but on the hills above the village are stones, cairns, and

THE NEW INN

Brampton, Appleby-in-Westmorland,
Cumbria CA16 6JS
Tel: 017683 51231

Despite its name, **The New Inn** is actually a pretty venerable establishment dating back to 1730. It's very traditional inside, with flagstone floors, beamed ceilings, real fires and plenty of interesting items from yesteryear adorning the walls. The hosts, bought the pub in the autumn of 2000 and have quickly made it a popular centre for locals and visitors alike. Open all day, every day, during the season, the inn has a cosy and charming restaurant which serves an imaginative and delicious menu of appetising meals based wherever possible on local produce. Food is served every lunchtime from 12.00pm until 2.00pm, and in the evenings from 7pm until 9pm. Choose from the regular menu or from the blackboard specials.

Real ale devotees will find a choice of 3 brews on tap plus a good range of draught keg bitters, lagers, stout and cider. Such is the popularity of the food and drink weekends are always busy and bookings are essential on Saturday evenings and for Sunday lunch. Meals are served either in the separate restaurant, in the bar or, in good weather, customers can enjoy their refreshments in the large beer garden at the rear of the inn. As we go to press, the refurbishment of the guest bedrooms is being completed. By the time you read this, four quality rooms, all en suite, should be available for bed & breakfast guests.

BRIDGE END INN

Main Street, Kirkby Thore, Penrith,
Cumbria CA10 1UZ
Tel: 01768 362180

Conveniently located beside the A66 Penrith to Brough road, the **Bridge End Inn** was originally built in the 1600s to serve the stagecoach traffic along this busy cross-Pennine route. In those days, it had its own smithy at the rear of the inn and was a popular meeting place for the local hunt. The present building is more recent but retains its hospitable atmosphere with its cosy surroundings and open fire. Open all day, every day, this free house is owned and run by David and Rosemary who took over here in 1998 and have more than 20 years experience in the licensed trade. Wholesome traditional food is available every day from noon until 8pm, (Sundays, 6pm), with the varied menu listed on the blackboard. Children are welcome and vegetarian meals are available on request. There's also an unusually extensive choice of well-kept ales, amongst them John Smith's Smooth, Worthington Creamflow, Boddingtons and Tetley Smooth, as well as 5 different draught lagers, Guinness and Strongbow on draught. At the time of writing, plans are under way to provide bed & breakfast accommodation at the inn, and this new amenity should be available by the time you read this. Please call for details.

the remains of what is claimed to be a druid's temple.

GREAT ORMSIDE
2 miles SE of Appleby-in-Westmorland off the B6260

This was once an important fort guarded by a pele tower, and the ancient **Church of St James**, which dates from the 11th century, occupies a site on the steep-sided defence mound. Relics of pre-Christian burials have been found in the mound, as well as a Viking sword (now in the Tullie Museum in Carlisle). A silver gilt and enamel bowl from the 7th century has also been found and is regarded as one of the most important pieces of Anglo-Saxon metalware to survive. A particularly beautiful piece, richly decorated with vine scrolls, birds, and animals, it is now on permanent display in the Yorkshire Museum in York.

From the village a path leads across fields to the village of Little Ormside, with its large cedar tree said to have been brought back from Lebanon as a sapling by General Whitehead. On the voyage home he grew it in his hat and shared with it his daily ration of one pint of water.

GREAT ASBY
4 miles S of Appleby-in-Westmorland off the B6260

This pretty village is set in a wooded hollow, its houses separated by Hoff Beck. Alongside the beck is **St Helen's Well** which is said never to run dry or freeze and nearby are the splendid almshouses of St Helen's, built between 1811 and 1820. Across a footbridge is Asby Hall (private), built in 1670. It was once the home of the Musgrave family of Edenhall whose crest and coat of arms can still be seen above the door.

BRAMPTON
2 miles N of Appleby-in-Westmorland off the A66

This village, along with the surrounding area, was said to be haunted by the ghost of Elizabeth Sleddall, the wife of a 17th century owner of nearby Crackenthorpe Hall. Elizabeth died believing that she had been cheated out of her share of the estate, so to shame the false inheritors her spirit was seen being driven around the countryside in a coach drawn by four black horses. Her ghost became so troublesome that the local people exhumed her body and reburied the remains under a larger boulder. Her ghost, whilst no longer troubling the local people, is still said to visit the hall.

DUFTON
3 miles N of Appleby-in-Westmorland off the A66

Behind this delightful hamlet lies **Dufton Gill**, a beautiful, secluded wooded valley through which runs a footpath. Also from Dufton there is a track carrying the **Pennine Way** up to High Cup Nick, a great horseshoe precipice at the edge of the northern Pennine escarpment that was formed by a glacial lake during the Ice Age.

LONG MARTON
3 miles N of Appleby-in-Westmorland off the A66

Visitors to this village can experience two very different forms of architecture, both of them equally impressive. The village church, with its carvings of knights and monsters over the doorway, is remarkable unspoilt and Norman, whilst nearby the **Settle to Carlisle Railway** sweeps across a grand viaduct.

TEMPLE SOWERBY
7 miles NW of Appleby-in-Westmorland on
the A66

Temple Sowerby prides itself on the title
"Queen of Westmorland villages", an
accolade justified by its lovely setting in
the Eden valley. (An added bonus: the
average rainfall here is half that recorded
in the Lake District National Park to the
west). To the north, the massive bulk of
Cross Fell, the highest point in the
Pennines, swells skywards to provide a
spectacular backdrop. The village itself,
picturesquely grouped around a sloping
green and an 18th century red sandstone
church, takes its name from the medieval
Knights Templar who owned the manor of
Sowerby until their Order was suppressed
in 1308. But the little community long
outdates those predatory Knights:
evidence of a Stone Age settlement has
been found and a Roman milestone just
outside the village marks the route of the
old Imperial highway, now the A66.

From Temple Sowerby there are
delightful walks through the Eden valley
or, if you prefer a gentle stroll, it's only a
mile to the National Trust gardens at
Acorn Bank where Crowdundle Beck
splashes beneath an elegant 18th century
bridge. The 16th century manor house is
how a Sue Ryder Home and not open to
the public, but visitors are welcome to
explore the attractive gardens planted
with a collection of some 250 medicinal
and culinary herbs.

NORTH EAST OF PENRITH

EDENHALL
3 miles NE of Penrith off the A686

An old tradition asserts that in the 8th
century the monks of Jarrow, fleeing from

Viking invaders with the body of St
Cuthbert, stopped here briefly. As a result
the village church is dedicated to the
saint. Part of the building appears to be
pre-Norman but most of the structure
dates from the 1100s.

Close to the church is the **Plague Cross**
which stands where there was once a
basin filled with vinegar. This acted as a
disinfectant into which plague victims put
their money to pay for food from the
people of Penrith. The plague of the 16th
century killed a quarter of the village's
inhabitants.

Edenhall is particularly famous for the
story of the "Luck of Eden Hall", a
priceless glass cup which, according to
legend, was stolen from some fairies
dancing round the garden wall by a butler
in the service of the Musgrave family back
in the 15th century. Despite the fairies'
entreaties, the butler refused to return the
6-inch high glass to them. As he departed
with the precious goblet, the fairies laid a
curse upon it: *"If ever this cup shall break
or fall, Farewell the luck of Eden Hall"*. On
inspection, the glass was identified as a
13th century chalice of enamelled and
gilded glass that is thought to have come
from Syria and may well have been
brought back by a Crusader. It was a
treasured heirloom of the Musgraves for
many generations and is now in the
Victoria and Albert Museum in London.
The goblet is still intact but Eden Hall has
long since disappeared and the Musgraves
no longer live here.

LANGWATHBY
4 miles NE of Penrith on the A686

Located on the opposite bank of the River
Eden from Edenhall, Langwathby's name
means "the settlement by the long ford"
and, though there are two prehistoric
pathways crossing here, the name of the
village and of its neighbouring

settlements suggests a Viking past.

Langwathby has a huge village green which still hosts maypole dancing on the third Saturday in May. The green is medieval in origin and would once have been surrounded by wood and mud houses, perhaps to protect cattle but also for defence against border raids. After the Civil War and the growth in prosperity in the late 17th century, these wattle and daub cottages were replaced by stone buildings. The drovers from Scotland passed through here to the market towns of England.

MELMERBY
9 miles NE of Penrith on the A686

Melmerby nestles at the foot of Hartside Pass, its spacious village green is dissected by three becks. Even today, every householder in Melmerby has grazing rights on the green. Horses are grazed more commonly now, but in the past it would have been more usual to see flocks of geese - indeed, there was once a cottage industry here making pillows and mattresses from goose feathers. Overlooking the 13-acre village green is **Melmerby Hall**, a defensive tower that was extended in the 17th and 18th centuries. The village church, with its tower, is a Victorian building, but the first known rector of the church came here in 1332.

A curious meteorological feature here is what are known as the Helm winds, localised gusts which sweep through the valley with the force of a gale whilst the surrounding countryside is perfectly calm.

From Melmerby the main road climbs out of the Eden Valley to the east and the landscape changes suddenly. The road passes **Fiend's Fell**, close to the highest point in the Pennine Chain, the summit of **Cross Fell**. Early Christians erected a cross on the highest point of the fell to protect travellers from the demons who haunted the moors. Today, a cairn marks the spot where the cross once stood.

ALSTON
26 miles SE of Carlisle on the A689/A686

For a few weeks in 1999 the small town of Alston, 1000ft up in the Pennines, became transformed into "Bruntmarsh", the fishing village in which the fictional Oliver Twist spent his early years. To recreate the squalid conditions of the poor in early 19th century England, production designers "dressed down" the town, so much so that anxious visitors noticing the soot-blackened buildings inquired whether there had been a major fire.

Alan Bleasdale's re-working of Charles Dickens' classic novel was for many the television highlight of 1999 and one of

Alston

the mini-series' many strengths was the authenticity of the locations. Alston proved to be ideal since the town centre has changed little since the late 1700s when the story is set and there are many even older buildings. The town council has created an **"Oliver Twist's Alton" trail**, with each of the 24 sites featured in the series marked by a picture of Mr Bumble.

The route includes some fascinating old buildings, a cobbled main street and, from the picturesque market cross, narrow lanes radiating out with courtyards enclosing old houses. Many of the older buildings still have the outside staircase leading to the first floor - a relic from the days when animals were kept below whilst the family's living accommodation was upstairs. This ancient part of Alston is known as The Butts, a title acquired by the need of the townspeople to be proficient in archery during the times of the border raids.

An unusual feature of Alston is the number of watermills in and around the town and the mill race was once the central artery of the old town. At High Mill, visitors can see the enormous **Smeaton water wheel** in action. The tall spire of St Augustine's Church is a well known local landmark and its churchyard contains a number of interesting epitaphs, as well as affording wonderful views of the South Tyne Valley.

Considering its small population, Alston supports an astonishing diversity of shops and "an almost Irish proportion of pubs to people". In addition the town is home to a wide variety of craftspeople, ranging from blacksmiths to candlemakers, wood turners to potters, and also boasts an outstanding art and crafts centre in the **Gossipgate Gallery** (see panel below).

GOSSIPGATE GALLERY

The Butts, Alston, Cumbria CA9 3JU
Tel: 01434 381806
e-mail: kempseys@gossipgate.com
website: www.gossipgate.com

Housed in a converted Congregational Church built in 1804 and with its original gas lights still intact, **Gossipgate Gallery** is the premier centre in the North Pennines for contemporary art and craft. Founded by Sonia and Peter Kempsey, the gallery specialises in displaying the work of contemporary artists and craftspeople from the North of England. A continuous programme of exhibitions runs from February to December. In the gallery shop, there's a huge range of artefacts for sale - original water-colours and prints, (many of them inspired by the spectacular scenery of the area), delicate jewellery handcrafted in silver and glass, striking turned wooden bowls from native hardwoods, and exquisite studio glass, ceramics and sculpture.

The shop also stocks a wide selection of local knitwear, hand weaving, hats, scarves, bags, belts and ties. There's more: greetings cards, CDs and books of local interest, artists' materials, delicious local honey, mustard, and preserves. When you're ready, make your way to the cosy and intimate Coffee Shop for a refreshing cuppa, or, on fine days, step outside and experience the peacefulness of the lovely Millennium Wildflower Garden. The garden is unique - a "Garden of Plant Ancestors" where commonly cultivated varieties bloom alongside their native wildflower ancestors. The garden also contains a tea terrace and a wide selection of local garden pottery. Gossipgate Gallery is open daily from Easter to October, 10am to 5pm; on winter weekends from 10.30am-4.30pm. For winter weekday hours, telephone for details: please note the Gallery is closed from January to mid-February.

Alston Motorcycle Shop

Another popular attraction in Alston is the **South Tynedale Railway**. This narrow gauge (2ft) steam railway runs regular services during the summer months and at the northern terminus of the 3-mile long track travellers can join a stretch of the Pennine Way that runs alongside the River South Tyne. From Alston's restored Victorian station there's also a bus service ferrying passengers to the Settle and Carlisle railway.

Alston Moor, to the south of the town, was once the centre of an extremely important lead mining region, one of the richest in Britain. Lead and silver were probably mined on the moor by the Romans, but the industry reached its peak in the early 19th century when vast quantities of iron, silver, copper, and zinc were extracted by the London Lead Company. A Quaker company, it was a

pioneer of industrial welfare and also built the model village of Nenthead to house the miners. Here, not only were the workers and their families provided with a home, but education was compulsory and there were some public baths.

LITTLE SALKELD
6 miles NE of Penrith off the A686

A lane from the village leads to **Long Meg and her Daughters**, a most impressive prehistoric site and second only to Stonehenge in size. Local legend claims that Long Meg was a witch who, with her daughters, was turned to stone for profaning the Sabbath, as they danced wildly on the moor. The circle is supposedly endowed with magic so that it is impossible to count the same number of stones twice. Another superstition is that Long Meg will bleed if the stone is chipped or broken. The actual name, Long Meg, has been the subject of debate. It has been suggested that Meg may be a corruption of the word "magus" meaning a magician.

There are more than 60 stones in the Circle, (actually an oval), which is approximately 300ft across. The tallest, Long Meg, is a 15ft column of Penrith sandstone, the corners of which face the four points of the compass. Cup and ring symbols and spirals are carved on this stone which is over 3,500 years old. The circle is now known to belong to the Bronze Age but no one is certain of its purpose. It may have been used for rituals connected with the changing seasons since the midwinter sun sets in alignment with the centre of the circle and Long Meg herself.

In 1725 an attempt was made by Colonel Samuel Lacy of Salkeld Hall to use the stones for mileposts. However, as work began, a great storm blew up and the workmen fled in terror believing that the

THE HIGHLAND DROVE INN

Great Salkeld, Penrith, Cumbria CA11 9NA
Tel: 01768 898349 Fax: 01768 898708
website: www.highland-drove.co.uk

Located in the heart of the picturesque Eden Valley, Great Salkeld stands on the old drovers road from Scotland. An impressive pele tower of 1380 is a reminder of the measures once necessary to repel less welcome visitors from the north, while the handsome 18th century **Highland Drove Inn** has been providing peaceful travellers with hearty hospitality for more than 200 years. Today, the inn is run by the father and son team of Donald and Paul Newton who arrived here in 1998 and have thoroughly refurbished the old hostelry while retaining all its olde worlde charm and atmosphere. An extensive selection of bar and restaurant meals, listed on the blackboard, is available every lunchtime from noon until 2pm (except on Mondays, unless it's a Bank Holiday), and every evening from 6.45pm to 9pm, (8.45pm on Sundays). There's a choice of 3 real ales - Black Sheep, Theakston's and a guest ale, as well as a range of other draught beers, lagers and other popular beverages. By the time you read this, a new 55-seater restaurant will be in service but even with this additional capacity you would be well-advised to book ahead for the weekends. An ideal base for visiting the Lake District, the Northern Pennines and the Scottish Borders, the inn has 5 guest bedrooms all of which are en suite and provided with television and tea/coffee-making facilities.

HOWSCALES

Kirkoswald, Penrith, Cumbria CA10 1JG
Tel: 01768 898666 Fax: 01768 898710
e-mail: liz@howscales.fsbusiness.co.uk website: www.eden-in-cumbria.co.uk/howscales
Dating back to the 17th century, **Howscales** is a charming old farmhouse which was built using the local red Lazonby sandstone both for the walls and the traditional tiled roofs. Quiet and secluded, the house enjoys an elevated position, looking across the pastures and woodlands to the hills of the Lake District and the Pennines. The former outbuildings, set around a cobbled courtyard, have been imaginatively converted, retaining many of the original features, and now provide quality self-catering accommodation in five self-contained cottages. "The Granary", "Geltsdale" and "Ravendale" are on two floors, having bedrooms and bathrooms on the ground floor and lounge, kitchen and dining on the first floor. "Hazelrigg" and "Inglewood" are entirely on the ground floor, each having bedrooms with en suite facilities and smooth level parking immediately alongside.

All the cottages, which can sleep between 2 and 4 guests, have full central heating, are fully carpeted and have well-equipped kitchens provided with everything you could possibly need. The lounges are comfortably furnished with sofas and armchairs with side tables and reading lights, colour TV and radio. Children are welcome, (a cot is available if required), and well-behaved pets are welcome by arrangement. Guests have the use of shared laundry facilities and pay phone, and are welcome to enjoy the garden and grounds. Each cottage contains an information pack to help you plan your holiday. The cottages have a 4-star ETC rating and Hazelrigg has a Category 2 rating from the National Accessibility Scheme for the disabled.

druids were angry at the desecration of their temple.

It was the same Colonel Lacy who gave his name to the **Lacy Caves**, a mile or so downstream from Little Salkeld. The Colonel had the five chambers carved out of the soft red sandstone, possibly as a copy of St Constantine's Caves further down the river at Wetheral. At that time it was fashionable to have romantic ruins and grottoes on large estates and Colonel Lacy is said to have employed a man to live in his caves acting the part of a hermit. Alternatively, the caves may have been intended to provide a wine store; Colonel Lacy used to entertain his guests here, and there were probably gardens around the caves. The rhododendrons and laburnums still flower every spring.

GREAT SALKELD
6 miles NE of Penrith on the B6412

The River Eden formed the boundary between the two old counties of Westmorland and Cumberland so while Little Salkeld was in Westmorland its larger namesake stood in Cumberland. The village is a picturesque collection of 18th century cottages and farmhouses built in red sandstone which are typical of this area. Great Salkeld is best known for the impressive church with its massive, battlemented pele tower built in the 14th century and complete with a dungeon. The Norman doorway in the porch is less than a yard wide and its arch has three rows of deeply cut zig-zags with five heads, one with a crown.

KIRKOSWALD
8 miles NE of Penrith on the B6413

The village derives its name from the Church of St Oswald: Oswald was the King of Northumbria who, according to legend, toured the pagan north with St Aidan in the 7th century. The church is unusual in having a detached tower standing some 200 yards from the main building.

This once thriving market town still retains its small cobbled market place and some very fine Georgian buildings. There's also a striking ruined 12th century **Castle**, formerly the home of the Featherstonehaugh family which, although not open to the public, can be seen from the road and footpath. In 1210 a licence was received from King John to fortify the original structure and enclose the extensive park. The castle was later destroyed by Robert the Bruce in 1314 but was rebuilt and extended in the late 15th century. The whole site covered three acres with the courtyard surrounded by a massive wall and a main gate with a drawbridge over the moat. The castle's splendour was due to the efforts of Thomas, Lord Dacre but, after his death in 1525, the panelling, stained glass, and beamed ceilings were transferred to Naworth and the castle became a quarry. Today, it is still protected by a wide moat and the great turreted tower rises 65ft above the remains of the vaulted dungeons.

One of Kirkoswald's most splendid buildings is the **College**, its name recalling the days when St Oswald's was a collegiate church. The two-storey house with its sloping-ended roof was originally built as a pele tower and converted into the college for priests in the 1520s. The manor house opposite has a particularly attractive entrance front in sandstone, which was added in 1696.

Just to the northwest of Kirkoswald are the **Nunnery Walks** which start at a Georgian house built in 1715 on the site of a Benedictine Nunnery founded during the reign of William Rufus. Narrow footpaths have been cut into the sandstone cliffs along the deep gorge of

The Dukes Head Hotel

Armathwaite, nr Carlisle, Cumbria CA4 9PB
Tel: 016974 72226
e-mail: HH@hlynch51.freeserve.co.uk

Quiet and secluded though it is, the peaceful, red sandstone village of Armathwaite is only a 15 minute drive from Junctions 41 or 42 of the M6. Located in the heart of the village, **The Dukes Head Hotel** is a delightful old hostelry which enjoys an excellent reputation for its outstanding cuisine. According to its brochure, the inn is "Home of probably the best Roast Duck in Cumbria"; most diners who have sampled this treat would say "Forget the *'probably'*". All items on the menu are prepared from only the finest and freshest of local ingredients and to complement this outstanding food there's a comprehensive list of unusual and appealing wines from around the world. Meals can be enjoyed either in the elegant non-smoking restaurant, in the lounge bar, warmed by open fires or, in good weather, in the garden. Landlord Henry Lynch, arranges themed cuisine nights once a month, (bookings are essential), as well as a variety of events designed to raise funds for local charities. This lively inn also offers its customers a game of boules during the summer, table skittles all year round and walkers will find details of a circular 6.5 mile walk contained in a leaflet the pub has produced, proceeds from which also go to charity. If you are planning to stay in this lovely part of the Eden Valley, the Dukes Head has 5 excellent letting rooms, 3 of which are en suite, the other two have private bathrooms.

Croglin beck and they pass through beautiful woodland to reveal exciting waterfalls. The walks are open to the public during the summer months.

ARMATHWAITE
10 miles NE of Penrith off the A6

Set on the western bank of the River Eden, the village has a particularly fine sandstone bridge from which there is a lovely view of Armathwaite Castle (private), the home of the Skelton family, one of whose forebears was Poet Laureate to Henry VIII. Close by, visitors to the **Eden Valley Woollen Mill** can see traditional looms rattling away and browse through a huge range of knitwear

produced from the finest wools and mohair. The Mill offers an inexpensive making-up service and accepts commissions for pile and rag rugs. It is open daily during the season but times vary during the winter months.

Also worth seeking out in Coombs Wood to the south is another of the **Eden Benchmarks**. Entitled "Vista" and created by Graeme Mitchison this remarkable sculpture seems to make the Lazenby Sandstone flow into liquid shapes.

North of Armathwaite, the River Eden approaches Carlisle and the Solway Firth; these lower stretches of the river are surveyed in the next chapter.

9 Carlisle and the Scottish Borders

For more than 350 years the area around Carlisle was known as the Debatable Lands, a lawless region where the feared Border Reivers sacked and plundered at will. Every winter, when their own food stocks were almost depleted, armed gangs from across the border would ride

Town Hall Square, Carlisle

southwards to seize the cattle and sheep of their more prosperous neighbours. Stealing and murdering, they wreaked havoc in this area and almost every village would have had a fortified structure, usually a pele tower, where the inhabitants and their animals could hide safely.

There are some 77 names on record as belonging to these disreputable reiver families - amongst them are the names Trotter and Maxwell - and anyone who wishes to find out if their family was involved should go to Carlisle's Tullie House Museum.

This is, too, the country of Hadrian's Wall and not only are parts of the structure still visible but Birdoswald gives an excellent insight into Roman border life. The wall was built as a great military barrier across the narrowest part of Britain, from the mouth of the River Tyne, in the east, to Bowness-on-

The Citadel, Carlisle

Solway, in the west. Guarded by forts at regular intervals, it was built between AD122-128 following a visit by the Emperor Hadrian who saw the then military infrastructure as insufficient to withstand the combined attacks of northern barbarians. Originally, much of the western side was built from turf, but by AD163 this had been replaced by stone. The wall was finally abandoned in the late 4th century.

CARLISLE AND THE SCOTTISH BORDERS

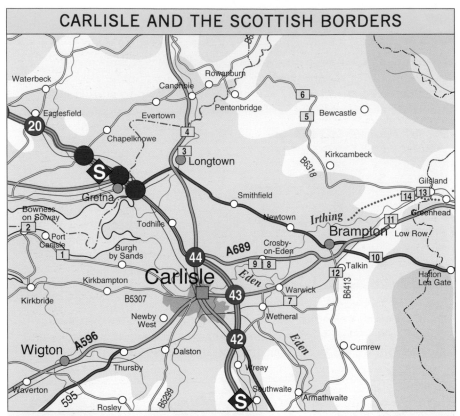

© MAPS IN MINUTES ™ (1999)

PLACES TO STAY, EAT, DRINK AND SHOP

1	The Highland Laddie Inn, Glasson	Pub, food and tea rooms	Page 187
2	The Kings Arms, Bowness-on-Solway	Pub, food and accommodation	Page 188
3	Briar Lea House, Brampton Road	Bed and breakfast	Page 188
4	The March Bank Hotel, Scotch Dyke	Hotel and restaurant	Page 189
5	Midtodhills Farm, Roadhead	Self catering	Page 190
6	Crossings Inn, Roadhead	Pub, food and accommodation	Page 190
7	Corby Bridge Inn, Corby Bridge	Pub, food and accommodation	Page 192
8	Crosby Lodge Country Hotel, High Crosby	Hotel and restaurant	Page 193
9	The Stag Inn, Low Crosby	Pub and restaurant	Page 194
10	The Belted Will Inn, Brampton	Pub, food and accommodation	Page 194
11	The Railway Inn, Low Row	Pub and restaurant	Page 196
12	Long Byres at Talkin Head, Talkin Head	Self catering	Page 196
13	Howard House Farm, Gilsland	Bed and breakfast	Page 198
14	Birdoswald Roman Fort, Gilsland	Roman fort and visitor centre	Page 198

CARLISLE

According to a recent survey, if you are born in Carlisle you are more likely to stay here than the inhabitants of any other place in England. Its castle, cathedral, many other historic buildings, parks, thriving traditional market, shopping centres and leisure facilities all combine to endow Carlisle with the true feel of a major city. Carlisle is the largest settlement in Cumbria, (with a population of around 100,000), and is also its county town. The city stands at the junction of three rivers, the Eden, the Caldew and the Petteril, and was already fortified in Celtic times when it was named Caer Lue, "the hill fort". It became a major Roman centre: the military base for the Petriana regiment, Luguvallum, guarding the western end of Hadrian's Wall, and also an important civilian settlement with fountains, mosaics, statues and centrally-heated homes.

Today, the squat outline of **Carlisle Castle** (English Heritage), high on a hilltop overlooking the River Eden, dominates the skyline of this fascinating city. There has been a castle at Carlisle since 1092 when William Rufus first built a palisaded fort. The Norman Castle was originally built of wood but, during the Scottish occupation in the 12th century, King David I laid out a new castle with stone taken from Hadrian's Wall. The 12th century keep can still be seen enclosed by massive inner and outer walls. Entered through a great 14th century gatehouse, complete with portcullis, and with a maze of vaulted passages, chambers, staircases, towers, and dismal dungeons. Children, especially, enjoy the legendary "licking stones" from which parched prisoners tried to find enough moisture to stay alive. The castle is everything a real castle should be and is still the headquarters of the Kings Own Royal Order Regiment whose Regimental Museum is located within the castle walls.

During the Civil War, the castle was besieged for eight months by the Parliamentarians under General Leslie. When the Royalists finally capitulated, Leslie began repairing the castle and the city walls. The Puritans were no respecters of Britain's ecclesiastical heritage; stones from six of the eight bays of the cathedral were used for the repairs and the building of block-houses for the Puritan troops.

Partially for this reason, **Carlisle Cathedral** is now one of the smallest cathedrals in England but it has many interesting features, including an exquisite east window that is considered to be one of the

Carlisle Castle

finest in Europe. Below the beautifully painted wooden ceiling of the choir, with its gold star shimmering against deep blue, are the carved, canopied choir-stalls with their medieval misericords. These wonderful carved beasts and birds include two dragons joined by the ears, a fox killing a goose, pelicans feeding their young, and a mermaid with a looking glass.

In the north transept is the superb 16th century Flemish Brougham Triptych which was originally in Cologne Cathedral. In the 19th century it was brought to Brougham Chapel near Penrith. The altar piece was later restored by the Victoria and Albert Museum in London and is now on permanent loan to Carlisle. It is a beautiful, intricate piece with delicately carved figures depicting scenes from the life of Christ.

Carlisle City Centre

It is hard to believe that it was here that Edward I solemnly used bell, book, and candle to excommunicate Robert the Bruce. It was here also that the church bells were rung to welcome Bonnie Prince Charlie in 1745. It is claimed that after the suppression of the Jacobite rebellion the bells were removed for their "treason" and only replaced in the 19th century.

Carlisle Cathedral is one of the few where visitors can enjoy refreshments actually within the precincts, in this case in the Prior's Kitchen Restaurant situated in the Fratry Undercroft. Seated beneath superb fan vaulting, customers have a good choice of home made soups, cakes and pastries, as well as morning coffee, lunches and afternoon teas.

Although an appointment is usually necessary, a visit to the nearby Prior Tower, if possible, is a must. On the first floor of this 15th century pele tower is a wonderful 45 panel ceiling incorporating the popinjay crest and arms of the Prior Senhouse. The 16th century Prior's gatehouse leads to a narrow lane called Paternoster which is named after the monks reciting their offices.

Like many great medieval cities, Carlisle was surrounded by walls. Guided walks and tours are available and the best view is to be found in a little street called West Walls at the bottom of Sally Port Steps, near the Tithe Barn. The walls date from around the 11th century and they remained virtually intact until the 1800s.

When the castle was under siege, the Sally Port allowed an individual to "sally forth". It was later used for access to the **Tithe Barn** to avoid paying city tolls. It is unusual to find a Tithe Barn within a city wall but this exception was probably made because of the Border raids. The barn dates from the 15th century and was used to collect and store taxes, or tithes, destined for the priory.

Close by is **St Cuthbert's Church**, the official city church of Carlisle and where the Lord Mayor's pew can be found. Although the present building dates from 1778, there has been a church on this site since the 7th century and the dedication is obvious since St Cuthbert was Bishop of Carlisle in AD680. It is a charming Georgian building with several interesting features including a moveable pulpit on rails.

The award winning **Tullie House Museum**, in the centre of the city close to the cathedral, is certainly another place not to be missed. Through skilful and interpretive techniques the fascinating, and often dark, history of the Debatable Lands, as this border region was called, is told. The museum's centrepiece is its story of the Border Reivers who occupied the lands from the 14th to the 17th century, with a law - or rather, a lack of it - unto themselves, being neither English or Scottish, unless it suited them to pledge, unscrupulously, allegiance to one or the other. These lawless, unruly people raged interfamily warfare with each other, decimating the lives of the local people and carrying out bloodthirsty raids. Their

treacherous deeds have also added such words as "bereave" and "blackmail" to the English language.

The horrific stories of the Reivers have been passed down through the generations in the Border Ballads, and many of the Reivers family names are still known - the museum even offers a genealogy service, so that visitors find out if their ancestry goes back to these people. (Armstrongs, Bells, Charltons, Dacres and Elliots were just some of them). Perhaps the definitive Reiving story has been told in *The Steel Bonnets* by George MacDonald Fraser, author of the Flashman books. The city of Carlisle dates back far beyond those desperate days and Tullie House also has an extensive collection of Roman remains from both the city and the Cumbrian section of Hadrian's Wall.

A short walk from the Museum brings you to the **Linton Visitor Centre** (free) in Shaddongate which provides an insight into the city's industrial heritage. Standing next to a 280ft high chimney built in 1836 as part of what was once one of the largest cotton mills in Britain, the Centre has displays of hand weaving on original looms, informative displays and a selection of world famous fabrics and designer knitwear to buy.

The Old Town Hall, now an excellent Tourist Information Centre, dates from the 17th century and once housed the **Muckle Bell**, an alarm bell which, it was claimed, could be heard 11 miles away. The bell is now housed in the Tullie House Museum.

The **Guildhall Museum** (free) is housed in an unspoiled medieval building constructed by Richard of Redeness in 1407. Originally a town house, it provides an

Covered Market, Carlisle

ideal setting for illustrating the history of both the Guilds and the City. Several rooms are devoted to creating the atmosphere of trade Guilds such as the shoemakers, the butchers, and the glovers. There is a splendid early 19th century banner of the Weavers Guild and an impressive collection of 17th and 18th century Guild silver. Displays also feature other items relating to the history of Carlisle and include a magnificent ironbound Muniment Chest dating from the 14th century. Conducted tours of this remarkable Guildhall are available.

Not far from the museum is the **Citadel** which is often mistaken for the castle. In fact, this intimidating fortress with its well-preserved circular tower was built in 1543 on the orders of Henry VIII to strengthen the city's defences. Much of it was demolished in the early 1800s to improve access to the city centre but what remains is mightily impressive.

Across the road from the Citadel is the railway station. The first railway to Carlisle opened in July 1836 and Citadel Station, which opened in 1850, was built to serve seven different railway companies whose coats of arms are still displayed on the façade. So elegant was its interior - and much of it remains - that Carlisle was known as the "top hat" station. Today it is still an important centre of communications; Intercity trains from Glasgow and London now link with lines to Dumfries, Tyneside, West Cumbria, and Yorkshire, and it is, of course, the northern terminus of the famous **Settle-Carlisle Railway** line.

One of the last great mainline railways to be built in Britain - it was completed in 1876 - the Settle to Carlisle line takes in some of the most dramatic scenery that the north of England has to offer. Scenic it may be but the terrain caused the Victorian engineers many problems and it is thanks to their ingenuity and skill that

the line was ever finished. During the course of its 72 miles, the line crosses 20 viaducts and passes through 12 tunnels, each of which was constructed by an army of navvies who had little other than their strength and some dynamite to remove the rock.

Located on the northwestern edge of the city, **Kingmoor Nature Reserve** occupies an area of moorland given to the city way back in 1352 by Edward III. Citizens enjoyed the right to graze sheep on the moors and to cut peat for fuel. Later, Carlisle's first racecourse was established here with annual Guild races being held up until 1850. Then in 1913, Kingmoor became one of the first bird sanctuaries in England and today provides a peaceful retreat away from the bustle of the city. A half-mile circular path wanders through the woodland with gentle gradients of 1 in 20 making it fully accessible to wheelchairs and pushchairs, and with seats every 100 yards or so providing plenty of resting places.

AROUND CARLISLE

DALSTON
4 miles SW of Carlisle on the B5299

Lying on the banks of the River Caldew, Dalston became a thriving centre of the cotton industry in the late 18th century, thanks to George Hodgson of Manchester, who used the river as a source of power for the flax mill and four cotton mills that were established here. The local economy was sustained still further by the emergence of a forge and two corn mills.

At the eastern end of the village square stands St Michael's Church, believed to date back to Norman times, which can be approached via a memorial lychgate. One of the few red brick buildings to be found in the village is the Victorian chapel which stands somewhat hidden between several Georgian houses along the village green. From the car park near the bridge there's a pleasant 2-mile circular walk along the banks of the river.

BURGH BY SANDS
5 miles W of Carlisle off the B5307

On 7th July 1307, the body of King Edward I was laid out in the village church: he was already a dying man when he left Carlisle to march against his old enemy, Robert the Bruce. A monument to Edward was erected on the marshes and a later monument still marks the spot. At the time of the king's death, the **Church of St Michael** was already well over a century old and is possibly the earliest surviving example of a fortified church. Dating from 1181 and constructed entirely of stones from a fort on the Roman wall, the church was designed for protection against Border raids which is why its

tower has walls seven feet thick. The tower can only be entered through a strong iron grille.

PORT CARLISLE
12 miles W of Carlisle off the B5307

At one time, sailing boats could make their way by canal from Port Carlisle to the heart of the city of Carlisle. Boats were towed there, a journey that took about 1 hour 40 minutes, enabling Carlisle to be reached within a day by sea from Liverpool. The canal was later replaced by a railway which brought many Scandinavian emigrants through the village on their way to the United States and Canada. But the building of the Bowness railway viaduct altered the deep water channels, causing Port Carlisle to silt up. The railway was eventually dismantled but its old course can still be traced and stretches of it form part of the **Cumbrian Cycle Way**.

THE HIGHLAND LADDIE INN

Glasson, Wigton, Cumbria CA7 5DT
Tel: 016973 51839

The little hamlet of Glasson is hidden away in wonderfully unspoilt countryside, only half a mile from the rugged beauty of the Solway Coastline. This stretch of the coast is one of the few places where you can still see local fishermen still practising the ancient skill of Haaf Netting. Small though it is, Glasson boasts an outstanding hostelry, **The Highland Laddie Inn**, a quaint, olde worlde tavern some 200 years old which is built over the Roman Vallum. The landlady, Irene Bell, is a cheerful and friendly Scottish lass who is also a superb cook. The inn enjoys an excellent reputation for its beef and steaks which come from local herds and are justifiably billed as "The Best of British". Lunches are served from noon until 2pm, (except Tuesdays in winter), when the appetising menu includes such tasty snacks as the inn's very own Roast Hot Beef Baguette with Onion Gravy. Something simple or more substantial is always available. A typical choice from the evening menu, (served from 7pm to 9pm on weekdays, 6pm to 9pm at weekends), might include a mouth-watering juicy 10oz Fillet or 12oz Sirloin Steak cooked to your liking and with a choice of sauces if desired, Half Honey Roast Duckling, many varieties of fish dishes, and locally-produced Cumberland Sauce. The inn also has a quality Tea Room serving home made cakes, scones, tray-bakes, tea and coffee which is open daily in summer, and on Thursdays and weekends out of season.

THE KINGS ARMS

Bowness-on-Solway,
Cumbria CA7 5AF
Tel: 016973 51426

From the beach at Bowness, (now in the care of the National Trust), an ancient footpath leads up the hill to **The Kings Arms**. In days past, this path was a well-frequented route for smugglers, (one of whom, Thomas Stoal, has a rather fine tombstone in the village graveyard). How much of the smugglers' contraband liquor found its way into the cellars of The Kings Arms is impossible to say but the inn was certainly already here since it was built in the late 1700s. Today, its owned and run by David and Margaret Wiseman, their daughter Janice and son-in-law David Milne, along with the Milnes' sons Christopher, Stephen and Jonathon.

Various members of the family look after the lunchtime menu but Margaret takes over in the evening. Whenever you eat here, however, you'll find an excellent selection of home cooked dishes with specialities that include fresh wild salmon, pheasant and wild duck in season, and delicious apple pie at any time of year. Food is available every lunchtime, from noon until 2pm, and in the evenings from 6pm to 9pm. This quiet corner of the county is a wonderful place for a restful holiday with all the major Lake District attractions within easy reach. The Kings Arms has 3 guest bedrooms, (2 family rooms, 1 twin), which are available all year round. Children are welcome and there are special deals for longer stays.

BRIAR LEA HOUSE

Brampton Road, Longtown, Cumbria CA6 5TN
Tel/Fax: 01228 791538
e-mail: briarlea@cltministries.co.uk
website: www.cltministries.co.uk

Only a minute's drive from the A7, **Briar Lea House** offers excellent bed & breakfast accommodation in a comfortable modern dwelling set in its own grounds and with its own heated swimming pool. With Gretna Green just 4 miles away and Hadrian's Wall about 8 miles distant, Briar Lea provides a good base from which to explore the Borders and the Lake District, or simply as a place to relax and recuperate. Alongside the B&B, Briar Lea is the base of Centre-Light Trust Ministries who plan to offer fellowship times of praise and worship, short conferences and training days. Alternatively, visitors can hold their own events here. Open all year round, Briar Lea has 3 guest bedrooms, all on the ground floor and all en suite with one having a jacuzzi bath. Children are welcome and high chairs and cots are available if required. A full English breakfast is included in the tariff and packed meals are available on request. Evening meals are not served but the owners Keith and Kathy Mashiter can guide you to good eating places in the neighbourhood. During the lifetime of this book, Keith and Kathy expect to have a caravan site in their paddock ready for tourers and also to be serving teas, coffees, cakes and snacks in the afternoon.

This stretch of the Solway coastline provided the setting for Walter Scott's novel, *Redgauntlet*, and the fortified farmhouse by the roadside at nearby Drumburgh is said to be the "White Ladies" of the novel.

BOWNESS-ON-SOLWAY
14 miles W of Carlisle off the B5307

Hadrian's Wall continues along the Solway coast to Bowness and many of the sandstone cottages around here contain stones from the Wall. Some of these stones can easily be identified, such as the small inscribed altar let into a barn near the King's Arms. The Roman fort of Maia once covered a 7-acre site here but today there's only a plaque explaining where it used to be. Bowness is sometimes said to be the end of the Wall but in fact it just turned a corner here and continued south along the coast for another 40 miles.

One local story tells that, in 1626, some Scotsmen crossed the Solway and stole the Bowness church bells. They were spotted, chased, and forced to lighten their boats by throwing the bells overboard. Later, the men of Bowness crossed the Firth and, in retaliation seized the bells of Middlebie, Dumfries.

LONGTOWN
9 miles N of Carlisle on the A7

Situated on the north side of Hadrian's Wall, only a couple of miles from the Scottish border, this is the last town in England. Its position on the River Esk and so close to the border, has influenced its history from earliest times. The Romans occupied this land and they were followed by other conquerors. The legendary King Arthur attempted to organise the Northern Britons against the pagan hordes who tried to settle and control this territory. In 573AD the mighty battle of Ardderyd was fought here and, according

THE MARCH BANK HOTEL & SPORTSMANS RESTAURANT

Scotch Dyke, North of Longtown, Cumbria CA6 5XP
Tel: 01228 791325

Set back from the A7, just 10 miles from Junction 44 of the M6, **The March Bank Hotel & Sportsmans Restaurant** enjoys the distinction of being the last property in England before crossing the Scottish border. This charming Victorian villa was built in 1870 by an American doctor who certainly selected an outstanding position for his spacious residence. It overlooks the beautiful Esk Valley, noted for its salmon and sea trout, and stands in four acres of mature gardens where banks of rhododendrons present a brilliant spectacle in early summer. The house became a hotel in the 1960s but it still retains a warm, country house atmosphere, its elegantly proportioned rooms attractively decorated and furnished with lots of period pieces, paintings and prints. Richard and Clair Moore bought the hotel in 1988 and it was they who created the Sportsmans Restaurant, noted quality cuisine with local game and smoked salmon dishes

among the specialities - and not a chip to be seen! The intimate licensed restaurant with its large window overlooking the garden seats just 20 diners so it's advisable to book, especially at weekends. Guests can also eat in the cosy bar, full of sporting trophies or, on warm days, outside. This outstanding hotel has 5 attractive guest bedrooms, all of them en suite and equipped with Teasmaids and television, and one of them with a 4-poster bed. Other amenities at The March Bank include a freezer and drying facilities and ample parking. Credit cards are accepted.

MIDTODHILLS FARM

Roadhead, Carlisle, Cumbria CA6 6PF
Tel/Fax: 016977 48213
e-mail:bewcastlecott@aol.com
website: holidaycottagescarlisle.co.uk

For a restful holiday surrounded by the magnificent scenery of North Cumbria, the self-catering cottages at **Midtodhills Farm** would be hard to beat. The 4 cottages overlook the beautiful Lyne Valley and Bewcastle Fells, an area rich in wildlife with moors, tarns, lochs, wooded river valleys and gentle pastureland to explore. Within easy reach are facilities for golf, fishing and bird watching, while at Kielder Water, almost on the doorstep, is an unrivalled range of water activities. Even closer, there are farm trails, two miles of river and a guided tour in which children can come face to face with rare breeds in the Pets Corner. In addition, the local school's swimming pool is available to guests between May and September. The cottages can sleep between 2 to 8 people. The largest, Arch View, which sleeps up to 8, is a splendid barn conversion

with an ETB Highly Commended 5 Keys rating. It has 4 bedrooms, one of them on the ground floor which is suitable for disabled guests. The 2-bedroomed Rigg Foot Cottage (Commended 4 Keys) sleeps 2-4, has a double bedroom with a 4-poster bed and, like the other cottages, has its own garden complete with furniture and barbecue. River View (4-6 guests) and Forest View (2-4 guests) both have a 5 Keys rating and are furnished and equipped to the same high standards. All the cottages are available all year round and pets are welcome by arrangement.

CROSSINGS INN

Roweltown, Roadhead, Carlisle, Cumbria CA6 6LG
Tel: 016977 48620

As its name indicates, the **Crossings Inn** stands at a country crossroads, apparently miles from anywhere but actually only a short drive from Carlisle and the Scottish border. When it was built as an alehouse, it stood on the old drovers' road which is now the B6318, the longest B road in England incidentally. Christopher Hogg, the son of a local farmer who has lived nearby all his life, bought the inn early in 2000 and has given it a new lease of life - The Crossings is now the hub of this hamlet and of the surrounding villages.

The inn has an inviting olde worlde atmosphere enhanced by its real open fires. Christopher is an accomplished chef whose across-the-board menu is available Friday, Saturday and Sunday evenings from 6.30pm until 9pm, and at Sunday lunchtimes from noon until 2pm. A speciality of the house is

the variety of tasty sauces Christopher has created to complement his appetising dishes. The range of excellent, well-kept ales includes Theakstons, John Smiths Smooth, Youngers, plus Theakstons Mild, Beamish, two draught lagers and bottled cider. If you are looking for somewhere to stay in this peaceful part of the county, the inn has 2 guest bedrooms, (1 double, 1 twin), both of them en suite and comfortably furnished and decorated. A hearty breakfast is included in the tariff and there are special rates for longer stays.

to legend, 80,000 men were slain.

Until 1750 Longtown was a small hamlet of mud dwellings. Dr Robert Graham, an 18th century clergyman, proposed the building of the Esk bridge which was completed in 1756, and it was this venture that led to Longtown's establishment as a bustling border town. These days it has some fine individual buildings and broad, tree-lined terraces of colour-washed houses.

On the outskirts of Longtown is **Arthuret Church**. The earliest records of the church date from 1150 and it was originally served by the monks of Jedburgh. But it is thought that the earliest church here may have been founded by St Kentigern in the 6th century and most recently, research has led people to believe that King Arthur was actually interred here after his last battle, Camboglanna, was fought a few miles east of Longtown at Gilsland. The present church, dedicated to St Michael and All Angels, was built in 1609, financed by a general collection throughout the realm which James I ordered after a report that the people of Arthuret Church were without faith or religion. The people that he referred to, of course, were the infamous Reivers, ungoverned by either English or Scottish laws.

Archie Armstrong, favourite Court Jester to James I and later to Charles I, is buried in the churchyard which also contains an unusual stone cross. It consists of two parts of an early medieval wheel-head cross clamped together onto a tapering shaft with 19th century decorations.

BEWCASTLE
14 miles NE of Carlisle off the B6318

Roman legionaries assigned to the fort at what is now Bewcastle must certainly have felt that they had drawn the short straw. The fort stood all on its own, about 9 miles north of Hadrian's Wall, guarding a crossing over the Kirk Beck. The site covered around 6 acres most of which is now occupied by the ruins of a Norman castle. Most of the south wall is still standing but little else does and the castle is best admired for its setting rather than its architecture.

A much more impressive survival dominates the village churchyard. Here stands the **Bewcastle Cross**, erected around 670AD and one of the oldest and finest stone crosses in Europe. Standing over 13 feet high, its intricate Celtic carvings have survived the centuries of weathering and much of the runic inscription can still be made out in the yellow sandstone. One of the carvings, a semicircle with 13 radiating lines, 3 of which have crossbars, is believed to be a sophisticated sundial which not only indicated the 12 hours of the Roman clock but also the 3 "tides" of the Saxon day - morning, noon and eventide.

WETHERAL
4 miles E of Carlisle off the A69

Wetheral stands above the River Eden, over which runs an impressive railway viaduct, carrying the Tyne Valley Line, that was built by Francis Giles in 1830. Wetheral Parish Church lies below the village beside the river and contains a poignant sculpture by Joseph Nollekens, of the dying Lady Mary Howard clasping her dead baby. Nearby, occupying a lovely riverside setting, is another of the Eden Benchmarks, a sculptured bench in St Bee's sandstone by Tim Shutter, entitled "Flight of Fancy".

St Constantine was the local patron and the church is dedicated to the **Holy Trinity, St Constantine and St Mary**. Constantine is said to have lived in caves in what are now National Trust

CORBY BRIDGE INN

Corby Bridge, Carlisle,
Cumbria CA4 8LL
Tel: 01228 560221

When it was built in 1838, the **Corby Bridge Inn** was known as the Railway Hotel since it was designed to cater for passengers on the main Carlisle to Newcastle railway which runs close by. Recognised as a building of special architectural interest, the inn has been awarded a Grade II Listed status.

Of great interest to railway enthusiasts, the inn will also be appreciated by anyone who values a good traditional hostelry with lots of atmosphere and many original features such as the open fires. Barbara and Les Griffiths have owned the inn since 1994 and have built up a loyal clientele for their cosy, warm and welcoming pub. All the time-honoured pub games - pool, darts, dominoes and backgammon are available and there's a pleasant beer garden at the rear where children can feed the chickens and goats. The inn enjoys an excellent reputation for its food, with a full menu of appetising and wholesome home cooked meals, including vegetarian options, available from noon until 8pm every day except on Mondays when only evening meals are served. To accompany your meal, there's a wide choice of beverages which includes 3 real ales and, during the summer, a potent Scrumpy cider. Conveniently located close to Carlisle and the Borders, the inn has 3 guest bedrooms, (1 family, 2 single rooms) available all year round.

woodlands alongside the river, a location known as Constantine's Caves. (The caves were also used later by the nearby Priory to conceal their valuables during the Reiver raids). Constantine died as a martyr in AD 657 and a life-sized statue of him can be seen in the grounds of Corby Castle to the south of the village. The castle, with its impressive 13th century **Keep** and terraced gardens overlooking the Eden, is usually open during the summer months.

During the reign of William Rufus one of his barons, Ranulph Meschin, founded a priory for Benedictine monks at Wetheral above a red-rock gorge of the River Eden. It was a dependency of the Abbey of St Mary at York and the prior and the monastery served the church and domestic chapel of Corby Castle. All that remains now is the imposing 3-storey gatehouse.

WARWICK
4 miles E of Carlisle on the A69

It is well worth visiting the village's remarkable Norman Church of St Leonard which consists of a restored nave and chancel with a curiously buttressed apse and a splendid arch leading into a modern vestibule. Warwick's other church, St Paul's, is reputed to have been commissioned by a wealthy Carlisle man who took umbrage at a sermon preached at St Leonard's.

CROSBY-ON-EDEN
4 miles NE of Carlisle off the A689

The tiny hamlet of High Crosby stands on the hillside overlooking the River Eden; the small village of Low Crosby sits beside the river, clustered around a Victorian sandstone church. Inside the church there's a modern square pulpit, intricately carved with pomegranates, wheat and vines. Apparently, it was carved from one half of a tree felled nearby; the other half was used to create a second pulpit which was installed in the newly-built Liverpool Cathedral.

A couple of miles east of Crosby, **The Solway Aviation Museum** is one of only a few museums located on a "live" airfield, in this case Carlisle Airport. Opened in 1997, the museum is home to several British jet aircraft of the 1950s and '60s, amongst them the mighty Vulcan.

Other exhibits include a wartime air raid shelter where a video presentation explains the story behind the museum, displays of the Blue Streak rocket programme, testing for which took place only a few miles from here, and a very impressive engine room which houses one of Frank Whittle's first development jet engines.

CROSBY LODGE COUNTRY HOUSE HOTEL & RESTAURANT

High Crosby, Crosby-on-Eden, Carlisle, Cumbria CA6 4QZ
Tel: 01228 573618 Fax: 01228 573428
e-mail: enquiries@crosbylodge.co.uk
website: www.crosbylodge.co.uk

"That excellent commodious MANSION called Crosby Lodge", - so begins a newspaper notice of 1831 informing readers that the Lodge is "To be LET and may be Entered upon at Candlemas next". Today, this commodious mansion has become the **Crosby Lodge Country House Hotel & Restaurant** but most of the particulars given in the old newspaper still apply. "The House is delightfully situated at a short distance from the River Eden, in a fine Sporting Country, has an extensive Lawn in front, and commands a fine view of the Vale of Eden and distant mountains". With its crenellated towers the Lodge has something of the appearance of a fortified manor but in fact it was built between 1807 and 1808 as a stately residence for David Kennedy, later a Deputy Lieutenant of Cumberland.

The present owners, Michael and Patricia Sedgwick, bought this lovely old property, now a Grade II listed building, in October 1970 and less than a year later, after major renovations, opened as a hotel restaurant in September 1971. Over the years, the Sedgwick family's personal attention has ensured that a high standard of service is maintained. In particular, the Crosby Lodge Restaurant has earned a well-deserved reputation for its first class cuisine. Chef James Sedgwick, aided by Roger who has been here for 26 years, and their team combine top quality, fresh produce with mouth-watering presentation, while the award-winning wine list, specially selected by Philippa Sedgwick to create an adventure, provides the perfect complement for any meal.

With its 4.5 acres of outstanding grounds and its charming walled garden, Crosby Lodge provides the perfect backdrop for weddings, anniversaries and parties, and is also well-equipped to cater for and accommodate business or social events. There are 9 superior guest rooms in the main building, plus two more in the converted stables overlooking the walled garden. All the bedrooms are en suite, individually designed and equipped with colour television, hair dryer, direct dial telephones and extra PC points. Guests can stay on either a bed & breakfast, or dinner, bed and breakfast basis. For those who take the latter option there are discounts for stays of more than three nights.

THE STAG INN

Low Crosby, Crosby-on-Eden, nr Carlisle,
Cumbria CA6 4QN
Tel: 01228 573210 Fax: 01228 573445

Located on the main road of this tiny hamlet, **The Stag Inn** is very eye-catching with its walls of warm pink local stone, hanging baskets and tubs of flowers. A listed building, it was originally a farmhouse before becoming an alehouse alongside what was then a main road with lots of stagecoach traffic. Inside, there's plenty of evidence of the inn's antiquity - flagstone floors, massive oak beams and an impressive old fireplace which brightens up any chilly evening. Peter and Carol Milnes are mine hosts at this delightful old hostelry. They took over here in 1999 but Peter, a chef by profession, has been in the hospitality business for more than 30 years. His appetising menu of traditional English dishes is

available every lunchtime (noon until 2pm) and evening (6pm to 9pm), and served either in the characterful restaurant upstairs or in the bar areas, one of which, the snug, is non-smoking. The regular menu is supplemented by a Specials Board which is changed every week. If you want to eat in the restaurant at the weekend, booking ahead is strongly recommended. Children are welcome and credit cards accepted. To accompany your meal, the bar stocks a wide range of popular beverages, including a choice of 4 real ales during the season, 3 out of season. In good weather, customers can take advantage of the pleasant little beer garden to the rear.

THE BELTED WILL INN

Hallbankgate, Brampton, Cumbria CA8 2NJ
Tel: 016977 46236 Fax: 016977 46900

No one is quite sure how **The Belted Will Inn** acquired its unusual name. The most likely explanation is that it refers to Lord William Howard (1563-1640) who lived at nearby Naworth Castle. His exploits against the invading Scots were celebrated by Walter Scott in his *Lay of the Last Minstrel* where he refers to Howard having a sword

> *Hung in a broad and studded belt:*
> *Hence, in rude phrase, the Borderers still*
> *Call'd noble Howard, Belted Will.*

Today, this charming old hostelry is owned and run by the Starkey family: Peter, who has lived in the village all his life, his partner, Lynn, his son Stephen and his girl friend Alyson. A free house, the inn offers a good range of quality ales and serves quality home cooked food every weekday evening between 6.30pm and 9pm, and from noon

until 9pm on Saturday and Sunday. Such is the inn's reputation for good food, it's definitely advisable to book at the weekends. Darts and pool are available at any time and if you're here on the first Thursday of the month, feel free to join in the regular Quiz Night. The Starkeys also lay on occasional live music sessions, usually on a Saturday. If you are planning to stay in this attractive corner of the county, the Belted Will has 4 comfortable guest bedrooms, two doubles, one family and one three-quarter single.

BRAMPTON

Nestling in the heart of the lovely Irthing Valley, Brampton is a delightful little town where the Wednesday market has been held since 1252, authorised by a charter granted by Henry III. Overlooking the Market Place is the town's most striking building, the octagonal **Moot Hall** topped by a handsome clock tower. There has been a Moot Hall here since 1648 but the present Hall was built in 1817 by Lord Carlisle. The iron stocks at the foot of a double flight of external stairs were last used in 1836.

Just around the corner, in **High Cross Street**, is the house (now a shop) which once witnessed one of the high points in Bonnie Prince Charles' rebellion of 1745. It was here that the Prince stayed during the siege of Carlisle and it was here, on November 17, 1745 that the Mayor and Aldermen presented him with the keys to the city. A few months later, following the Prince's defeat, six of his supporters were hanged on the Capon Tree on the south side of the town and in sight of the Scottish hills. The tree survived until the last century and in its place there now stands a monument commemorating the event.

Just off the market place is **St Martin's Church** which was rebuilt in 1878 and contains one of the undiscovered secrets of the area - some magnificent stained glass windows designed by one of the founder members of the pre-Raphaelite brotherhood, Edward Burne-Jones. It was his fellow-member of the brotherhood, Philip Webb,

who designed the church and insisted that contemporary stained glass should be installed.

AROUND BRAMPTON

LOW ROW
3 miles E of Brampton off the A69

Within easy reach of the town is **Hadrian's Wall**, just 3 miles to the north. If you've ever wondered where the Wall's missing masonry went to, look no further than the fabric of **Lanercost Priory**, just outside the town. An impressive red sandstone ruin set in secluded woodland, the priory was founded in 1166 by Robert de Vaux. In 1306, Edward I spent six months at the priory recuperating after his skirmishes with the Scots. Lanercost is well preserved and its scale is a reminder that it was a grand complex in its heyday. However, the priory suffered greatly in the

Hadrians Wall

border raids of the 13th and 14th centuries. One such raid is known to have been led by William Wallace, an early campaigner for Scottish independence from English rule. When the Priory was closed in 1536, the sandstone blocks were recycled once again for houses in the town. But much of the Priory's great north aisle remains intact, set in a romantic and hauntingly beautiful position in the valley of the River Irthing.

Also most impressive is **Naworth Castle**, built around 1335 in its present form by Lord Dacre as an important

The Railway Inn

Low Row, Brampton, Cumbria CA8 2LE
Tel: 016977 46222 Fax: 016977 46927
e-mail: railwayinnlowrow@aol.com
website: www.therailwayinn.org.uk

Built as a byre and converted around 150 years ago to an inn, **The Railway Inn** is hidden away in its own grounds in the picturesque village of Low Row. It takes its name from the main Carlisle to Newcastle railway line which passes nearby. Steve and Val Doughty bought this charming old tavern in late 2000 and have made it the centre of village life, popular with locals and visitors alike. The restaurant is open Friday and Saturday evenings, and also at Sunday lunchtime when a traditional Sunday roast dinner with all the trimmings (and with a vegetarian option) is available. (Booking is advisable). During the week a snack menu is served. Steve

and Val vary the menu from time to time but you'll always find a good choice of wholesome and appetising choices. Meals are served in the separate restaurant or, in good weather, you can take your drinks to one of the picnic tables outside. Credit cards are accepted.

A visit to the Railway Inn can easily be combined with two nearby visitor attractions. Lanercost Priory is an impressive red sandstone ruin which was founded in 1166 and built largely with stones cannibalised from the other historic attraction close by, Hadrian's Wall. Despite the depredations, this is one of the most impressive stretches of the 1800-year-old Wall.

Long Byres at Talkin Head

Talkin Head, Brampton, Cumbria CA8 1LT
Tel: 016977 3435 Fax: 016977 2228
e-mail: harriet@talkinhead.demon.co.uk
website: www.talkinhead.demon.co.uk

Visitors to **Long Byres at Talkin Head** will find themselves sharing this 120 acre working farm with a herd of Exmoor ponies, another of young cows, as well as red squirrels, hares, badgers and foxes. Yet more wildlife can be seen in the nearby RSPB Geltsdale reserve. Guests at Long Byres are welcome to explore the farm, especially the lovely stream which is ideal for picnics, paddling and dam building. Long Byres has been offering self-catering holidays in this lovely part of Cumbria since 1979. There are 7 cottages, all ingeniously converted from old farm buildings and all featuring attractive quarry tile floors and exposed beams with pine panelling. The bathrooms all have a bath with shower; the kitchens are very well equipped, and a colour TV is provided, along with all bed linen and towels, and a cot if required. The cottages all enjoy charming views across the surrounding countryside and sleep from 2 to 4/5 people. Wonderfully peaceful and relaxing, Long Byres is nevertheless within easy reach of many visitor attractions such as Hadrian's Wall and the historic city of Carlisle.

border stronghold. The castle passed through the female line to the Howard family after the last Lord Dacre was killed as a child, improbable as it might seem, by falling off his rocking horse. Now owned by the Howard family, Earls of Carlisle, the Castle is private but there are good views from the minor road off the A69 that passes in front of it - the scene is particularly attractive in spring when the lawns are ablaze with daffodils. Pre-booked parties are welcome all year round and the Castle has become a popular venue for weddings and corporate events.

The Castle's supreme glory is the Great Hall, hung with French tapestries and guarded by four unique heraldic beasts holding aloft their family pennants. The Long Gallery extends for 116ft and was used as a guardroom. It now houses an interesting collection of paintings, many brought together by the 9th Earl, George Howard. He entertained many pre-Raphaelite painters here, but the only surviving example of their work is Burne-Jones' *Battle of Flodden* - the rest were destroyed by a fire in 1844. In the courtyard there are some intriguing medieval latrines!

The area around Brampton had good reason to be grateful to the Dacres of Naworth, who as Wardens of the Northern Marches protected it against marauding Scots. However, the townspeople of Brampton in Victorian times must have had mixed feelings about a later descendant, Rosalind, wife of the 9th Earl of Carlisle. An enthusiastic supporter of total abstinence, she contrived to get most of the small town's forty public houses and drinking rooms closed.

South of Brampton are **Gelt Woods**, lying in a deep sandstone ravine carved by the fast-flowing River Gelt. By the river is an inscribed rock called **Written Rock** which is thought to have been carved by a Roman standard bearer in AD207.

TALKIN
2 miles S of Brampton off the B6413

Talkin Tarn, now the focus of a 120-acre country park, has been a popular place for watersports for over 100 years. Glacial in origin, the Tarn was formed some 10,000 years ago and is continually replenished by underground streams. Modern day visitors can sail, windsurf, canoe or hire one of the original wooden rowing boats. Fishing licences are available, there's a Nature Trail and an orienteering course, a play area for children under 8, and guided walks are also available. The park is a peaceful place but, according to legend, beneath the surface of the lake there is a submerged village destroyed by a wrathful god, the ruins of which can still be seen below the water surface in a certain light.

GILSLAND
7 miles E of Brampton on the B6318

Located in one of the most picturesque setting along the whole length of Hadrian's Wall and overlooking the River Irthing, **Birdoswald Roman Fort** (English heritage) is one of the best preserved mile-castles along the Wall and unique in that all the components of the Roman frontier system can be found here. Set high on a plateau with magnificent views over the surrounding countryside, the early turf wall, built in AD 122, can be seen along with the fort. Originally, this fort would have covered five acres and it may have been the base for up to 500 cavalry and 1000 foot soldiers. During its 300 year occupation, the fort underwent substantial alterations and the turf wall, the stone wall, Harrow's Scar Milecastle, and the fort itself are all visible reminders of the occupation (see panel on page 198).

HOWARD HOUSE FARM

Gilsland, nr Brampton,
Cumbria CA8 7AJ
Tel: 016977 47295
website: www.stayonafarm.co.uk

One of the best-preserved sections of Hadrian's Wall runs for several miles to the east and west of Gilsland and visitors at **Howard House Farm** enjoy a grand view of this famous World Heritage Site. Located only half a mile from the Northumberland border, the 150-year-old farmhouse stands 600ft high on the hillside and is surrounded by a 250-acre working beef and sheep farm. Swaledale ewes crossed with a blue-faced Leicester ram comprise the main flock but also on the farm are 20 Jacob ewes, a very ancient breed which was mentioned in the 1599 translation of the book of Genesis. As a hobby, Elizabeth Woodmass spins the fleeces which produce an attractive brown and cream mixture.

Elizabeth and her husband John, the fourth generation to run the farm, have been welcoming bed & breakfast visitors to Howard House since the early 1970s and they both place great emphasis on making their guests feel at home. Children are encouraged to help feed the goats and to watch a working farm in action. The spacious old farmhouse has 3 guest bedrooms - a ground floor family room, and a double en suite and a twin room upstairs. These upstairs rooms command magnificent views across thousands of acres of unspoilt countryside. A full English breakfast is included in the tariff, (with fresh free range eggs from the farm, naturally), and pets are allowed in the downstairs room.

BIRDOSWALD ROMAN FORT

Gilsland, Carlisle, Cumbria CA8 7DD
Tel: 016977 47602 Fax: 016877 47605 e-mail:
birdoswald@dial.pipex.com

Located in one of the most picturesque setting along the whole length of Hadrian's Wall and overlooking the River Irthing, **Birdoswald Roman Fort** is one of the best preserved mile-castles along the Wall and unique in that all the components of the Roman frontier system can be found here. This World Heritage Site is set high on a plateau with magnificent views over the surrounding countryside. The early turf wall, built in AD122, can be seen along with the fort, and a superb stretch of the Wall stretches from the fort for a third of a mile. Originally, this fort would have covered five acres and it may have been the base for up to 1000 soldiers. During its 300-year occupation, the fort underwent substantial alterations and the turf wall, the stone wall, Harrow's Scar Milecastle, and the fort itself are all visible reminders of the occupation.

Between April and October, history comes to life at Birdoswald with a wide variety of events - battle re-enactments, music and drama, and the site also has an interactive Visitor Centre, a gift and tea shop, and a picnic area. In 1999, a residential study centre with a range of excellent study facilities as well as accommodation was added to the site's amenities.

It is thanks to Henry Norman, a Victorian romantic and owner of the land on which the fort stands, that today's visitors can see these wonderful remains. An enthusiastic archaeologist, Norman extended the farmhouse, built the tower, and carried out the major excavation work to the fort, walls, and gates.

Gilsland village is also known for its sulphur spring and there was once a convalescent home for miners and shipyard workers here. It is now owned by the Co-operative Society and people still drink the waters as a cure for arthritis and rheumatism. Near the spring is the **Popping Stone**, traditionally the place where a man "popped the question" to his lover. It was here that Sir Walter Scott successfully proposed to Charlotte Carpenter.

List of
Tourist Information Centres

ALSTON MOOR TIC

The Town Hall, Alston, CA9 3RF

Tel: (01434) 382244

AMBLESIDE TIC

Central Buildings, Market Cross, Ambleside

Tel: (015394) 32582

APPLEBY-IN-WESTMORLAND TIC

Moot Hall, Boroughgate, Appleby

Tel: (017683) 51177

BARROW-IN-FURNESS TIC

Forum 28, Duke Street, Barrow-in-Furness

Tel: (01229) 894784

BOWNESS-ON-WINDERMERE TIC

Glebe Road, Bowness-on-Windermere

Tel: (015394) 42895

BRAMPTON TIC

The Moot Hall, Brampton

Tel: (016977) 3433

BROUGHTON-IN-FURNESS TIC

Town Hall, The Square, Broughton-in-Furness

Tel: (01229) 716115

CARLISLE TIC

The Old Town Hall, Carlisle

Tel: (01228) 625600

COCKERMOUTH TIC

The Town Hall, Cockermouth

Tel: (01900) 822634

CONISTON TIC

Ruskin Avenue, Coniston

Tel: (015394) 41533

EGREMONT TIC

Lowes Court Gallery, 12 Main Street, Egremont

Tel: (01946) 820693

GRANGE-OVER-SANDS TIC

Victoria Hall, Main Street, Grange-over-Sands

Tel: (015395) 34026

GRASMERE TIC

Red Bank Road, Grasmere

Tel: (015394) 35245

HAWKSHEAD TIC

Main Car Park, Hawkshead

Tel: (015394) 36525

KENDAL TIC

Town Hall, Highgate, Kendal

Tel: (01539) 725758

KESWICK TIC

Moot Hall, Market Square, Keswick

Tel: (017687) 72645

KIRKBY LONSDALE TIC

24 Main Street, Kirkby Lonsdale

Tel: (015242) 71437

KIRKBY STEPHEN TIC

Market Street, Kirkby Stephen

Tel: (017683) 71199

LONGTOWN TIC

74 Swan Street, Longtown

Tel: (01228) 792835

MARYPORT TIC

Maryport Maritime Museum,
1 Senhouse Street, Maryport

Tel: (01900) 813738

PENRITH TIC

Robinson's School, Middlegate, Penrith

Tel: (01768) 867466

POOLEY BRIDGE TIC

The Square, Pooley Bridge

Tel: (017684) 86530

SEATOLLER TIC

Seatoller Barn, Borrowdale, Keswick

Tel: (017687) 77294

SEDBERGH TIC

72 Main Street, Sedbergh

Tel: (015396) 20125

SELLAFIELD TIC

Sellafield Visitor Centre, Seascale

Tel: (019467) 76510

SILLOTH-ON-SOLWAY TIC

10 Criffell Street, Silloth-on-Solway

Tel: (016973) 31944

ULLSWATER TIC

Main Car Park, Glenridding, Ullswater

Tel: (017684) 82414

ULVERSTON TIC

Coronation Hall, County Square, Ulverston

Tel: (01229) 587120

WATERHEAD TIC

Waterhead Car Park, Ambleside

Tel: (015394) 32729

WHITEHAVEN TIC

Market Hall, Market Place, Whitehaven

Tel: (01946) 852939

WINDERMERE TIC

Victoria Street, Windermere

Tel: (015394) 46499

WORKINGTON TIC

Carnegie Arts Centre, Finkle Street,
Workington

Tel: (01900) 606699

Index of Towns, Villages and Places of Interest

List of Advertisers

Hidden Places Order Form

To order any of our publications just fill in the payment details below and complete the order form *overleaf*. For orders of less than 4 copies please add £1 per book for postage and packing. Orders over 4 copies are P & P free.

Please Complete Either:

I enclose a cheque for £ [_____] made payable to Travel Publishing Ltd

Or:

Card No: [_____]

Expiry Date: [_____]

Signature: [_____]

NAME: [_____]

ADDRESS: [_____]

POSTCODE: [_____]

TEL NO: [_____]

Please either send or telephone your order to:

Travel Publishing Ltd   Tel : 0118 981 7777
7a Apollo House   Fax: 0118 982 0077
Calleva Park
Aldermaston
Berks, RG7 8TN

	PRICE	QUANTITY	VALUE

Hidden Places Regional Titles

	PRICE	QUANTITY	VALUE
Cambs & Lincolnshire	£7.99	....	....
Chilterns	£8.99	....	....
Cornwall	£8.99	....	....
Derbyshire	£7.99	....	....
Devon	£8.99	....	....
Dorset, Hants & Isle of Wight	£8.99	....	....
East Anglia	£8.99	....	....
Gloucestershire & Wiltshire	£7.99	....	....
Heart of England	£7.99	....	....
Hereford, Worcs & Shropshire	£7.99	....	....
Highlands & Islands	£7.99	....	....
Kent	£8.99	....	....
Lake District & Cumbria	£8.99	....	....
Lancashire & Cheshire	£8.99	....	....
Lincolnshire	£8.99	....	....
Northumberland & Durham	£8.99	....	....
Somerset	£7.99	....	....
Sussex	£7.99	....	....
Thames Valley	£7.99	....	....
Yorkshire	£7.99	....	....

Hidden Places National Titles

	PRICE	QUANTITY	VALUE
England	£9.99	....	....
Ireland	£9.99	....	....
Scotland	£9.99	....	....
Wales	£9.99	....	....

Hidden Inns Titles

	PRICE	QUANTITY	VALUE
South	£5.99	....	....
South East	£5.99	....	....
South and Central Scotland	£5.99	....	....
Wales	£5.99	....	....
Welsh Borders	£5.99	....	....
West Country	£5.99	....	....

For orders of less than 4 copies please add £1 per book for postage & packing. Orders over 4 copies P & P free.

Hidden Places Order Form

To order any of our publications just fill in the payment details below and complete the order form **overleaf**. For orders of less than 4 copies please add £1 per book for postage and packing. Orders over 4 copies are P & P free.

Please Complete Either:

I enclose a cheque for £ [_____] made payable to Travel Publishing Ltd

Or:

Card No: [_____]

Expiry Date: [_____]

Signature: [_____]

NAME: [_____]

ADDRESS: [_____]

POSTCODE: [_____]

TEL NO: [_____]

Please either send or telephone your order to:

Travel Publishing Ltd
7a Apollo House
Calleva Park
Aldermaston
Berks, RG7 8TN

Tel : 0118 981 7777
Fax: 0118 982 0077

	PRICE	QUANTITY	VALUE

Hidden Places Regional Titles

	PRICE		
Cambs & Lincolnshire	£7.99	....	....
Chilterns	£8.99	....	....
Cornwall	£8.99	....	....
Derbyshire	£7.99	....	....
Devon	£8.99	....	....
Dorset, Hants & Isle of Wight	£8.99	....	....
East Anglia	£8.99	....	....
Gloucestershire & Wiltshire	£7.99	....	....
Heart of England	£7.99	....	....
Hereford, Worcs & Shropshire	£7.99	....	....
Highlands & Islands	£7.99	....	....
Kent	£8.99	....	....
Lake District & Cumbria	£8.99	....	....
Lancashire & Cheshire	£8.99	....	....
Lincolnshire	£8.99	....	....
Northumberland & Durham	£8.99	....	....
Somerset	£7.99	....	....
Sussex	£7.99	....	....
Thames Valley	£7.99	....	....
Yorkshire	£7.99	....	....

Hidden Places National Titles

England	£9.99	....	....
Ireland	£9.99	....	....
Scotland	£9.99	....	....
Wales	£9.99	....	....

Hidden Inns Titles

South	£5.99	....	....
South East	£5.99	....	....
South and Central Scotland	£5.99	....	....
Wales	£5.99	....	....
Welsh Borders	£5.99	....	....
West Country	£5.99	....	....

For orders of less than 4 copies please add £1 per book for
postage & packing. Orders over 4 copies P & P free.

Hidden Places Reader Reaction

The *Hidden Places* research team would like to receive reader's comments on any visitor attractions or places reviewed in the book and also recommendations for suitable entries to be included in the next edition. This will help ensure that the *Hidden Places* series continues to provide its readers with useful information on the more interesting, unusual or unique features of each attraction or place ensuring that their stay in the local area is an enjoyable and stimulating experience. To provide your comments or recommendations would you please complete the forms below and overleaf as indicated and send to:

The Research Department, Travel Publishing Ltd,
7a Apollo House, Calleva Park, Aldermaston, Reading, RG7 8TN.

Your Name:

Your Address:

Your Telephone Number:

Please tick as appropriate: Comments ☐ Recommendation ☐

Name of *"Hidden Place"*:

Address:

Telephone Number:

Name of Contact:

Hidden Places Reader Reaction

Comment or Reason for Recommendation:

....

....

....

....

....

....

....

....

....

....

....

....

....

I tried to listen, but Clive's voice was like a tiny trickle of water in the rushing rapids of my anger.

Powerless to stop myself, I squeezed until my soul screamed out in rage, until my teeth ground together with a sickening crunch.

Clive looked down at my arm and took hold of it with both his skeletal hands. But I continued to close the vice on Cheapteeth.

A gasp went up from the audience in the clearing.

Then it happened.

My clawed, nine-fingered hand crushed the light from Kambo Cheapteeth. The clown's dirty, mud and paint-encrusted face sagged suddenly, and a glowing blue light drifted from between his lips and floated upwards.